E ENEMIES WITHIN

Rodney Tyler is a 43-year-old freelance journalist and author. He was born in Reading and attended Reading School before going to Manchester University where he graduated in Psychology. After a brief period on local papers he joined the *Daily Mail* in 1966 and was a writer and executive on national papers for the next sixteen years. He now contributes articles across a wide range of topics to many of our leading newspapers and magazines. His work appears regularly in *The Times* and is syndicated widely abroad. His special interest is politics, particularly the personalities of the contemporary scene. He lives in London with his wife and daughter.

THE ENEMIES WITHIN

The Story of
the Miners' Strike, 1984–5

IAN MacGREGOR
with RODNEY TYLER

Fontana/Collins

First published by William Collins 1986
First issued in Fontana Paperbacks 1987

Copyright © Ian MacGregor 1986

Made and printed in Great Britain by
William Collins Sons & Co. Ltd, Glasgow

To the many coal miners
who had the courage
to stand up for their rights

and to the managers who supported them

CONTENTS

ILLUSTRATIONS

ACKNOWLEDGEMENTS

This book has been prepared and written at some speed in order to coincide, as nearly as possible, with Ian's departure from British Coal. Both of us would therefore like to thank all those people who helped, not only for the information they gave but for the time they gave up, often at very short notice, in order to assist in its preparation.

Within British Coal Jimmy Cowan, John Northard, Ken Moses, Bert Wheeler and Kevin Hunt deserve particular mention; and, for their staffwork on the endless dates and details of documents, Caroline Crouch and Sheila Mann. Sheila also kept the two of us in touch with each other and juggled with airline timetables and cars to make sure we were, at least occasionally, in the same place at the same time.

For further details of the dispute we are indebted to David Hart and Tommy Thompson and Andrew Fearn. David Prior and Albert Frost were a great help in dealing with the BSC years. And the librarians of *The Times* and the *Daily Express* helped Maggie Tyler fill in many tiny details.

It was mostly written at Ardifuir Farmhouse, opposite Crinan on the remote coast of West Argyll, and thanks are due to friends in Lochgilphead, who kept Rod sane, and in food and clean clothing during his isolation – especially all the MacLeods for the former, and the Fletts for the latter.

In the later stages Lucinda McNeile, of Collins, dealt

swiftly and expertly with the manuscript despite all the problems created by expiring deadlines. Mike Salem provided the technical help with data transmission and word-processing difficulties for both Rod and his secretary, Sally Louis, without whose work the book could literally not have been written.

Finally, the original encouragement to embark on the project came from Tim Bell, who was of great help and assistance throughout.

PREFACE

On 4 July 1983 Arthur Scargill declared war.

'We have two choices,' he told the assembled delegates at the National Union of Mineworkers' Annual Conference. 'We can give in, as many German people did in the 1930s, and allow the worst to happen — we can watch social destruction and repression on a truly horrific scale, and wait for the inevitable holocaust. Or we can fight back.

'A fight back against this government's policies will inevitably take place outside rather than inside parliament ... I am not prepared to accept policies proposed by a government elected by a minority of the British electorate. I am not prepared to quietly accept the destruction of the coal-mining industry, nor am I willing to see our social services utterly decimated.

'This totally undemocratic government can now easily push through whatever laws it chooses. Faced with possible parliamentary destruction of all that is good and compassionate in our society, extra-parliamentary action will be the only course open to the working class and the Labour movement.'

It was another nine months before battle commenced: but Scargill left neither the prime minister, nor me, nor many other right-thinking people in any doubt that day of his intentions. His army of 'storm-troopers' was ready to bring the government to its knees if it dared stand in his way.

I had not yet taken up my three-year appointment as chairman of the National Coal Board, but Mrs Thatcher had already made it clear in a long and detailed discussion about the future of the industry what she wished me to do. Already, in 1981, in her first term of office, the miners under Joe Gormley had come to the brink of confrontation with her government. Wisely, having been caught totally unprepared, she backed away and, unlike her predecessor Ted Heath, had lived to fight another day.

Now she knew that, with the NUM led by Arthur Scargill, there was very little chance of avoiding another encounter. Indeed, if there was to be any attempt to stop the drain of taxpayers' money being poured into the pits at the rate of £875 million in the current year, that battle was inevitable. Scargill was spoiling for a fight; and on this basis she discussed with me the steps it would be wise to take in preparation for his onslaught.

Judging from Scargill's own words, the 1983 general election giving her a 141-seat majority had elevated his ambitions. There was plenty of evidence to show that he intended to impose his will on the NCB, but now he saw it as his mission to defeat the ballot box in the pretence of being the great saviour of the working-class movement in Britain – and topple her government.

As we sat in her study at Downing Street, Mrs Thatcher asked me what I thought would happen if Scargill were to manage to mobilize the miners into all-out confrontation. I told her that that would depend on how well she was prepared to cope with it. She wouldn't want to get into the same position that her predecessor had been faced with in 1974 – having no alternative but to give in.

'However, I gather that since your last encounter with the NUM you have encouraged the accumulation of substantial stocks of coal,' I said.

'Naturally,' she replied. 'It was the only prudent thing

to do – especially since Arthur Scargill took over as the miners' leader. The threat of confrontation is now far greater. But it would be tragic for this country, just as it was beginning to see some progress towards economic recovery, to be brought to a standstill by a man like Scargill, who is, after all, a Marxist revolutionary – going under the guise of a normal trade union official.'

'Well,' I said, 'if he does come head-on at us – then I have three golden rules for the conduct of strikes. First, you should never have a long strike where the issue is only money – such disputes always end in a compromise and any ground that is lost can be made up over a period of time. Second, you should never have a major strike unless it is over a crucial issue like the right to manage or the efficiency of the business. It is my experience that once you abdicate the right to manage you never get it back without a major struggle. And third, most importantly, never go into a strike if you aren't prepared to see it through.

'It is a bit like poker, Prime Minister. If you aren't prepared to lose, you will never win.' I don't know if the quizzical look on her face was because she didn't know how to play poker. I prefer to think it was because she was wondering what sort of oddball doctrine this was. But I went on: 'It seems obvious that if Scargill is heading for a confrontation, first of all he will try to prevent the further accumulation of coal stocks in the next year – then challenge us with a set of demands we can't meet as the next winter comes on.

'Therefore, Prime Minister, I think we should realize this and try, if a confrontation comes, to make sure it happens at a time suitable to us rather than to him.'

'How can you manage that?' she asked, still looking puzzled. 'It seems you are going to dictate when this strike is going to happen.'

'That will be part of my job. We have to face the fact that the miners' leaders will almost certainly use any attempt to put the industry in order as an excuse to launch an assault on the NCB and, through us, on your government. We have to be totally prepared for that contingency.

'But I must warn you that it could be a long and rough ride. And I would suggest that if you don't see it that way, you should tell me now, before we start down the path.'

Indeed, in the succeeding months the situation did begin to hot up. We offered the miners a wage deal and, as I had suspected, Scargill turned on the emotive outcries and started an overtime ban. Thus, early in 1984, I had to tell Peter Walker, the secretary of state for energy, that Scargill was now clearly itching for a fight – even though saner counsels in his union were not so keen on the idea. It was already obvious to me that he was going to do everything to push his union into a confrontation but was not prepared to have a ballot. He clearly wanted to do something without being constrained by his membership. The evidence was suggesting that, backed by his army of flying pickets which had brought him national notoriety when they had appeared under his banner in the 1972 Saltley Gasworks riots, he planned to override democracy within his own union, force the miners out on strike and use these carefully trained storm-troopers to smash down the duly elected government of the country. It was my job to try to stop him. But if Britain's coal industry was to mean anything – if we were to stop the rot of waste and inefficiency – then the irresistible force had met its immovable object.

By the spring we had accumulated more than 50 million tonnes of coal stocks – almost six months' total supply. It was obvious something had to be done to bring production into line with the country's actual needs. This first step was incorporated in a plan to cut a modest 4 million tonnes a year from the rate of more than 100 million tonnes at which we had been running. As the Monopolies and Mergers Commission had pointed out in its recent report, the NCB had a number of high-cost pits and should begin to close some of them.

That was why, on 6 March 1984, it was inevitable that when we told the union our plans to start reducing production from high-cost pits, Mr Scargill should start his strike. As it turned out Mrs Thatcher did see it the way I had described. She could see what was coming. She did see it through. And, to her credit, she wavered only once – despite having few people in her cabinet who really understood what it was all about.

1

From Kinlochleven to Muskegon

I was twenty days short of my seventy-first birthday, I had spent many years in America and I had just presided over the drastic but wholly necessary restructuring and rationalization of British Steel (which had involved the shedding of many thousands of jobs) when, at eight o'clock on the morning of 1 September 1983, I walked into Hobart House to start my three-year term as chairman of the National Coal Board.

The amalgam of epithets which had greeted my appointment – and was to continue throughout my tenure – hurled by both the supposed great and the good, from Arthur Scargill to the Bishop of Durham, could best be summed up as portraying me to be a 'geriatric American butcher'. But, like the Holy Roman Empire, which we were taught at school was neither holy, Roman nor an empire, none of these pejoratives was strictly true of me.

I was born and lived the first twenty-eight years of my life in Scotland, before going to America to help with the British war effort. I stayed there after the war because that was where the opportunities seemed to be – opportunities which, in fact, resulted in my creating many, many more jobs all over the world than I have ever had to shed. When the time came to 'retire' at sixty-five, in good health and with the confidence of forty years of a satisfying and successful career, I honestly felt I was just reaching the peak of my abilities in management; a feeling that is surely justified by the fact that both British Steel and British Coal (as the NCB is now called) have never been in better shape than they are now, or offered their employees as much security as they do.

Perhaps the most widespread misconception of the three (Mr Scargill had launched an effective propaganda campaign long before I ever entered the doors of Hobart House), and the most foolish, was that I was there to butcher the coal-mining industry. I have a straightforward and robust attitude to unions. I do not compromise on the principles of good management I have learned over the years. I believe the success of an enterprise is the only path to prosperity and security for workers and management alike. I have no time for those union leaders, and there are many of them, whose guiding light is ideology rather than the interests of their members. I have plenty of respect for men like John Boyd of the engineers (whom I asked to join the BSC board), who have the interests of their members at heart but are not a soft touch. They can see the short and the long term in any deal and get the best out of it for their members.

I did not take on the Coal Board in order to butcher the industry, or to smash the miners. But there was no way I was going to let their leadership stand in the way of establishing the management's right to manage the business and make it a going concern. Any government that hired a man just because he had a record as a strikebreaker would be a foolish government indeed. A lifetime of accumulated management skills across the whole spectrum was needed at the NCB, though it must be said that an ability to handle confrontations looked as though it was going to be high on the list of requirements.

It is an ability that I discovered almost fifty years ago to the day as I write this. I don't know why I was hired as a metallurgist in the armour department of Beardmore's works on Clydeside in the spring of 1936, but I used to see distinct amusement on the face of our chairman, Sir James Lithgow, at the thought of this 23-year-old waif, only five foot nine and weighing less than nine stone, careering round doing his bidding among some of the biggest, strongest and toughest workmen in the land. Sir James always had a twinkle in his eye when he talked to me, and by good fortune I was set a number of tasks which were fairly important for someone of my age. Although I wasn't conscious of it at the time, I realize now that I was being submitted to a series of challenges to see how I rose to them – the best form of training you can possibly have.

To be honest I was appalled by the sight of the Beardmore Parkhead Forge the day I arrived to start work. It was like an abandoned factory – which in a sense it was, since very little had been done there since the crash of 1929. Great rusty sheets were hanging off the buildings, swinging and banging in the wind, and the rail tracks inside the property were overgrown with weeds. I rapidly became involved in the work of reorganizing and reconstructing the factories. Ultimately, by the time war broke out, I was managing a plant of my own in the complex with a workforce of about 1500.

One of Sir James's great abilities was to let his managers manage. You were expected to fight your own battles and solve your own problems on a day-to-day basis. He was a man of immense personal confidence and he communicated this to those under him. Of the half dozen or so men who have influenced my life, he was one – my first great mentor. I learned a lot from observing his optimism, his forceful attitude and his willingness to tackle problems.

Some of this must have already rubbed off on me when, after a few months at Beardmore's, I was confronted with my first strike. The plant where I was working made armour plating for tanks. There were three unions, representing the boilermakers, who to my recollection cut up the plates, the engineers, who machined the plates ready to be fitted, and the steelworkers, who did the heat treatment and drove the cranes. On this occasion it was the steelworkers who walked out, immobilizing the whole plant. It never occurred to me that there was any solution other than to shin up on to the roof and run the overhead crane myself to keep the job going. This I did for a fortnight until the men returned to work. No great victory had been won, only wages lost which they could ill afford to pass up.

I had been too young to be involved in the General Strike of 1926, but I remember my father's concern that a few union leaders should not be allowed to use their men to hold the country to ransom, and that my two elder brothers drove tramcars in Glasgow to keep things moving. From this experience at Beardmore's, I began to see for myself that striking was rarely, if ever, the solution to a problem because the motives for striking were nearly always a show of power on the part of union officials, and the victims were inevitably the working people. The issue in the Beardmore's strike, as far as I can remember, was trivial, but the officials got the men all steamed up. Only when things subsided did they realize that the plant was working on without them and that all the wounds were self-inflicted. I began to see, even at that young age, the difference between those union leaders who are motivated by ideology and the few who have their members' best interests at heart. You could negotiate with the latter, but not with the former. Nothing much has changed.

I suppose it was inevitable that I should have gone to work in a factory like Beardmore's. The practical arts were probably in my blood from the day I was born, within sight and very definitely within sound of the British Aluminium works at Kinlochleven – a remote place on a forbidding fjord on the borders of Argyll and Inverness – where my father worked as an accountant. The site was necessarily remote for large amounts of hydroelectric power were needed in the processing of the aluminium. My first memories are of the vast pipes which brought the water, impounded from the incessant rain in huge dams, down the mountain to power the generators, and of the day a car from the cable railway up on the mountain broke free and crashed into one of these pipes, splitting it open and causing a great flood to sweep down on the village.

We moved to Edinburgh when I was five and I was enrolled at the primary school of George Watson's College. Shortly afterwards, I developed an unfortunately favourable attitude towards air raids. A Zeppelin came over the city and, amidst great excitement as we watched from the ground, jettisoned a bomb which was clearly meant for the castle, or some such strategically important target. It only managed to break the windows in my school half a mile away.

School and I were not on the best of terms in my early years. I had had several sessions with the local school in Kinlochleven in the early attempts to start my education, but I found it confining. In between times I had the good luck to be sent off to my godfather, the Reverend John McCaskill, at Onich, fifteen miles away down the loch. He contributed greatly, and very entertainingly, to my early education and development. Later on I used to go and stay with my aunt who was married to the minister at Kilmelford, and I was always happy to escape from the rather grim surroundings of Kinlochleven.

I was lucky to have parents who believed that their children should have as good an education as possible – even if it strained the family budget – and that they should be able to stand on their own two feet. From this early age, aided by the fact that my two brothers were somewhat older than me and my younger sister was frequently ill, I was encouraged to be independent, and the trips to Kilmelford first kindled my lifelong love for the region of western Argyll. My father's interest in and keen membership of the county's education authority also helped because it took us back there summer after summer, long after we had moved away to Edinburgh and subsequently to Glasgow.

On the day we were due to start our holidays we would get up early to be at the Broomielaw to catch the handsome paddle steamer, the PSS *Columba*, which left on the dot of 7.11. I don't know why it was that particular minute, but it always was – perhaps one of the MacBraynes, who owned the fleet which served all the coast and isles, was at heart a crapshooter. Anyway, we would call at towns and villages like Gourock and Dunoon all the way through the Kyles of Bute to Ardrishaig, where we would transfer to the *Linnet* to go through the Crinan canal. This we did licketysplit, because, by God, those lock-keepers did not dare hold up His Majesty's mail. By tea-time we would be in the harbour house at Crinan ready to start our summer holiday. It was my childhood recollection of heaven.

Most of the holidays were spent with my mother – my father joined us at weekends and for his holidays. She had been a school teacher before she married and she was a really big pusher to make sure we were all trained and educated. We were supposed to do our homework before we went out to play and we were supposed to do our share of chores around the house. On rainy days in the holidays she used to take us into the living room, push all the furniture back, and spread four packs of cards out face down on the floor. Then we would play pelmanism, which she said not only kept us occupied but was good for us as it trained us to remember things. My mother was the driver behind us, having tremendous energy and working like a Trojan. She managed the family and my father never really disagreed with her. My father was quite religious and we attended the United Free Church. Our upbringing was happy but quite strict, and the family income was modest. None of us had any surplus pocket money.

Most people remember a place in which they were happy or which had some particular meaning for them. For me it was Argyll. I particularly remember summer evenings when my father was there. He and my brothers and I would go out fishing and he would do the rowing while we would catch all kinds of fish. Every now and then we'd run into a shoal of mackerel and the excitement would nearly tip the boat up. Then we'd come home tired and probably wet and the catch of fish would have to be disposed of. My mother would clean and dress the fish, roll them up and stick them in a pie dish, cover them with water, vinegar and a little salt and parboil them ready to be eaten cold the following day. While she was doing it we would tell her stories about our adventures in the boat, drink our hot Ovaltine and then be off to bed. We didn't need any rocking to sleep. Under the windows of that house the walls were covered with climbing tea roses, and after the sun had gone down and the wind had died the scent of those roses would drift into the room. I can still smell it now.

I remember another, less romantic, smell from my childhood. After the First World War the region became slightly less remote and MacBrayne's steamers began to give way to MacBrayne's buses, but they were just as much of a spit-and-polish operation, painted red, with tan canvas tops held on by great leather straps, and great brass headlamps and radiators polished till they shone. Each bus had a name on the back – Fox, or Tiger or Wolf – and I remember being at Kilmelford, hanging on the garden gate waiting for the daily bus to come down through the village, raising clouds of dust as it whisked by. I can still savour the smell of the dust and the petrol of the day, probably made from alcohol, and the hot oil, probably made from castor oil, as it hung in a haze in the air. My fascination with the engineering of the emerging motorcar was clearly coming out early!

By the time I was in my early teens I found myself responsible for the repair and maintenance of my brothers' various and much-used second-hand cars. On more than one occasion I was called out in the middle of the night to go and repair one or other of the vehicles about which they had no clue. My eldest brother became a chartered accountant and the second one a lawyer – but sadly he died of pneumonia in the 1930s before we had discovered the importance of sulpha drugs. It seemed only natural after school that I should read a practical subject at university and, after consultation with my father who I think was worried that I might not get a job in those depressed times, I chose metallurgy. I was given a place at Glasgow University where the course was run in conjunction with the Royal Technical College.

I enjoyed the course and got a first. For a while I thought of staying on to do a higher degree, but the economic pressures on the family, with two brothers still struggling as beginners in their professions, were such that I felt I had to go out and get a job. My parents were just about comfortably off – but by no means able to afford the drain of three sons living off them. One of the people who tried to persuade me to stay on and do research for a Ph.D. was a student a year ahead of me, who was my instructor for practical work in my last year. Harold Montague Finniston and I became close friends. He was regarded as an intellectual even then, and we used to tease him because in his excitement his brain would seem to work faster than his mouth and he would start garbling his words. I don't think he has changed very much – he's still a great enthusiast and gets easily worked up. But I think he was too intellectual for the job at British Steel, which he held some years before me. I think the horny-handed sons of toil who had come up through the ranks of BSC were somewhat suspicious of his obvious mental capabilities.

Thus it was I started work in 1935 immediately after getting my degree. Before going to Beardmore's, I went to British Aluminium in Warrington as a management trainee. When I had completed the course I learned that they were thinking of putting me into the research department, which sounded like a dead end. I wanted to be in the mainstream where the career opportunities were, but, as one of the people I worked with pointed out to me, I had not been to Oxford or Cambridge so, no matter how good my degree, I stood little chance of getting any of the plum postings. Who you were was still much more important at that time than what you were. This, I think, was one of the key factors in my decision not to come back to Britain after the war. It was also one of the key factors in my decision to move to Beardmore's.

Throughout my four years on Clydeside I noticed that, as the business tempo of the place, indeed of the whole country, increased, so too did the amount of union activity. Unions, like businesses, have a cycle of ebb and flow – in the 1920s, there had been a surge of union power, building up to the General Strike, which tended to polarize the population. Then there was a movement against all-out union power and in the recession union activity was pretty muted. You would assume that at times of high unemployment and job insecurity there would be less aggressive union activity – but the lesson did not seem to have been learned in the 1980s by Arthur Scargill. With the might he believed he had behind him, and the fact that the NCB was a nationalized industry, he undoubtedly thought that the normal rules did not apply.

It must have been the way I rose to Sir James Lithgow's challenges – as well as the amusement I caused him – that kept me moving up the ladder. But nothing could have prepared me for the next little management task he put my way. In 1940 he was co-opted by and joined the Ministry of Supply under Lord Beaverbrook and I was summoned, first to Canada, then to the United States, to help arrange alternative production of heavy armaments – particularly the tanks we so desperately needed to replace those we had lost at Dunkirk.

My title was technical assistant to a man called Michael Dewar, who was chairman and managing director of British Timken, an associate company of a large American firm. As such, he was reckoned to be in a position to get things moving quickly and time was very obviously not on our side. But scarcely had we arrived in Washington than the British contingent ran into a major problem. The US National Security Council, aware that many firms had been left high and dry with French orders unpaid for after the fall of France, now feared that Britain was in for the same fate. They therefore barred us from placing orders that might never get paid for and might get in the way of their own slowly accelerating rearmament programme.

To simplify matters they ruled that we could place orders, but that they must be for American designs – the theory being that if Britain did fall, then at least they would be left with equipment they could use in their own defence effort. This, however, was of little use to General Douglas Pratt, who arrived directly from Dunkirk, and promptly pronounced the American M3 tank, which had just been developed by the US army ordnance engineers, totally unsuitable in the light of his recent experiences at the hands of the German Panzer divisions in the Low Countries. The problem was simply that, while the American tanks had superb running gear, the top 'fighting' half, as had been shown by recent British experience, was totally inadequate. It would be like facing the powerfully armed and gunned German tanks with peashooters. We needed heavy armoured turrets with big guns capable of firing large, high-velocity, armour-piercing shells.

For a while relations were strained, but the solution which evolved was a classic of British compromise. The British welcomed the design of the US running gear. If the US army ordnance would put our design of heavy-duty turrets on the top, the result would be fine by us. It is a credit to the Dewar mission that the compromise was adopted – and subsequently became the Sherman tank. But first we desperately needed just to get production going, so the British mission ordered a number of M3s and got lines set up and moving inside nine months – against the two years it would have taken in Britain to get tooled up and ready. In the meantime lend-lease had come in and the Americans were working much closer with us. The new tank, the M4, got the go-ahead and the Sherman tank, which was used throughout the war, was a credit to the collaboration between us. I still feel proud to have been part of the Dewar team.

Getting production under way was a task taking eighteen hours a day and seven days a week. I was twenty-eight years old and entrusted with enormous responsibility. The constant pressure kept the adrenalin going, but I was also very aware that I was lucky to be doing what I was doing – there were many others in the field who had been whisked off into the army – so it therefore seemed to me my duty to work around the clock. In March 1941, however, the workload and poor bachelor nutrition caught up with me and I got a cold which turned into a severe throat infection. Before I knew what was happening I woke up in hospital, where I was kept for a month. After this Mr Dewar made us all ease up at least one day a week and we used to take a boat out into Chesapeake Bay near Washington and swim. It was while sitting on the deck eating breakfast one beautiful morning that the news, which had always up to now been so discouraging for the British, came on that Germany had invaded Russia. As Churchill said, it was the beginning of the end, but that seemed very far away that morning. I'll never forget it.

By then I had been transferred to working in the US Department of Ordnance because, when lend-lease became effective, the Americans were responsible for all the buying for the British and needed someone to advise on our requirements – particularly with regard to the problems of production and specifications. Gradually I was drawn into other aspects of the defence programme until, in October, I was suddenly summoned back to London. The purpose of my journey, it transpired, was to prepare a report for the minister of supply, Lord Beaverbrook, estimating what the US was capable of in terms of producing military hardware – a report which was later used by Mr Churchill when he went to Washington to meet Roosevelt after Pearl Harbor to hammer out the so-called Victory Plan.

The trip gave me a short time at home with my parents, whose house had been bombed. Everywhere there was the awful devastation of the Blitz. Apart from giving me a chance to see my parents and to work at a high level in the Ministry of Supply, it also afforded me two of the strangest journeys I have ever undertaken in a lifetime of travel. Being summoned back to England was one thing, but getting there was quite another in wartime. Eventually I was found a place on a B-24 Liberator on a delivery flight from Montreal, via Gander in Newfoundland, to Prestwick. We set off on a clear autumn day, but at Gander the weather closed in and I spent two days in a tent with a blizzard blowing outside, ice on the walls and only a pot-bellied stove for heating in the middle. This meant that as you lay on your bed one side roasted while the other froze.

If I had known my problems were only just beginning I would probably have found an excuse to stay, but, complete with flying suit, I got back on the plane two nights later and, laden with fuel, we took off for Prestwick in strict radio silence. As the only passenger I was given a straw palliasse and told to bed down behind the bomb bay. After a couple of hours we began to ice up, so we descended slowly until the de-icers worked and we could then climb laboriously back up again – only for the same thing to happen again and again, all of which used precious fuel and slowed us up considerably.

As dawn was breaking I was summoned to the cockpit, where the pilot explained our predicament. 'As it's getting light could you go to the rear turret,' he asked, 'and keep an eye out for Messerschmidts?'

I went, more than a little anxious, and looked for Messerschmidts. A little while later I was called once again up front where the pilot told me: 'We have another problem. Perhaps you could help us?'

'I'll do my best,' I volunteered. 'What now?'

'We're all New Zealanders and Canadians and we've

never been on this side of the Atlantic before. We can see land through the cloud, but we haven't a clue where we are and we're getting low on fuel. We thought perhaps you might look out and see if you recognized anything.'

For what seemed like hours I strained to see through the clouds, till finally, by the grace of God, I spotted Ailsa Craig in the Firth of Clyde and could give the pilot directions for Prestwick where we landed with about a cupful of fuel left.

The journey back to America combined the ridiculous with the sublime. Lord Beaverbrook had had dinner with Averell Harriman the night before I was ordered to go. Harriman had just been seconded to London as Roosevelt's special representative and had offered any help he could in moving people to and from the States. Hence, thanks to the two of them, I was given a priority place on a Pan Am clipper out of Lisbon – the ultimate in luxury, I had a bed of my own, and breakfast, lunch and dinner served in the dining room by white-jacketed waiters. There was something to do for every one of the thirty-five hours we were flying via the Azores and Bermuda to New York – when we weren't eating or sleeping, we played cards and drank in the plane's state room!

Shortly after I arrived back I found myself working quite closely with the British Iron and Steel Corporation headed by a man called Ian Elliott and his assistant, Frank Saniter, a metallurgist from Sheffield. They were in the US buying critical war materials and shipping them to England. We got to know each other, through helping each other overcome shortages and bottlenecks, and became very friendly. One day I got a note from Frank inviting me for dinner at his place with two young ladies. One of them was called Sibyl Spencer, who was British and Ian Elliott's PA, and the other was her assistant, called Helen MacGregor. I only found out later that it was a set-up job. Sibyl Spencer recalls Frank's invitation to dinner on Saturday, which she found in her typewriter, as saying: 'If you'll bring your MacGregor, I'll bring mine.'

We had a marvellous dinner and in return I suggested that I should buy them all brunch the following day. We were in the middle of that meal, at about midday, when the radio cut in with the news of Pearl Harbor, and we all sat around, shocked, listening to the story unfold.

The difference that day made to America had to be seen to be believed. Things that had taken months now took weeks. The nation was electrified into action. Decisions were made on the spot and everyone had a singularity of purpose. You could feel the whole place starting to throb. If we had worked hard before, we now redoubled our efforts. There was never any question about long hours, inconvenient travel, or shortages – the whole country was mobilized.

The difference that day made to me was that less than six months later in the chapel of St Margaret's, in the basement of the unfinished Washington Cathedral, Sibyl Spencer became Mrs MacGregor. I am sure it did not escape her notice that even on that day of all days she was stepping out for the first time as my wife through an unfinished building site!

As everything speeded up at work after Pearl Harbor one of the critical factors in the manufacture of tanks turned out to be the production of armour plate. So, together with two Americans, Reuel Warriner and Paul Queneau who had been seconded from the International Nickel Company, we were set the task of expanding production of alloy steel armour plate while at the same time devising ways to conserve critical alloy materials as far as possible and improve specifications. We eventually put together a pool of companies, with one at the head and the rest subcontracting to do the job, and it was through this work that I formed my lifetime's friendship with Reuel and Paul. They were good engineers and scientists and also very fine and impressive men. They have had an enormous influence on me and their friendship has been invaluable. Reuel died about seven years ago, but I still regularly see Paul, who returned to INCO and, after retiring, became a professor at the prestigious Dartmouth College in New Hampshire.

My last major project before the end of the war arose out of the anticipated need for trucks as a result of the saturation bombing which it was expected would destroy the railways of Europe. These 'six-by-sixes', as they were called, because all six wheels were driven, were to be built in their hundreds of thousands and shipped across the Atlantic ready for D-Day and after. The problem, however, was a shortage of heavy-duty axles, gearboxes and transfer cases, and I became part of a team to overcome the bottleneck. Nobody had ever built such heavy-duty lorries at that rate, and certainly nobody had ever needed to mass-produce such a complicated axle and gearing system. Eventually another pool system of companies was set up – under the same controlling aegis of the Standard Steel Spring Company – and the problem was finally overcome. By 1945, with Standard Steel Spring management, I had had the satisfaction of working on two major successes and I had thoroughly enjoyed being part of them. I had also learned a great deal about organizing effective management, which stood me in good stead throughout my career.

With the end of the war in sight I made several inquiries about the prospects of jobs back in England, but they were all somewhat discouraging. On the other hand I had grown to like America. I had travelled the length and breadth of the country and got to know many of its people. I loved their warmth and friendliness and above all their optimism. Everyone expects the light will shine on him and he'll be the big winner. And if it doesn't happen for him, he works damned hard to make sure his children have a chance of it happening to them. The millionaire is not a figure of envy; people don't knock the man who makes a fortune – they admire him and want to be like him.

So when Ira Wyant, of Campbell, Wyant and Cannon, started to woo me to stay in the US and work for him, I needed very little winning over. I had met Ira back in 1940 when I worked with him on the technical problem of making steel castings for tank tracks. We had continued to keep in touch. Now, as the war came to a close, he was looking forward to getting back into the car component business and asked me to join his company. His foundry made cylinder blocks and heads, gearbox casings and the like – a business which had fascinated me since I was a boy with my brothers' cars.

Thus, on VE Day, Sibyl, our young son Ian and I were in Muskegon, Michigan, to start our new life, but not before I had been told most firmly by the US government that, as a prospective employee of an American firm, rather than an envoy of the British government, I would have to get permission from the British government to resign, leave the country and apply at the US border for an immigrant visa. Hence our detour on the way from Detroit to Muskegon through the tunnel to Windsor, Ontario, in Canada and back again – as American immigrants.

2

American Opportunities

Ira Wyant and his partner George Cannon became two more of my mentors. I soon found that there was a world of difference between working as a Briton on loan to America and actually working for a living in the USA. It was largely due to their warmth and generous treatment of us that we settled in so quickly. In business they taught me a lot: Ira was calm and analytical, but very strong and forceful when he needed to be; George was an impatient perfectionist who could not stand low productivity or sloppy work. Both of them had the great knack, which I strove to emulate as I rose to the top, of managing by encouragement. I always felt I was being encouraged to go out and do things myself – a marvellous way to learn.

Very soon I was in the thick of the automobile business – and the outcome of the 1945 general election in Britain only served to confirm my feelings that I was wise to stay where I was. I was promoted to marketing manager of CWC and found myself banging on the doors of, and negotiating with, all the major car, truck and heavy plant manufacturers – everyone from Ford and General Motors to International Harvester and Caterpillar Tractor. It was a marvellously broad education in the whole of the automotive industry at a time of great creativity and expansion.

It was during this period that I witnessed my first

American labour dispute and watching Ira Wyant and George Cannon handling it taught me a lot. American unions were at that time divided into two groups. They still are to a great extent, though they are united in name. On the right, and more republican than the Republicans, were the craft unions led by George Meany. The plumbers, the electricians – all the skilled workers – were in the American Federation of Labor (AFL). They had always enjoyed higher wages, better conditions and more restrictive practices than the 'industrial' unions in the Confederation of Industrial Organizations – which were more like our big labour unions. The CIO was based very much on the same socialist theories as British unions and claimed to represent the 'working class' in conflict with the bosses, management, and all the trappings of capitalism. They had always been envious of the political power of British unions through their close association with the financing and domination of the Labour Party. They had, for historical reasons, never had the same influence over the Democratic party. But their leaders, men like Phil Murray of the Steelworkers and Walter Reuther of the Automobile Workers, were essentially British in their outlook on union affairs – indeed a number of their top men were British. Even then we did not discriminate between our exports! The USA was in receipt of some of the less attractive as well as the best aspects of our way of life.

Hence the presence on our doorstep one day in 1949 of the agent of the United Automobile Workers – Mr Leonard Woodcock, a distant relative of George, who was for some years the general secretary of the TUC. He was demanding that we abolish our piecework system and incorporate it in straight hourly payments. Apparently it was demeaning for one man to work harder than another in order to earn more, so the union had decided that in future we should just pay a straight wage. Everyone could then work as hard, or as little, as they felt inclined. Rather than go headlong into battle with the big car giants over this piece of egalitarian dogma – a battle they suspected they might lose – they were hoping first to pick off one by one all the smaller suppliers, who had fewer resources to fight with.

The strike lasted about three months and was very bitter. In a sense it was a classic of its kind because it could be clearly demonstrated that the men had been worked up by the ideologists into a frenzy to carry the banner for a cause far beyond their local ambitions. But when they came to examine things in the cold light of day they began to realize that the strike was actually against their own interests – at least against the interests of those who wished to work and make a good living.

The company succeeded, but not before the salaried staff had gone in to work the plant themselves.

The important lesson I learned from Wyant and Cannon through the dispute was that management has to maintain its resolve, preserve its right to manage and not to have this right abridged: to have that fundamental right compromised inevitably leads to loss of efficiency and competitiveness and can threaten a company's very survival. It was a lesson I took with me, three years later, when I was forced out of CWC and joined a company called Manning, Maxwell and Moore. I was sad to leave CWC, but through a boardroom wrangle Wyant and Cannon had lost their influence and the company had been taken over by what we would nowadays call asset strippers or conglomerators, and my position as part of the original management was made increasingly difficult. This was my first experience of the American way of hiring and firing and for a while I was quite deflated – but I talked to friends and they told me it happened to many good people and that I shouldn't let it worry me. They advised me to recharge my confidence and go out and get another job.

MM & M was based in New England; it had been founded in the nineteenth century essentially as a railway supply business. It had gone through a difficult period during the depression, but it had had a profitable period during the war and was quite well set up making a broad spectrum of products from process control instrumentation and valves of all sorts to cranes and hoists. Unfortunately it was being brought to the brink of ruin by increasingly severe labour problems, which were the product of weak compromises. In addition, the company had begun to suspect that at their main plant in Stratford, Connecticut, their union, an obscure branch of the teamsters union, had recently been taken over by the Mafia. They asked if I would take it on. Why not? I thought.

When I got there I discovered that the union had virtually taken over, and that the management was under great pressure. The piecework system had run out of control and their costs were escalating rapidly. In short order I tackled the union and demanded we get things sorted out. I offered them a formula which would still keep the company in business and would give them a fair wage, but they rejected it out of hand and we went straight into a strike.

This one lasted longer than three months and was bitter and violent. On one occasion when I was arriving at the plant, pickets attacked my car and turned it over before the police could beat them back and rescue me from inside. Another time a state mediator came to my house late at night with a warning that the union saw me as the only thing that stood between them and victory and that they were thinking about getting their friends in the Mafia

to take out a contract on me. 'What's that supposed to do
for me?' I asked. 'You should maybe think about your
position,' he said. 'Well,' I said, 'you go back to them
and tell them that any such action would probably
solve all my problems – but it would only be the start of
theirs.'

A week later the strike was over. It was resolved by the
use of an interesting technique. Throughout the dispute
we ran a publicity and letter-writing campaign to encourage our people back to work and to discredit the union
leadership. We had the feeling early on that many of the
men were not happy with what had happened to their
union and had come to distrust its leadership. They were
normal, decent working folk who didn't like being used
as strike fodder – but were, in many cases, too frightened
to say so. We knew that eventually the dam of their feelings
would break if we kept the pressure up, so we wrote regularly to them individually at home, laying out the financial
peril of the company and promising them that their jobs
could only be secure if we got back to work – soon,
as the company was in danger of losing its major business
because of the strike. Finally, when we thought they were
about ready, Dwight Fanton (our labour attorney and
legal adviser) and I worked out a scheme to jolt the union
leaders. We went off quietly one afternoon to the National
Labor Relations Board in New York, making sure to
arrive just as the bureaucrats were leaving. Over their
protests that it was closing time we insisted that we file
'unfair labour' charges against the union right then –
knowing that, as good bureaucrats and anxious to clock
off, they would have to accept our petition but would
leave it in a desk drawer until the following morning
when they would inevitably tell the union. Our charge
was that the union had, contrary to the labour laws, been
denying their members details of the various offers we

had made. But what was in the charges – though genuine – did not matter as much as the timing and the impact of the charge of illegal union action.

That night we met the union again to try to negotiate, without any success – since the union leaders were confident they did not have to concede a thing. We said nothing about our visit to the NLRB, but afterwards we told the local press that we would have a statement for them just before the deadline for the morning edition, when we hoped it would be too late for them to get hold of the union to alert them and give them a chance to respond.

As we thought, the announcement, splashed over the front page of the local morning paper, that the union leadership was being challenged for breaking the labour laws, tipped the balance. The workers put pressure on the union leaders, attitudes in negotiations became conciliatory, the union eventually agreed to changes in the piecework system and the men came back. It did not take the workers long to realize that the union leadership had been rejecting quite reasonable proposals without telling the men and the company soon found its feet again. I heard nothing more from the Mafia, but when I left the company a few years later I received a beautiful leather-bound album with a message of thanks and good wishes signed by every employee in the factory.

I don't want this to seem as though my whole life was a conflict with the unions. I tell these stories to illustrate some of what I had learned by the time it came to March 1984 and my dealings with Arthur Scargill. During many years as a top manager labour problems were but a small part of my life. I was a builder, not a destroyer. But if a union leader wanted to challenge the good management of the business and wanted a scrap – then he could have it. I never backed away from that kind of confrontation.

I had learned that sometimes it was better to make a strategic withdrawal if I thought I couldn't win the day. But then I would regroup and come back to fight another day. Over the years I spent a lot of the time in dealing with labour problems trying to differentiate between those conflicts which involved the ideologies of the leaders and those which genuinely were about the interests of the individual employees. I found, by and large, that as soon as a union leader became concerned with the former, the latter tended to go out of the window.

I stayed at MM & M for five years and became general manager of the enterprise, but by this time I was forty-five years old and getting impatient. I wanted to be a bigger fish in a bigger pond. The company was very good to me, but the owners were very cautious and wanted to go slowly, whereas I was in a hurry to get on.

America really is a country of opportunity. If you are reasonably self-confident and believe in your own capabilities then you can compete with anyone. It was a very exciting place to be in the 1940s and 50s – you felt the whole country had ambitions. The nation had come through the war with a sort of collective understanding of its mission: to be the defender of the ordinary man against any system of dictatorship or any form of authoritarianism. The Americans identified in the Soviet Union the same basic threats to the individual as they had seen in Hitler. They could see it also in men, of whatever political shade, who would seek to impose their political will or ideological beliefs upon them. But they also had the self-reliance and strong desire to do well for their children that has been the characteristic of all upwardly mobile immigrants to any country. They did not want to lean on the state or have the state or anyone else lean on them. That is why Kennedy's words, 'Ask not what your country can do for you; rather what you can do for your country', struck such a responsive chord with so many Americans.

The system does not work because of a particular ideology. It works at the lowest common denominator of the ordinary man who wants to get on with his life and by his own efforts take his opportunities, without anyone or any organization interfering.

As far as my opportunities were concerned I very definitely wanted to paint on a bigger canvas than the one at MM & M. I put these musings to my old friend Reuel Warriner one day over lunch. He had recently joined a company called Climax Molybdenum as head of marketing. The timing was perfect, because within a few weeks his chairman, a man I came to admire greatly called Arthur Bunker, had expressed interest in finding a senior executive who was keen on diversification and expansion and had a broad industrial training. As Bunker later explained to me, he felt vulnerable because he had a one-product company (Molybdenum, as its Latin translation says, is 'lead-like' and it is used as an additive to steel to make it stronger and tougher) and any major discovery of the ore elsewhere by another company would severely threaten Climax – hence his desire to diversify into other businesses.

One of the things, however, that was holding him up – apart from not having the right executive to do it, which they tried to put right in 1957 by asking me to join the company – was a continuing series of labour problems. Two were particularly aggravating and, in solving them, taught me some lessons that were to prove invaluable later.

Arthur Bunker was not the only one to realize that the company, as a one-product outfit, was vulnerable. The particular section of our old friends the United Automobile Workers, who represented the workers in the plant where Climax converted the molybdenum ore into a usable product for the steel industry, were aware of it also. And they had stuck the management up against the wall with a series of escalating demands, which now threatened the whole basis of the company. There were only about 250 workers involved, but their union was as aware of the power of their monopoly as any bunch of airport baggage handlers or cross-channel ferry crews or dockers, who so regularly seem to ruin so many people's holidays.

The workers in the converting plant near Pittsburg were already on strike when I joined the company and Bunker, knowing my previous labour relations experience, asked me to handle it. After a couple of weeks analysing the situation I decided to set about finding alternative installations that would be capable of handling the conversion process – whatever the cost – for a few months. We came up with two: one in Salt Lake City and one in Canada. After a while Bunker called me in and asked if I had started to negotiate with the men at our plant in Pennsylvania. 'No,' I answered. 'I don't intend to do that until I am ready.' 'How long will that be?' he asked, clearly worried at the delay. 'I will be ready when I don't need them to come back at all,' I told him.

It took me two months to get things organized. Then I called in the union and told them I was ready to negotiate, but that we had some contract demands to settle before they could return to work. What I wanted was simply to restore to the management the right to manage the plant and to make the operation reasonably economic once again. It was the same old story. The union leaders had virtually hijacked the role of management and hemmed it in with restrictive practices and impossible terms. Finally they saw that the company position was strong and after three more months they came back and we were able to get the operation back into production on a reasonable basis. The strike taught me, if I should ever need to know it, the power of the union in a one-product industry and the value of having alternative strategic arrangements lined up, if possible before facing confrontation over unreasonable demands. 'Always get your ducks lined up' became a maxim of mine.

The other problem arose at the Climax mines in Colorado and cropped up just as the Climax Co. was about to merge with the American Metal Co. – into what was to become Amax. I was sent out to Colorado by Bunker to see if I could assist the local manager, Frank Coolbaugh, solve the problem. First, however, I had to deal with Mr Coolbaugh who, naturally, resented the presence there of a newcomer and outsider and made it clear that he thought he didn't need my help. In a speech that I was reminded of many years later when addressing a British government minister, I sat him down in his own kitchen one night and told him over a beer: 'Look, we both work for the same company. The chairman has asked me to do these things. If you have a quarrel, it is not with me, it is with the chairman. So why don't you go to him and get it sorted out? And in the meantime why don't we both get on with doing what we have to do to sort out the strike?'

He didn't go to the chairman and we got the strike settled in about two months. One of the techniques we used, which I was to find useful later at British Leyland, was recommended by one of our industrial relations people called Larry Kelly.

The Climax mine was started just after the First World War and was on top of the Freemont Pass on the Continental Divide some 11,000 feet above sea level. It had grown over the years and with it the small mining camp around it. Conditions were severe and isolated and a frontier mining camp spirit prevailed. Every now and then a bunch of troublemakers would get on the payroll and stir things up. Larry suggested that we should keep a careful record of what these guys did any time they caused trouble or broke the rules. And we should keep these records quite openly, and if necessary call the individual in to check the details of any infraction with him so he knew that our records were accurate. It had a salutary effect on the troublemakers and a couple of documented warnings would quieten down all but the most frequent offenders whose ultimate departure was achieved with very little fuss.

The Climax/American Metal company merger came within a year of my joining Climax – and within another year the whole of the new company was thrown into turmoil by the death of its first president. American Metal was much bigger than Climax: it had copper, zinc, lead and potash mines in the US, Canada, Mexico and Africa. Both companies were rich, however, so a merger was agreed and, although I was made a vice president of the new company, the Climax people were, by and large, treated like the poor relatives for some years. The American Metal executives felt that, as major partners, they should take over the direction of the new company.

Not only did the first president – Hans Vogelstein – die, setting in motion quite a scramble for succession, but soon after that the situation was further complicated when Arthur Bunker, who had become the first chairman of Amax, contracted leukaemia. His death at the comparatively young age of sixty-three was a great loss to the company, for he was intellectually a man of great understanding and vision, and also to me personally, as he had become a strong friend, ally and mentor.

In the turmoil of 1959 and 1960 the infighting that went on was quite something. But I sensed my time was not ripe and went off into a corner, so to speak, and got on with what I had been hired to do in the first place, which was organizing a management structure for the business and planning its diversification. From where I was I could watch the battle for succession rage – and predictably it ended up with a compromise candidate between the warring camps. My old associate Frank Coolbaugh from Colorado became president and managing director, and Walter Hochschild, a member of one of the American Metal founding families, became chairman.

The first major area of diversification I concentrated on was aluminium, followed by iron ore. After considerable effort these new ventures added substantially to the company's turnover and profits. In due course the board approved of my activities and appointed me chief executive. Soon after, in 1967, I became chairman as well as chief executive. At last I felt a great satisfaction and thought this was just a beginning. There were lots of things to do and now I had the opportunity to do them. I suppose I had developed a certain self-confidence – maybe even to the point of vanity – but I felt at home being where I was. I would have been surprised if the board had done otherwise than to appoint me. That is not to say that I hadn't taken part in all the usual politics and scheming to get there. In all big organizations, particularly nowadays in large dynamic companies, there are internal politics, which in some respects make normal politics look like a beginner's game, because for individuals there is so much at stake. The winners win big, though perhaps some of the losers live to fight another day.

Provided it is a live organization going somewhere, it may not do all that much harm to have competition among the people at the top jockeying for position and power. It toughens the temperament and prepares for the hard disciplines needed to exercise power successfully. Some people are just bullies. They are soon found out when they reach the very top and do not succeed for long. Power is, after all, the great aphrodisiac – it is what motivates politicians, union leaders and executives too. It is that strange urge felt by them all to command. I am sure it is a form of egotism or vanity to want to command the people and situations around you. Most people try to rationalize it away – but quite frankly I enjoyed it. And over the years I came to understand some of my own motivations, and also those of other people.

I was helped in this understanding of myself and other people to a certain extent by an experience I had some years ago at Reuel Warriner's urging. I spent a week at the Menninger psychiatric clinic in Kansas. Reuel thought that all of us could learn from knowing more about our own motivations. The Menningers were two of the top American psychiatrists and they had decided that it might be useful for top government and corporate officers to learn something about the basics of psychiatry. They organized a week-long course, starting off with analysis of each of the participants. I went, somewhat sceptically, but it turned out to be a remarkable, and completely shattering, experience.

They took each of the individuals in groups of eight and really took us to pieces – but, more importantly, they had us analysing each other, so that, by the end of the second day, they had us pretty well down on the floor in terms of self-esteem. You began to realize all the things you did wrong and all the base motivations for what you did. If you survived that crushing experience (and some of the group didn't – it had so depleted their vanity that they actually quietly slipped out at night and went home), then the next three days were spent in building up a rather simple and empiric understanding of your own and other people's behaviour.

I managed to stay the course. The experience turned out to be enormously valuable in later years because I found I could work with people and have a basic understanding of the mechanics of their behaviour. This has enabled me to sort people out fairly well in my mind. Many companies now send their senior managers to headshrinkers of one sort or another – but the danger is, like all the so-called management tools, that you become over-reliant on them. When I was at British Leyland I discovered that Michael Edwardes wouldn't hire a soul unless he had sent them to, and they had been passed by, his favourite headshrinker. That's probably how he may have lost one or two really good people, because they either failed or refused to go through with this exercise.

I felt my experience in Kansas was only a preliminary introduction to the subject; I had learned some of the simpler working rules. I gleaned something about people's characters by observing them for a while and looking at their backgrounds. I used it in the selection of managers – and, needless to say, it also came in handy from time to time in assessing the motivations of people on the other side of the bargaining table.

No system, or human, is infallible and none of these useful insights helped me, after I had been chairman for a few years, to anticipate the struggle precipitated by Don Donahue, the Amax president. When I took over as chairman and chief executive I had been happy to endorse his appointment as president under me. He was a very bright and capable man. At the time of the oil crisis in the early 1970s, however, he thought he saw an opportunity. He worked on the concerns of the brothers Hochschild, who were the two dominant private shareholders in Amax. He was afraid that our enormous aluminium investment, which had grown to over $200 million and, of course, had been my baby, was about to turn into an albatross. His reasoning was that the cost of the electricity needed to make the aluminium would soar as OPEC started to raise the price of petroleum. He produced figures to demonstrate the increasing cost of aluminium which turned out to be reasonably valid, and he had his own particular set of supporters on the board whose loyalties tended to support the old American Metal men, of which Donahue was seen as one of the most promising. I began to worry that not only did I have faint hearts to cope with but also activists who were keen on Donahue, and who saw in this situation a promising opportunity to curtail the chairman's power and perhaps even depose him.

I suddenly realized that I was in for a real boardroom power scrap and there had to be a fast and decisive response. I told the board, who by this time sensed blood, that I fundamentally disagreed with this argument about the future of aluminium. In fact the natural outcome of the increased cost of energy must be the increase in the importance of light metals. I went on to say: 'Not only do I think our aluminium company was a good investment, but I'll prove it. I will find a partner – somebody who will take half of it off our hands – who will pay us more than half the book value of the business to prove you are wrong.' Well, the response from the activist board members was, 'Put the money where you mouth is'. My proposition was not in my view all that much of a gamble.

Over the years I had followed the evolution of the world aluminium industry and it was as clear as daylight to me that if energy costs were to rise dramatically the people in the greatest difficulty would be the Japanese. And so it was that frantic phone calls were made to get hold of my old friend Mr Tatsuro Goto of Mitsui. On the phone I told him to expect Bob Marcus from our aluminium company. Then I told Bob, who was the best negotiator I knew: 'Go to see Goto and sell half the company to him for not less than $120 million and don't come back until you've done it.' Meanwhile, I kept up efforts with Tatsuro on the phone. Within a week Bob called me and said he had a deal. I quite relished the next board meeting. Not long afterwards Don Donahue and I came to an amicable parting of the ways and he left. Don had not realized that the oil crisis was hitting Japanese energy costs far harder than it was hitting ours, so the prospect of Mitsui buying into our aluminium businesses with its much lower costs, by comparison to theirs, was quite attractive. Nor did he give enough credence to the long-term prospects for the industry. By the time I retired from Amax in 1977, our 50 per cent of the aluminium company, now known as Alumax, was worth more than the 100 per cent we had invested in it a decade earlier.

I had learned from Arthur Bunker, who had been an inspiring leader at Climax and in the early days of Amax, that to run a large enterprise one has to study the global economics and politics of the business world, especially in the fields in which your business is engaged. He taught me the value of keeping an eye on world industrial and commodity markets.

It was such long-term thinking that led me in the late 1960s to get Amax into coal mining – a business which in the end has become one of the cornerstones of the company's profits. In the sixties I read a lecture given by Charles Kettering, the chief engineer of General Motors. We were still very much in the era of the big gas-guzzlers, but in his talk Kettering explained that GM's recent bid to make smaller cars, which had been such a market failure, was in response to his anticipation that the price of fuel would rise as the US ran out of oil reserves. The cars had failed to sell despite their excellent design, it was explained, only because GM's ideas were ahead of their time. Sooner or later, the price of oil would go up and the US would be increasingly at the mercy of other oil-producing countries.

That set me thinking that it would not only be the size of cars and car engines that would be affected, but that anyone who had a source of energy other than oil could be on to a winner. Mr Kettering was, of course, proved absolutely right in 1973 and my actions in buying into coal in a big way in the late sixties were simultaneously vindicated. Over the years Amax built up its coal production to 40 million tonnes a year – most of it going to supply electricity-generating stations, with whom we did long-term deals to help them over the traditional, and worrying, cycles of fluctuating costs. These long-term contracts didn't help me with certain members of the Amax board, who were critical of our contracts when coal prices shot up in the spot market, but those same people couldn't be heard when the spot market declined.

As we pushed forward with coal expansion at Amax there was an episode I was to find myself ruefully recalling a decade later as I sat with the prime minister and her home secretary early in the Scargill strike. Amax started up a huge opencast mine in Gillette, Wyoming. It wasn't long before we had the United Mine Workers camping at the mine entrance trying to sign up all our new employees.

Eventually, when they had collected enough membership cards, the UMW registered under the National Labour Relations Act and served us with their demands, – particularly a cents-per-ton pension contribution – which, for a try-on, were identical with those for mineworkers in the relatively low-production underground pits in the Appalachian coal-mining areas. The nego-

tiations were long and protracted but there was a fundamental gulf between us. Eventually the talks collapsed,
so the UMW called the men out and we had a strike on
our hands.

My feeling was that these local employees in Wyoming
would not back a strike to win pension contributions far
beyond anything we paid elsewhere but which would not
give them another penny in their own pockets. They
had good jobs and were earning good money, and were
obviously being directed by the union leaders from back
east – but naturally they would be scared to go against
anything the mighty union ordered. My industrial relations man, Roger Sonneman, arranged for his people to
talk to the men and found this to be true – most of the
men wanted to get back to work, he reported. But the
Wyoming men were afraid that as soon as they came back
to work a bunch of goons might descend on them from
Pennsylvania and try to force them back into line with
threats of violence and intimidation.

So I sent Roger out to chat with the local law enforce-
ment authorities such as the sheriff and the local judge.
I suggested he should find out whether the sheriff was
some kind of pussycat or whether he was a real red-
blooded western sheriff. Roger reported back to me that
the sheriff had indeed insisted that he was red-blooded
and that no bunch of foreigners from the eastern USA
would come into his county and try to break the law.
Roger then told the sheriff he was going to have an
opportunity to test his mettle against a bunch of hell-
raising miners from Pennsylvania. Roger reported back
that the sheriff was fully prepared to defend his fine local
western people from any rough types that might arrive
from the east. He also reported that the judge was a nice
orderly old American lawyer, who was now righteously
concerned for the good name of Gillette County, and he

too wasn't going to have it spoiled by a bunch of imported hell-raisers.

We told the men that we had been assured they would be protected by the local lawmen and named the day when we were going to reopen the mine for them. Sure enough, there were the world's first genuine flying pickets – they'd arrived by plane from the east – ready to impose the union's will, if necessary at the end of a baseball bat. As soon as the first carload of men going back to work turned up at the mine this mob started moving menacingly towards them; but, true to his word, the sheriff had got up a real posse of his own and they emerged from the sage brush and in no time at all had the pickets rounded up and off to jail for the night.

Next morning, the judge delivered his verdict, which can be paraphrased thus:

Boys, I'm required to pass sentence on you for the crimes you've committed in our county. We could lock you in the hoosegow here for quite a time. However, I'm going to be kind to you, because, after all, you are visitors here and we should be friendly. So I think we should do this: I'm afraid I'm going to have to find you guilty – but I'm going to suspend your sentence in jail, because that would be terrible for you to have a long period of incarceration away from your homes. So what I am going to do is give you a chance to make it right for both of us. I want you to sign an affidavit that you will leave our county and not come back – particularly not come back representing the UMW and cause any more harm to the citizens of our county nor prevent them from going about their lawful business. And of course I will also want you to put in that paper you'll all sign that you agree that no other person from the UMW will come here as a proxy for you. In other words, I don't want you going back to Pennsylvania and handing the job on to another bunch of fellows, because if that happens I will assume you have breached the conditions of your release and I will send the federal marshal after you to bring you here to serve your sentence.

At the height of the violence on the picket lines and the threats and intimidation of the forces of law and order in March 1984, I had this incident in mind when I told Mrs Thatcher and Leon Brittan, who was then home secretary, that I never thought the day would come when I wished I had some of my scruffy, sometimes ill-disciplined, sometimes loud-mouthed American police by my side in this country and some of the curious ways of the law to back them up.

It had surprised me to find that in Britain people at all levels seemed to accept the totalitarianism of the left, that violence had become almost a legitimate expression of opinion and that law-breaking was let pass with little more than a collective shrug of the shoulders and a slap on the wrist. I resent the thought of ideology trampling over the individual. All my upbringing and instinct was offended by union leaders using their members for their own ends, suffocating democracy to establish a diktat. I had always been a zealous supporter of the rights of individuals and it made me frustrated and angry to see how easily the rights of individual union members could be suppressed.

Thus, by the time I retired in 1977, I had taken the company from nowhere to among the top 100 in the *Fortune 500* list of US businesses. In ten years revenues went up from $275 million to $1.1 billion, net earnings up from $60 million to $150 million, shareholders' equity from $436 million to $1.56 billion. These are the factors by which you might judge a company – and I suppose that is what my record up until then should be judged by. But I wasn't just proud of guiding a group of people and a company to great success – I was proud of the growth and expansion of our company and the many tens of thousands of jobs created all over the world, as well as the careers and the security that the wealth they had created gave to them too.

The left-wing attacks on multinationals such as Amax conveniently forget the wealth and benefit those companies are able to create. I suppose it stems from the multinational company being the antithesis of communist theory. Marxism has it that the capitalist corporation is a total exploiter of the working man. It must be a matter of great chagrin to communists all over the world to see that the multinationals are, by and large, great success stories in providing jobs; and in training and extending the knowledge of technology, consequently creating goods and expanding the wealth of communities wherever they go. Most people understand this in a vague way. Just as most people fundamentally want the dignity and satisfaction of work and to make the best of their opportunities for themselves and their children. All too often it is the ideologues who get in the way.

It is essential to have a broad grasp of all the problems involved in any industry. One of the great deficiencies of modern management is that too few people have a sufficient grasp of the total technological background against which modern society has to function to realize the implications of the system within which they work.

One man I admired perhaps more than any other – and who was certainly of great help to me – was H. J. Szold. Jim Szold, a Lehman Bros partner, was perhaps the wisest man I knew. At Amax when Szold was one of our senior directors, he was able to take a broad look at everything, and he never got ruffled. No matter what the panic, he would just smile and say, 'Gosh, well let's just sit down and think about it for a bit,' and in no time we'd have a solution to the problem. I have always tried to emulate him and sit back and look the form over when things get rough. He was a wonderfuly wise old man and for years I never did anything without getting his blessing.

When he was over seventy he said that all directors should retire at a certain age – and he thought seventy was about right. So he set an example and stood down, and in his place from Lehman's came George Ball, who had been under-secretary for economic affairs, with secretary of state Dean Rusk, in the Kennedy administration.

Strangely enough, and by sheer coincidence, I was also presented with the possibility of serving as secretary for economic affairs in the US government – but under Henry Kissinger. Over the years I had been active in various businessmen's international economic groups both in Europe and in the Far East. Through these I got to know Robert Ingersoll, former chairman of Borg–Warner company. When he retired he was appointed US ambassador to Japan. Over the years I had built up an acquaintanceship with Mr Ingersoll and when Henry Kissinger became secretary of state in the second Nixon administration, Ingersoll was appointed his deputy in Washington and given the task of finding a secretary for economic affairs. He invited me, I suppose because I had been pretty active in international business economic councils.

I went to Washington and spent a couple of days going over the job from soup to nuts with Henry and Bob Ingersoll. I was very tempted, but the sad truth was that I couldn't afford to take it. The adjustments necessary to one's financial affairs when contemplating public office in the US are quite extensive.

It was with regret that I had to decline the offer. Although, as it turned out, shortly afterwards Nixon became increasingly embroiled in Watergate, and though that did not involve Henry Kissinger or the State Department, nonetheless it weakened and reduced the effectiveness of the whole of the Nixon administration. So perhaps it was divine providence.

Had I gone to Washington I am sure my subsequent career would have denied me the other great opportunity to serve – in my native land – which was to come along later. The invitation to return to Britain arose in a large way as a result of my 'post-retirement' job. Post retirement is such an odd phrase to use, because the truth was that I never had any intention of retiring in the conventional sense of the word. I was just getting into my stride. I was fit, healthy and raring to go – so much so that my wife Sibyl used to joke that the young executives who accompanied me on business trips would always need a week off to recover when we returned, whereas I would go straight to the office.

George Ball was aware of my reluctance to be put out to grass and take up gardening. As I approached sixty-five, he had openly suggested that I might like to pursue my interest in what you might call the financial engineering side of industry – by joining the Lehman Brothers Bank. In the spring of 1977 I finally agreed and was appointed chairman of Lehman International and a member of the executive committee of Lehman Brothers. It was an honour, an exciting prospect – and of course I was expected to create business opportunities on my own which would justify my membership of the firm.

As it turned out I was there less than a year, because the bitter feud between Peter Petersen and Lew Gluxmann, which ultimately erupted some years later into one of the greatest Wall Street sensations, was even then in its early stages. It made life uncomfortable not only for me but for a number of other partners and in 1978 I became one of what was known as the 'Gang of Four' who achieved notoriety when we resigned in a body and went up town to join Lazard Frères at Rockefeller Plaza.

Lazard Frères had achieved a reputation as an imaginative and aggressive investment bank under André Meyer. But the years had taken their toll and he had become ill. Michel David-Weill, a descendant of one of the Lazard founding families, had just taken over. He was keen to restore the partnership and it seemed a good idea to him to take some refugees from the Lehman Brothers struggle. This new opportunity gave me the chance to work in a much more attractive climate and I enthusiastically set about trying to develop my share of the business.

An example of the high-powered projects for which bankers get large fees came in the urgent request I received one day from the Lykes family to help find a solution to their problems with a failing steel enterprise called the Youngstown Sheet and Tube Company. Ultimately, after lengthy negotiations with the LTV Corp. and also with the justice department of the US government, Youngstown was merged with the Jones and Laughlin division as part of the massive LTV group. In the process I learned a great deal, and quickly, about the state of the world steel market. Not only was there a slump in demand for steel in the US, but America seemed to be getting left behind in technology and productivity. These were just some of the changes that had landed Youngstown in such trouble.

Banking is very interesting but I was not entirely happy as I missed the day-to-day direct hands-on activity that went with the excitement of running a normal business. In banking you can spend a lot of time spinning your wheels and then have a short period of frenetic activity.

Thus I was intrigued by a conversation I had one night at a dinner party in New York, just as the Youngstown business was coming to a close. I described the problems with which I was wrestling in the US steel industry to a fellow guest, Sir Hector Laing of United Biscuits. He suddenly turned to me and said: 'My God! You may be the person we need. I was talking to the prime minister just the other day and heard her concern as to how she could find someone to get British Steel into better shape. Maybe you're just the man she's looking for.'

3

British Leyland: the Disease

My chat with Sir Hector, about which I wondered, but did nothing, was the second in a number of apparently chance meetings and encounters which, though I did not realize it at the time, seemed to be drawing me inexorably back to Britain and Britain's problems. I had been lucky enough to have had a satisfying career in business – a career which most men would regard as one of accomplishment. I had in my time all the recognition any man could want – chairman of the International Chamber of Commerce, chairman of the American Mining Congress, the Fritz Gold Medal from the American Institute of Mining Engineers (which numbered Marconi and Alexander Graham Bell among its previous recipients), recognition from France for the joint ventures in aluminium undertaken with Amax when I was awarded the Chevalier of the Legion d'Honneur, as well as numerous honorary degrees.

I was healthy and felt in the prime of life. As I told a reporter at the time, 'Some people of my age run after girls. Some take up golf. And some go fishing. But I prefer to go on working, because I feel there is so much yet to accomplish.' And somehow, increasingly, the focus of my attention came to rest on Britain's terrible industrial problems and the thought that I might perhaps make a contribution and be able to help.

The process had started in 1975 – ironically at another cocktail party, this time in London – when I had a chat with Ronnie Grierson of Warburg's. He is a renowned figure in the world of merchant banking, as well as being a director of many enterprises on both sides of the Atlantic, including deputy chairman of GEC. Our conversation naturally drifted round to the escalating problems faced by the Labour government with the country's industry in rapid decline. It all seemed to bear a close resemblance to a bath out of which someone had pulled the plug. The task in front of its newly-created National Enterprise Board, under Sir Don (later Lord) Ryder, looked monumentally daunting. Into this dismal prognosis Ronnie threw the fact that one of the worst of the problems was British Leyland, which, under Lord Stokes, had recently been heading for the plughole at the rate of knots.

Only vast injections of money, a takeover by the NEB and a new chairman, Professor Ronald Edwards, had pulled it momentarily back from the brink. My experiences in and around the car industry in the US, and what I knew of the British scene from my frequent visits here and many business contacts, excited my interest and we discussed together what was wrong at British Leyland and what could be done. Grierson said finally, 'Would you be interested in helping Don Ryder?' To which, as my enthusiasm and imagination welled up, I replied, 'You bet I would.'

Thus it was, in short order, I found myself, first, talking to Don Ryder and offering what help I could, and second, being offered a full-time top executive post at British Leyland (which I really hadn't expected to come so suddenly out of such a brief exchange). In the cold light of reality, I still had obligations to the Amax board and so I had to say that I couldn't just drop everything and come running. However, I agreed to join the board of British Leyland, as it then was, as a non-executive director to advise and counsel as best I could. A monthly, or sometimes more frequent, trip to London therefore became a regular part of my agenda.

You didn't need to be an expert to know that British Leyland was in trouble: a cursory glance at the figures was enough. In the previous year it had lost £123 million and the losses looked as though they were getting worse. There had been 44 major strikes in 1975, losing 8.8 million man hours and 137,000 vehicles. Five years earlier British Leyland had been selling 40 per cent of the cars in the UK, now the figure was below 30 per cent. Toyota could produce 2.3 million cars a year with a workforce of 43,000; BL could only manage 1.9 million yet had a workforce of 170,000. The place was a grim tragedy of low productivity, overmanning, union disputes, obsolescence, lack of investment, and management's inability to cope – all the usual ingredients of failure – into which the government was now proposing to pour £1.5 billion to try to make things better.

Far from being the exception in Britain, the crippled car firm was more the rule. Its troubles were a symptom – if a large one – of the general industrial slide in the mid- to late seventies. My subsequent experiences during four years at British Leyland were to be the foundation for my next three years at British Steel and latterly three more at the Coal Board. At root, each of those industries' problems were broadly the same. They were the nation's problems – as were the solutions – though I fear that, except in the most general of terms, very few of our politicians understood either the questions or the answers.

I have often thought about the British problem and many analyses of these complex matters have been made.

I prefer to think of some of the simpler strands of this involved situation and am attracted by one facet. For years British labour costs were very cheap by international standards. It was cheaper to pay ten men's wages than it was to invest in machinery to do those ten men's work. The low cost of labour in Britain made it very difficult for British management to justify labour-saving investment. When Henry Ford first announced his $5 a day wage everyone thought it was a huge amount of money. But it was linked to the installation of all sorts of devices in production and assembly which substantially reduced the number of men needed to build cars. His competitors were soon forced to do the same – raise wages but still reduce labour costs.

In Britain there seems to have been less incentive to improve efficiency or scrap outdated methods. Jobs proliferated, because the costs were low. I remember on Clydeside before the war, for example, the huge payrolls in the shipyards where teams of men had finely demarcated jobs which required their presence – even though much of their time was spent waiting until another man had carried out his part of the work – as laid down strictly by his union. What is more, no craftsman ever worked on a job without an unskilled mate, whose function was little more than carrying the tools and holding the work while it was being done.

All this was deemed to be acceptable, and was rationalized away, because the cost of labour was so low. In the long stretch of full employment we had had since the early 1950s firms had taken it even further by, I suspect, starting to hoard people. Maybe they grew to be like tribal chiefs of old, who measured their wealth in the number of slaves they had. British employers came to measure their wealth in the number of people they had on the payroll. Indeed there was apparently good reason for this.

In a full-employment and low-efficiency economy people were the limiting factor on production. If you couldn't get the people, you couldn't produce the goods. Instead of looking for more efficient ways of doing the job – by investing in labour-saving equipment – these low labour costs, low economic incentives and low tax incentives to invest, coupled with the general spirit of the fully-employed society in which we lived, all served to preserve the status quo. The tendency was to hoard the people for a rainy day while in the meantime their numbers showed how prosperous your company was.

Consequently, throughout the years that we were slowly falling behind the rest of the industrialized world in efficiency, the problem was masked by the fact that our labour was so cheap. A German factory with modern machines and fewer people being paid higher wages could just about be matched by an outdated British factory with more people on lower wages.

All this came to a shuddering halt with the oil crisis and the consequent inflation of the 1970s. One of the first effects of inflation was that, justifiably, wages went up. The second thing it did was to erode capital and savings. The effect was particularly devastating to our manufacturing industries. British companies' labour and other costs escalated in the late seventies by three or four times as much as those of German and Japanese campanies, and they died like flies.

British Leyland was just one of hundreds of companies trapped in the vice of inflation; squeezed on the one side by their inability to afford ever-increasing wage demands, and, on the other, by their inability to invest in the capital required to survive because of the erosion of their savings. Whereas, for years, it had been difficult to justify investing in capital projects to use labour more efficiently, now companies could not afford to. They were able neither to retain, nor to generate, enough capital to make the desperately needed new investments.

Within a few years, for example, the white goods industry virtually vanished – it became almost impossible to walk down a British high street and find a fridge, or a washing machine, or a cooker that had been made in Britain. We were now experiencing the devastating effect of hoarding all that labour instead of investing capital in new products or processes. No longer could we survive as a labour-intensive economy. Instead we had to begin the slow and painful change to a capital-intensive economy. The change was imperative. There was no way the King Canutes of labour and industry could stop the inexorable tide.

I remember attending a conference of dump trucks operators in Harrogate in the early 1980s and, incidentally, sharing the platform with Joe (later Lord) Gormley, who had just retired as miners' leader. In an analysis of the effects of inflation some of them offered the example of a 20-ton dump truck bought five years earlier for £25,000. If an operator made a profit out of the work he did for the Coal Board, who paid him to use it, he could get his £25,000 back in depreciation allowances in five years. Alas, by that time the useful life of the truck would be over. It would be virtually worn out and would have to be replaced. Our operator would have his £25,000 in depreciation allowances, but when he went to buy a new truck he would find that inflation had put the price up to £60,000! The only way for him to stay in business would be to go into debt to get the extra money to replace his truck. That was the nature of the problem that faced individuals and companies. The only way to survive was to use savings or to borrow to maintain the capital he originally owned.

The situation was, of course, made worse by the innate

conservatism of the country and the resistance to change shown at most levels. This was born principally out of an almost complete failure to understand what was going on. Unfortunately, many of the people who lost their jobs were, in my view, victims first of a world recession and of these rapid changes in circumstances, and the total failure of many businessmen and politicians either to understand them, explain them or, most importantly of all, do anything about them. Among the few who grasped the general outline of the nature of the threat of inflation, only Margaret Thatcher seemed to understand what it was all about. Too few of our leaders in politics and the Labour movement, even in business, realized what had caused the damage as high-cost Britain rapidly lost its place in the shrinking world markets of the early 1980s. Most of them buried their heads in the sand and either blamed someone else or pretended it wasn't happening while they waited for it to go away.

That imperative switching from a labour- to a capital-intensive society meant my involvement, for the first time in my life, in the shedding of jobs on a large scale, rather than their creation. It was difficult because, on the one hand, I understood and sympathized with the cruel problems of those we had to let go, and I worked hard to ensure that the terms under which they went were as generous as they could possibly be, but, on the other hand, it was my job to ensure the survival of the industry and therefore these changes had to be made as urgently as possible.

In California, where the two vast continental plates rub together, there is a great crack in the earth's surface known as the San Andreas Fault. Most of the time, as these two plates move slowly against each other, nature accommodates the changes between them with a number of small slips and minor tremors. These do not alarm and create only the minimum of fuss and disturbance. But sometimes these minor movements stop and a blockage builds up. Then vast underground distortions take place and pressures build up before the whole thing clears with a big bang – in other words, a major earthquake.

The change from a labour-intensive to a capital-intensive economy taking place in our society over the last decade or so has demonstrated a similar San Andreas effect. The change is inevitable for many reasons. No politician or union boss can order those pressures to disappear. Attempts to resist it can only result in a bigger bang when the pressures finally break through to a new and different economic balance. It was my job to try and manage the change – to be a sort of midwife to it – in such a way as to ensure it caused the minimum of discomfort. And also, where these blockages seemed to be building to intolerable pressure, to find a way of clearing them.

Three principal factors impeded us, and still do, in dealing with the problems – all of them interrelated.

First: government intervention can only delay change and confuse the issue. By intervening and by subsidizing the shipbuilding industry, for example, the government helped delay essential change, and that delay ultimately saw the industry so dependent on aid that, once the support was withdrawn, it virtually disappeared. British Leyland and British Steel both very nearly went that way too, but strong efforts to eliminate the inefficiencies that had required them to be financially supported may have saved them now.

Until the Thatcher government forced rigorous efforts to stamp out waste and inefficiency in the running of those companies, the money pouring in was, in effect, delaying the day of reckoning, preserving the illusion that we could go on hoarding labour and using it inefficiently without considering the economic realities of the situation.

Nationalized industries were created by well-meaning people, but are, in the main, inefficient, overmanned and heavily dependent on public funds. Mrs Thatcher has been right to seek to make them more responsive and efficient and to seek to keep them that way by privatizing them. Even a good socialist like President Mitterand of France now wants to turn many of his nationalized industries back to private ownership – to reduce the drain they have imposed on the public purse. But they can only be sold off when they are in profitable shape, or near enough so for people to want to invest their hard-earned money in them. Far from being the 'family silver', as one articulate but perhaps ingenuous politician described them, most of them are – or were until recently – family millstones, dragging down not only themselves but also the whole economy.

Nor can you build walls to keep change out. One of the more appealing and wistful ideas politicians suggest is to erect tariff barriers to keep out cheaper foreign goods. The danger is that if you use such devices to protect, say, the British car industry, which is not as competitive as some of its foreign rivals, thus perpetuating some of the overmanning and lack of efficiency, you may only be putting off the day when you will ultimately have to come to terms with the cost to the public of that protection.

Second: Britain has always had a world reputation as a nation of administrators – indeed our former colonies bear testament to this. But I am by no means sure that we can claim the same respect as a nation of managers. One of the most enlightening experiences I ever had was in Council House Street, in Calcutta, in the early 1960s.

I was taken there by an Indian friend to be shown a building like a huge warehouse, which was six or seven storeys high with a vast room on each floor. It was furnished like an examination hall with row upon row of desks and a sort of dais at one end with bigger desks on it where people could clearly supervise what was going on. But these people were not invigilators of that sort – they were taxmen. At each of the hundreds of individual desks there was an in-tray and an out-tray with a dozen or so manila files each bound with pink ribbon. 'There you are,' my Indian friend laughed as I gazed at the sight. 'Britain's most important legacy to India – red tape!' That moment came back to me many times in later years when I came face to face with the numbing realization that the British penchant for administration may have swamped its ability to manage.

Administration is the perpetuation of existing systems and the status quo. It is the essence of management to change and to improve things; management has to seek efficiency, identify the need for change and have the will to effect it. Administrators, by their nature, do not make changes; they set up a committee to consider them. Perhaps the greatest postwar manifestation of the growth of administrators was in the field of personnel and industrial relations. Whole new departments were set up whose job it was to administer relations with the workforce and the unions. They were full of worthy people who saw it as their role to attempt to accommodate the union hierarchy in order to achieve the compromises necessary for smooth and continuing administration. In fact, the growth of these personnel and industrial relations departments too often meant that management was willing to abdicate a large measure of its responsibility for communication with and the efficient direction of the workforce.

Between the people who made the management decisions and the men who were expected to carry them out there now emerged the IR department. It also became increasingly convenient for management to communicate with their employees through union representatives, so that the important chain of communication became further distorted, diffused – and finally ineffective in many cases.

The growth of the role of the union hierarchy in an enterprise naturally encouraged the development of the union's function, so it set itself up in the business of communicating and interpreting to the workforce what it claimed it knew the management was up to. Not only did the management gradually lose touch with their individual employees but also their intentions were increasingly distorted and sometimes wilfully misrepresented to them. The real tragedy was that the management's junior arm, the foremen and the overseers who had to get the job done – the NCOs, if you like – were often left out of the system of communications and frequently remained completely in the dark. Their personal dignity and morale was steadily eroded as a result of being the last to know anything. To protect themselves, it is not surprising that they too organized unions – despite the fundamental conflict of interest that this led them into – further adding to the chaos and further increasing the numbers and authority of IR people needed to administer it all.

The final stage in this process arrives when the industrial relations administration becomes paramount and it becomes compelling for the company, through its IR department, to have good relations with the unions, as an end in itself – irrespective of the compromises on economics or efficiency which may have to be made to achieve it.

At British Leyland there was a classic case of this. Pat,

now Sir Pat, Lowry, chairman of the Advisory, Conciliation and Arbitration Service, had devoted most of his
life to achieving the desired harmony in this field. Pat was
a very decent and sympathetic man, who had risen to be
IR director of British Leyland. He had under him an array
of people doing all the functions described above. Pat,
I was told, enjoyed an excellent reputation with the
workforce. Financial crisis in the company followed financial crisis and from where I stood it seemed that the whole
company might be going down the drain. We were also
having almost daily strikes. Yet I believe that Pat's paramount duty to maintain good relations with the workforce made it almost impossible for him to make much
progress in getting them to perform better.

In nationalized industries there are always demands
from external forces that the management have 'good
industrial relations'. At the hands of ambitious or ideological union leaders, such pressure may make the task of
management almost impossible. Questions can be asked
in the House of Commons and a determined and dedicated ideological union leader can easily put pressure on
the management of a nationalized industry by implying
that the unwillingness of the management to fall into line
and concede to his demands is 'creating bad industrial
relations'.

Thus the poor devil in charge feels the heat and sees
the recognition by the nation of a lifetime's successful
administration slipping away from his grasp, just because
he has had the temerity to say 'no' to some absurd demand
from some sanctimonious union official who can easily
project what is 'good for his boys' as sweet reason in the
face of uncaring and obdurate management. It is not hard
to see how these pressures may produce decent and
well-intentioned compromises today – at the expense of
tomorrow's reality.

Third: the unions are also responsible for helping to prevent the inevitable change, particularly when their leaders are suspicious of anything that might undermine their power. A reduction in their membership, as is often caused by these changes, is just such a threat to them. The number of members is critically important to a union: starting with the simple arithmetic of union dues and the revenues they supply, which enables it to maintain a strong permanent staff. But reduction in membership also affects a union's power in the higher councils of the movement such as the TUC. Indeed membership of these higher councils – and through them impact on the Labour Party – depends not so much on money (though that helps) but on numbers, which mean votes.

In many cases unions had merely expanded to fill the vacuum created for them by the gap between management with their IR departments and the workforce. The unions assume great power as principal communicators with the workforce and take it upon themselves to criticize the management freely. As in the case of some nationalized industries, unions claimed – and were given – a voice in the direction of the enterprise. This, I believe, leads to power without responsibility. For thirty years, in an expanding economy, union leaders had succeeded on the basic and very simple premise that their members were automatically entitled to a living. Why not? It seems perfectly reasonable to persuade your members to support you as their leader, on the strength of this premise – especially when you could invariably demonstrate that it was indeed so by successfully threatening the profitability, and in some cases even the survival, of the company.

The fact that this attitude helped ease this great nation down the slippery slope in the process was not a union concern. The times tended to prove them right. From 1946 to 1976 union power always seemed to come out ahead. Those who had the temerity to stand in their unions' way for any length of time paid an enormous price. When change inevitably came, it was difficult for that arrogance to give way to reality. Defeat was not a word they were very used to, nor retreat a response to which they were accustomed.

But while success and power can breed arrogance, they can also provide opportunities for the unscrupulous, the dishonest, and even the evil, to use their power to gratify their own needs. Sometimes these needs can come from straightforward personality problems, quirks in a man's make-up; a need to be seen and to impose his will on others. Sometimes this springs from an inverted inferiority complex, sometimes just from the wish to excel, or to be noticed, or to perform.

There is a type of man who needs to perform, who needs a stage, who needs an audience and who needs applause. Not all are actors or pop singers or politicians. Some are union leaders. It is an understandable human urge to want to express oneself through demonstration – in other words, to occupy the centre of the stage.

But political motivation can also be a driving force and there were those who saw it as their role in the union movement to find a way to destroy the present economic system. The whole ragbag from Marxists to anarchists could be found in union leadership by the early 1970s. And the most dangerous of all were those who combined both these drives – the craving to be a star plus the desire to destroy. They wanted to achieve a new era through the destruction of the present system and were usually able to operate from the centre of admiring and loyal coteries. They were contemptuous of the union rules and cared little for the true interests of their oft-vaunted 'working-class' members, whom privately they respected only as the source of the power which helped them achieve their political ambitions. The workers, sometimes misled and exploited, whose uncritical loyalty to their union was often blind, could easily become mere cannon fodder in the supreme battle of the 'working class' with the bosses. Defeat was simply not in the vocabulary of these union leaders and retreat was impossible.

At all levels of society there has been a widespread failure to understand this sea change that is taking place as we move from a labour- to a capital-intensive economy, and, understood or not, an equally widespread failure to accept it. As I have said, government, until Margaret Thatcher, failed to understand it. Large parts of the Civil Service, if they understood the problem, failed to accept it. Managements, if they understood it, frequently had neither the human nor the financial resources to deal with it. Union leaders, with a very few outstanding exceptions, have neither understood it nor been willing to accept it. No wonder we ended up with over three million poor souls unemployed. They are the real victims. And the greatest lie of our age is that Mrs Thatcher's policies are designed to destroy British industry and the workers. They are exactly the opposite; the only attempt even being contemplated – let alone being made – to save both it and them. They represent enormous changes. Perhaps what is really surprising is that, with such reactionary forces attempting to stand in the way of the changes, so much has been accomplished so far with so little distress and so little social and political unrest.

British Leyland was one of the first industries to go through this traumatic change. As labour costs soared, so the prices of the cars rose. Customers began to turn away when they found they could buy virtually the same thing elsewhere – even cheaper, because it had been made by fewer people, being paid lower wages and using more efficient machinery. Between 1975 and 1980 British labour costs went up by around 80 per cent, whereas those in Germany went up by only 13 per cent and the Japanese actually went down by 1 per cent. In addition, whereas the Japanese were producing something like forty cars per man per year, Leyland could only manage around ten.

BL's labour problems were so bad that the company and its products became the joke of the nation, contributing hugely to the impression throughout the world that British quality craftsmanship had disappeared and British industry was almost permanently strikebound. Morale at British Leyland was extremely low. There was no sense of mission or of urgency about the place. It was generally assumed that things would go on as they were indefinitely. Whatever was happening in the rest of the world, the feeling was that the company would somehow muddle through and go on forever. The executives seemed well motivated, but harassed and distracted from their proper function by the endless stoppages and the constant round of industrial relations' meetings.

At my first board meeting I asked what Pat Lowry and his staff could do about it. I thought he seemed resigned to all this hassle and he more or less shrugged his shoulders and explained to me, as a newcomer, that it was endemic and there really wasn't much the company could do about the troublemakers. I related the experience I had had in the US car industry and suggested that he might institute a system of publicly keeping records of the problems stirred up by some of the more hot-headed union shop stewards. If he hadn't already arranged it, I believe he may have taken this suggestion to heart, because use of 'the record' was I think to prove beneficial when the problem of 'Red Robbo' arose.

Nevertheless, the general attitude seemed to indicate that management had been forced to abdicate much of the right to manage, and that the resolution of the constant flow of grievances could only be achieved through endless rearguard actions and management concessions – with very little contribution to shop-floor peace coming from the unions. Too many shop stewards suffered from the wrecker syndrome – a few with the theatrical overtones thrown in such as are demonstrated at their most dangerous in Arthur Scargill. Derek 'Red' Robinson was certainly no shrinking violet and, as chairman of the shop stewards at Longbridge when Michael Edwardes set about trying to bring some sense to British Leyland, he continued his long record of creating considerable trouble.

British Leyland's problems in 1975, however, were further exacerbated by its ageing range of cars. It had nothing new to compete with the growing Japanese and European invasion. The Marina, the Allegro, the Maxi and the Princess had all been around for several years and none of them was a totally satisfactory car. Great hopes were pinned on the new Rover, but I was afraid that it was going to be a disappointment. The hatch-back styling might have been the craze of the moment, but there didn't seem to be enough legroom in the back – essential for an executive fleet car, which was, after all, supposed to be the target market for its sales.

My first visit to Land Rover left me with two sentiments: respect and concern. Respect for the dedicated craftsmen who laboured skilfully to put it together, literally piece by piece; and concern because I could not see how you could go on paying them for that kind of work and keep the vehicle at a price people would want to pay.

The sports cars – MG and Triumph – were also low-volume, high-cost models. It was doubtful whether they could continue to hold a place in the market either inside or outside the UK. In addition, the TR7 plant at Speke, near Liverpool, had proved, alas – like so many other factories set up in or near that city – to be an industrial relations nightmare. On some Mondays the absenteeism was more than 30 per cent. Productivity was low and the quality often so poor that the body shells had to be completely reworked before final assembly in Coventry. Even Jaguar, the former jewel in what was now a crown of thorns, looked like falling from its setting, so bad were its after-sales mechanical problems.

Shortly after I joined the British Leyland board I was buttonholed by Randall Pearson, then president of Pepsi Cola, at a party in Greenwich, Connecticut. He told me how his wife had recently been driving her Jaguar home one night in the rain on the busy Merritt Parkway, when suddenly all the car lights had gone out. She had managed not to panic and to get the car out of the traffic and on to the verge, where she had sat shivering with shock until she was rescued. Somebody had gone to a lot of trouble to persuade Pearson to buy a Jaguar but, along with thousands of others, he swore he would never buy a second one. I asked at a board meeting soon afterwards how much British Leyland were paying out on warranty repairs for Jaguars and the figure was astronomical. But that inquiry may have started Jaguar on the long road back to trying to restore its reputation for quality.

Alex Park, who was chief executive of British Leyland, was charged with implementing the famous, but probably too optimistic, 'Ryder Plan' for British Leyland, but he was having trouble grappling with the sheer magnitude of the problems. Sir Ronald Edwards, the non-executive chairman when I arrived (who sadly died soon after), did not have the chance to give the strong guidance required. Again I was asked if I could take some form of full-time executive role, but once again I could not abandon my commitments and leave Amax. However, I did talk to Lord Ryder about possible alternative candidates and I was able to help him recruit Sir Richard Dobson to take Edwards's place. I also agreed to try to give more of my time to British Leyland. I ended up working with Sir Richard and took part in a sort of unofficial support group which met before each board meeting to help Alex Park resolve some of his, essentially personnel, problems.

Alex Park was the victim of a situation which would have been difficult for even the toughest man to handle. He was too nice, much too much of a gentleman, and in a way his previous financial career had sheltered him from the ruthless and tough decisions which he, as chief executive, had to face in the car-making business. The pressure on him was also greater because by this time the Labour government were showing signs of becoming increasingly concerned about Leyland's continuing downward spiral in competitiveness and market share, as well as their increasing costs. In the atmosphere of post-IMF realism, I presume even a Labour government realized that British Leyland's increasing requirements from the taxpayer's pocket could not be politically sustained.

Then things changed dramatically, precipitated by Lord Ryder's sudden resignation from the NEB in July 1977 and the appointment in September of Sir Leslie Murphy as chairman. A few days after he had started, I received a transatlantic call from Sir Leslie. He asked me if I could arrange to spend some time with him in the UK. Although I was at the time quite busy with Amax affairs, I agreed to meet him the following weekend. I spent most of Saturday with him and gave him my impressions of the state of British Leyland, the management and the board.

He decided that we should meet some of his NEB directors. We had lunch the next day with the late Bill Duncan, who was then a senior director of ICI and an acquaintance of mine from Greenwich, Conn., when he had headed ICI in the USA. It was agreed that it was appropriate to try to help Alex Park by getting hold of a strong, aggressive, 'hands-on' executive, while Alex continued to try to hold together the steadily worsening financial situation. Several names were discussed, but only when Bill Duncan reminded us that recently one of the NEB directors had been named 'Executive of the Year' did I react, because I realized he was referring to Michael Edwardes, the chief executive of Chloride. I was well aware of Edwardes's prowess as a tough, uncompromising chap. I had heard graphic accounts of his management conquests from my retired brother, a life-long officer of The Chloride Company.

Thus a campaign was started to woo Michael Edwardes to take on the task of deputy chairman and chief executive of British Leyland. I undertook, among others, to talk to him. Our most important meeting took place in the first-class lounge at the Air France terminal at Kennedy Airport in New York. I was going in one direction and he in another, so we sat down in a quiet corner to talk things over. It was clear straightaway that Edwardes reckoned we had a tough set of problems at British Leyland and that it was going to be even tougher for us to entice someone to step into what he recognized was a real can of worms. I remember suggesting to Edwardes that if he had the confidence in his own capabilities that I expected of a man classed as 'Executive of the Year', he must recognize the British Leyland task as the opportunity of a lifetime. This was no humdrum advancement in his career but a chance to show that he really was the tops. I speculated that success would probably see him recognized in the usual way by a grateful government, Civil Service and populace at large.

Edwardes's reaction encouraged me. I reported to Leslie Murphy that I thought he was really interested and suggested he should follow it up. While Murphy was keen to get on with management changes, the hurried timetable for Edwardes's transfer to British Leyland which he had in mind was further shortened from weeks to days when very soon afterwards Sir Richard Dobson made his now celebrated speech to a private club dinner in London.

Sir Richard, a wonderful man but with some frankly controversial views, included what he regarded as some witty, rather personal remarks in a speech on the problems of British Leyland. He had the misfortune to be tape-recorded by the son of a member of the club who was attending in place of his father. This young man took the liberty of sharing the confidence of the tape with some less tolerant activists at college, and soon those remarks were broadcast far and wide, to the embarrassment of Sir Richard's employers, the government. By Friday he was handing in his sword with apologies to his minister. After a frantic weekend completing the recruitment of Michael Edwardes, on Monday morning British Leyland had a new chairman and chief executive.

Within days the board was reconstituted. As is so often the case in modern American-style management, the executive officers, apart from the chairman and chief executive, no longer had board seats. Two new non-executive directors, Austin Bide from Glaxo, and Albert Frost, who had just retired as chief financial officer of ICI, joined Edwardes, Sir Robert Clarke and myself. I took on the post of deputy chairman. There are many arguments about running an enterprise like this, but I have always felt that it speeds up decisions and, provided the non-executives monitor the situation closely, it gives the chief executive more freedom to act. It was clear to Edwardes that he should lose no time in dealing with British Leyland's overheads, and should do something immediately about getting the labour relations situation under control and speeding up the programme of new models which was already under way.

He set about his task with vigour and, by and large, did a very good job. But some credit for his success must be given to the unique quartet of board members who were able to lay down clear guidelines and support for him and his management. When it came to major decisions, they very firmly participated in setting goals. The 'Red Robbo' crisis was just such a confrontation. The board had made clear to Edwardes from the day he took the job that some issues would have to be met head-on or the enterprise would not get anywhere. Edwardes had a mandate to get the union problem straightened out and not to be afraid of confrontation if that was the only way of restoring sound policies and practices. He was to try to persuade them, but if they were not willing to be persuaded he had to have the courage to face up to them, and to what would no doubt be the agony of achieving proper productivity. It was a crisis situation.

As the story unfolded it was a good job that the board had some tough characters on it, for Edwardes continued to need a lot of support when the going got rough. For example, when it was decided to close Speke, which, after years of aggro and no apparent improvement in plant attitudes, had become a large financial wound in the side of the company, Edwardes had to explain the decision first of all to Eric Varley, the industry secretary, and then to James Callaghan, the prime minister. This was an important, crisis decision for a Labour government. Only brave and well-briefed Labour politicians could possibly agree to such a closure. Edwardes would need to have good arguments to go in with. At the board meeting beforehand the directors were completely firm and several suggested a key point to make – notably that the continued existence of Speke was in a way an insult to the other good British Leyland people of the Midlands, who were beginning to cooperate, were working reasonably well, and were trying to get out a good product.

Later, in 1979, the board intervened again when the 'Edwardes Survival Plan' to combat BL's last huge crisis was announced – a plan which involved shedding 25,000 more jobs, the final scrapping of Triumph and MG and a further all-round cost-cutting exercise, just to hold the situation until the new models (Metro, Maestro and Montego) could come in. He planned to negotiate with the unions for the acceptance of his proposals, but the board were keen that he should write directly to the workforce, to point out the true facts and that the company was in the gravest of danger. He was also to explain his plan and to poll the workers' response to it, asking them to vote for it even though it was clear that some would lose their jobs as the company tightened its belt.

I can't say there was universal enthusiasm for this idea. The IR people had severe reservations and assured us that the union officials would be horrified. But in the event it seems clear that the direct approach saved the day. Eighty per cent of the workforce responded and of them 87.2 per cent were in favour of the plan, thus taking the wind out of the sails of the more reactionary trade union officials who, predictably, wanted to stop it.

The remaining opposition came from some of the more militant shop stewards, and by all accounts only a small number of them. It was at the November board meeting that we first got news that they were showing their hand. Pat Lowry sent in a note to Edwardes stating that a leaflet was being distributed at the main Longbridge plant calling on the workers to sabotage the plan. It was signed by four shop stewards – including 'Red Robbo'.

This sudden news of a revolt jolted both Edwardes and Lowry, neither of whom came up with any suggestions as to what should be done next. Derek Robinson and his pals were planning to overturn months of work and the democratic wishes of the workers, and to undermine the last chance for the company to survive – but there was nothing either of them could apparently think of that would stop him and his associates.

Albert Frost and I found ourselves drawn into conversation in a corner of the small boardroom. It seemed we were of like-mind that Robinson and his ilk were throwing down the gauntlet. We decided that this should not be seen as a conflict between personalities and that perhaps it was best that the board, not Edwardes, should be seen to pick it up. The issue at stake was a challenge to the management of the company – and that was clearly the board's concern, not the management's. If decisions had to be made which could jeopardize the survival of the company at this stage in its difficult history, then the board had to be involved and had to be decisive. The board had to insist that the management had the right to manage, otherwise there was no way it could recommend any further infusions of money from the government. Therefore it should, and indeed did, instruct Edwardes to sack Robinson.

I suspect Michael Edwardes was somewhat relieved that the board was prepared to make such an issue out of its responsibility for management. We were aware that failure in this could lead to the liquidation of the business, but we did not believe that, with the results of the poll so much in favour of the plan, there could really be that much lasting support for Robinson – especially, as it subsequently emerged, since his dossier contained a long history of disruptive activities at Longbridge.

Michael Edwardes was pushed very hard that day. The board had to take over the responsibility for two reasons. First, because the issue was who had ultimate control of the business, and second, because, while a lot had been done in his first two years, we were very conscious of the contracting field of options open to British Leyland. The company was still going downhill at a fast clip. I was convinced about what we should do. You can go on trying to sell your policies to the unions and their members, but when push comes to shove you have to reassert the fundamental right to manage. At British Leyland I got my first glimpse of the extent to which that right had been let slip and had to be won back after years of decline and abdication. The problem was to be precisely the same at the Coal Board – we had to reassert the right to manage – only then the struggle was far tougher.

I have great respect for Edwardes's achievements – even though we disagreed during our time together on some fundamental points. Strains developed in our relationship and I was sad that, when it was announced I was to go to British Steel, he felt I should leave the board. But I learned once again that he, like many high-fliers, seemed to be of the opinion that 'if you are not with us – you are agin us'.

In the end he too left BL in 1982. When he did so, he left a company which had seen much improvement but still perhaps did not have as strong a management as I would have hoped. I fear, as I write this, that competitive and political pressures will cause its troubles to begin all over again.

To survive in the 1980s as a volume car-maker you have to have three ingredients. A car designed for good performance and high reliability. A car which can be built at a cost competitive with any of the others around. And, lastly, a large enough base market to sell it in. BL will be hard pressed to do the first two of these in the next generation of cars without huge injections of cash from somewhere. BL's share of the British market alone is not big enough – BL's mass-market competitors are world competitors and BL has not even achieved a sufficient role in the European market to joust with the Fords, GMs, Volkswagens, Renaults and Fiats. It seems to make sense to make common cause with Ford, General Motors or one of the Japanese companies who might at least be able to help it survive. GM were doing what appeared to make economic and market sense in the deal that the government was forced to abandon in spring 1986. In our modern, highly industrialized democracy there are not many who really know much about these complicated subjects and the public statements on the subject all too frequently come from emotion rather than hard reason. Fewer and fewer people – least of all many of the politicians – know how the world production and economic system works, yet more and more think they can dictate how things should be done.

4

British Steel: the Cure

The public is almost completely ignorant of what goes on behind the veil put up by those industries in receipt of state funds – whether nationalized or not. We are hardly privy at all to the secrets of what they do with our money, let alone what it is intended to accomplish and how. Yet, with such large amounts of cash leaving our pockets to keep some of these enterprises going, everyone seems to feel he has a right to have a say about them. That goes for government, opposition, civil servants and many members of the public.

I think the present government probably has the best answer for these industries – each of them should be put as quickly as possible on a sound economic footing, then freed from the frequently contradictory pressures they attract from government, opposition, and various sections of the public. In recent years I have gone straight from one publicly owned industry to another, perhaps becoming a victim of the Don Quixote syndrome. The affairs of each of these businesses has become for me the next windmill at which to tilt.

When the call came it seemed natural that I should take the job at British Steel. BL taught me several important lessons – most notably that the British working man is not necessarily a bolshie, nor an anarchist. He is a good operator and if he can be led positively, with his talents effectively harnessed, he can compete with anyone in the world.

But sometimes when things get badly out of kilter, when the crisis mentality is so deeply ingrained and when the economic problems seem at their very worst, an organization or a country needs an inspiration. A gesture has to be made that transcends the problem and gives everyone new hope. When I arrived at British Steel in May 1980 the situation was pretty bad. BSC had just come through a complete stoppage which had lasted more than three months during which the market-hungry European steel industry had swamped the UK with its product. The settlement to the dispute, which gave the workers a massive increase in wages, was one of those British compromises which merely increased the problems of British Steel. It substantially increased costs and made our price disadvantage far worse – already affected by the rising value of the pound against European currencies. I had thought things were pretty bad at BL, but BSC, in addition to being a high-cost producer, had lost a lot of its market in just a few months. As I began to get the feel of this depressed and demoralized management group, I thought I could see the need in Britain for what I called a 'Queen Mary' gesture – something which would give everyone, not only in BSC but in Britain too, some hope and inspiration.

I remembered my days during the Depression on Clydeside. When I was attending university in Glasgow there were parades into the centre of the city made up of all those sad figures of the unemployed. In those days unemployment threatened families with total poverty and deprivation. Few who were not trapped in that holocaust can really appreciate the utter devastation of those times. The symbol of this human tragedy was to be seen dominating the landscape of the Clyde valley near Clydebank. Standing several floors high above the Clydeside tenements for all to see was the nearly completed but rusting hull of what was meant to be a proud symbol of Britain's domination of the seas and shipbuilding. It was John Brown hull number 534. But, come the Depression, it had been abandoned and lay there as a monument to the collapse of the economy. Then, when continual gloom seemed to be all that could be predicted, it was suddenly announced that the government was going to lend the shipowner Cunard the money to finish it. I think the credit required was astronomic at the time – the figure of £9 million comes to mind. The SS *Queen Mary* was finally launched in 1935. The psychological boost that gave the whole region was incalculable – it was proof, visible for miles around, that the recession was over even if the reason for the rush was the shadow of impending conflict in Europe.

As we began slowly to make progress with the vast problems at Steel, my mind turned to the need for such a gesture for the 1980s. But when I ran into it, and had to fight it, I came to realize that the power of innate conservatism which pervades all institutions, not only the unions, but the very establishments of government too, also contributes to the national malaise.

I don't know if Sir Hector Laing followed up his suggestion at that party in New York, or whether my appointment to Steel came through some contacts I had with James Prior (whose son worked with me at Lazard's in New York) when he was employment secretary – or whether it was Sir Keith Joseph's own idea, as he must have known of the part I played at BL; but I do know that shortly afterwards I was approached by David Norman of Russell Reynolds Ltd, who had been entrusted with the task of finding the right man to succeed Sir Charles Villiers as chairman of British Steel. An appointment was made for me to see Sir Peter Carey, the permanent secretary at the Department of Industry, on my next visit to London. The interview quickly expanded to include Sir Keith. He struck me as ascetic and reserved – but I found him very straightforward and understandable and we quickly developed an empathy with each other. In all the time of our relationship, I found him to be an intelligent, warm and easy person to work with.

I suppose that my career, as well as my recent UK exposure, may have impressed them – right up to my recent experiences with J. & L. and Youngstown Sheet and Tube – because it wasn't long before I heard that they were willing to negotiate with me.

It was then that matters became complicated. The management consultant had suggested that the new Tory government was going to be prepared to pay salaries and match terms and conditions that commercial concerns would have to expect to offer around the world. There was a lot of debate and it soon became apparent that somewhere in the government machine the idea of American-style salaries was vetoed. I quite frankly told the management consultant that I would not cut my connection with Lazard Frères to take on for three years what was obviously a pretty unattractive project for any normal candidate. How otherwise would there have developed so much enthusiasm at the Department of Industry for my candidacy? As one of the government's advisers told me, 'They have plenty of applicants but no candidates.'

I became quite discouraged as it began to look as if the economic terms would be quite inadequate. It was at this point that several of my partners, sensing my keenness to take on the job and the frustration of totally unacceptable financial conditions, came up with an idea which subsequently solved the problem. I owe a lot of gratitude to my Lazard Frères partners, and especially Michel David-Weill in New York, and the great imaginative skill of Ian (now Sir Ian) Fraser who was then chairman of Lazard Brothers in London. Soon all that remained was for Sir Keith's people to convert Ian Fraser's good ideas into a satisfactory arrangement with Lazard Frères and with me so that I could come and serve the three years of my contract on 'lend-lease'.

A great fuss was made at the time about that deal, which, I hasten to add, was struck without involving me at all. People seemed to be blinded by the sum of money involved and the deal was not really made too clear when it was presented in the House of Commons. Poor, honest and brave Sir Keith sat down after making a good try to explain its details. Barry Jones, Labour's shadow employment minister, at once rose to his feet and merely asked: 'Is the Right Honourable Gentleman well?'

Let me explain it. When I retired in 1977 I had put a substantial amount of my capital into Lehman Bros. When I transferred to Lazard's, this capital bought me my partnership in the bank and the return on it provided an important part of my retirement income – but, if I was going to receive a return on my capital, then I was expected, like other partners, to work to 'service' that capital. My capital helped keep the firm running on a day-to-day basis – but there would be no profits unless I went out and helped earn them, which is what each partner does by creating deals and receiving fees for their services.

My partnership in Lazard's had been rewarding to me and I felt a loyalty to them – as well as wanting to keep what was essentially my retirement capital in a company with a good potential for return and income. So, if the British government wanted me to run British Steel for them, I was willing to accept their ideas on salary but Lazard's had to be compensated for the three years I was going to be out on loan from them. After all, if I had worked full time for an American client of Lazard's to overcome some management problem they would expect substantial fees based on the company's performance. The deal finally worked out by Ian Fraser and the Department was based on just these principles. I gave up my full partnership and became a limited partner. Certain targets for British Steel's performance during my stewardship were agreed and a two-part fee would be paid to Lazard's, partly for my yearly service and partly on the basis of a bonus on how well a five-man committee judged the performance of the corporation. At the end of the day the Department paid in bonus to Lazard's a total of £875,000.

I was quite excited at the prospect of taking on the problems at British Steel. I did not feel daunted by them, massive though they were. In a way I felt I was doing something important for my country and that I would have a real chance to tackle some of the underlying difficulties it faced. I was helped in that decision – as I was when I agreed to go to Coal – by the fact that, in the Thatcher government, the country seemed to have at last a leadership which believed in trying to get some of the chronic inefficiencies under control. It also seemed to have some real understanding of the great changes that were taking place and the urgent need for us to respond to them. People presumed Britain was a leading capitalist society – with corresponding advantages – but to me this did not seem to be so. Britain was now quite dramatically poor – excessive dependence on labour in a world where capital investment, education and training had become the keys to ensuring competitiveness and the creation of new jobs.

There was no greater example of this profligate use of

unskilled labour than the British Steel Corporation which had been nationalized, for the second time since the war, by the Labour government in 1968. It had made small profits in the early 1970s and – as with British Leyland – it started to generate larger and larger losses from 1975 onwards, until, in the year I took over, they reached £668 million. Somebody worked out that, at one stage, the taxpayer was paying at the rate of £30 a second to keep the show on the road.

The problems were threefold. First, there had been a worldwide collapse of the steel industry. This was caused initially by the explosion in the cost of energy in the seventies. In 1972 the average price of a ton of petroleum was $15. By 1981 the price had peaked at $250. If you assume that the 1972 price had continued up to 1983, the difference between that and what the free world actually had to pay for its energy was $2.75 trillion. Now that is $2.75 trillion taken out of the world cash flow and directed to the OPEC countries in just a decade. Money which would have normally been spent on growth and development now had to go to pay for the huge increase in the cost of energy.

The principal contributors to OPEC's new wealth – and therefore the very people who paid the price – were of course the big consumers of petroleum, the world's major industrial countries who over the years had evolved a pattern of world trade and development which was the engine for steady and continuous growth. What OPEC did was to take away all the money which had provided the resources for savings, investment, growth and development. When you drain sums of money of that magnitude out of the world's cash flow, the first thing to be abandoned is the normal programme of expenditure on forward growth, development and investment. Sure enough, by the second half of the seventies, there was a worldwide slowdown in forward plans for capital investment to modernize and to build and to expand – the very sector which normally accounts for two-thirds of the world's steel production. There was an enormous shift in resources to the OPEC countries and we no longer had the money to invest in machinery, buildings, and so on.

The second problem was that, at the same time, these vast new OPEC resources which were coming from increased oil prices were being channelled through the major banks in places like New York, London, Paris and Frankfurt into projects in such countries as Mexico, Brazil, Iran and Korea. Much of it went into local consumption but in many cases it went to financing favourite expansion programmes. These often included modern steel mills, for whose products there was a limited immediate local market. Thus we saw many traditional markets for our steel, on which we in Britain and the rest of Europe had depended, now disappear – a problem which was exacerbated because not only did much of that steel have a limited market at home, it was also being made with the latest state of art technology and dramatically lower labour costs. Over these years we found this Third World steel pushing into Europe and North America – and even Japan had problems.

BSC's third problem was the same one that BL had – only worse. In the 1960s British Steel had been a leading producer of steel – and indeed we had invested in much up-to-date plant to produce it. But we had failed to realize the full advantages of the labour savings which should have resulted from the new investments. Efforts to reduce the manpower up to the time when the crisis became more serious were predictably resisted by the unions. In the late seventies the government had taken a very protective role with the unions. They could see a vote vanishing with every job that went, since most of the steel-producing plants were in heavy industrial areas, all of them Labour strongholds.

As if to demonstrate their obduracy and their lack of understanding of the generally disastrous state of the industry, the leadership of the steelworkers' union, the ISTC, had just concluded their destructive three-month strike on the basis of more pay and no redundancies! The management realized that they would have to draw the line somewhere because already the company was completely non-competitive. It seemed of no consequence whatsoever to the unions that BSC had lost £450 million in the previous year and that their wage claim – and those of others – would have added £210 million to the BSC wage bill, £65 million to its coal bill, £25 million to the cost of its electricity, £50 million to iron ore and £100 million to other charges.

Thus, as world markets were declining if not vanishing, and world competition was increasing, the British Steel Corporation conveniently withdrew from the race for three months just when competition had become most fierce. Naturally the sudden disappearance of BSC as a competitor was a godsend to the hard-pressed European steel industry which was glad to service what was left of the UK steel-consuming industry. Not that there was much; for it was the same story in all Britain's traditional labour-intensive industries. One by one the old home markets for steel were collapsing. Shipbuilding went. The heavy railway equipment industry went. The construction industry slumped. Even our consumer goods industries – everything from cars to washing machines – came under intense competition. Few could handle the marketing pressures and the dramatic cost disadvantages. Everywhere British consumer industries were in retreat and the casualties were immense.

The steel industry also had one other particular competitive problem to handle. The Japanese had developed techniques for low-cost, high-quality steel which quickly placed them and their steel-consuming industries at a great advantage. It also enabled Japan to attack markets with costs that completely undermined the rest of us.

Luckily, as I said, we had some modern capacity – largely thanks to my old friend Monty Finniston who had understood the Japanese threat and tried to cause a rebirth of the British steel industry. But we also had much that was outdated, overmanned and often ill-positioned. Monty was not permitted to abandon aged and outmoded sites and he became tangled up in all the compromises that political pressures forced on him. Apart from the initial attempt at Teesside where he had built the first 14-metre, Japanese-style blast furnace, the whole concept was slowly swept away in the flood of claims and counter-claims about where the industry's future lay and the primeval bureaucratic urge to avoid change, risk and uncertainty. Britain was not ready for a Japanese-style revolution.

It was clear to me when I started at BSC that we were not going to be able to solve problems as formidable as these without upsetting quite a few apple carts. The big imponderable to me was not whether we could get BSC right, but how strong was the government's resolve? Were the prime minister and her industry secretary going to be able to carry the rest of the cabinet with them when the going got tough? Fortunately for me, in the initial period at least, she remained absolutely steadfast. I had met her for the first time just before I started the job, when she invited me over to Downing Street for a chat. She came pretty well as advertised: very impressive, very clear, very forceful. Most successful families have one like her. She didn't beat about the bush. In some ways she was like my mother – who always had a clear idea of what she wanted to do. I guess she wanted to look me over too, to make sure I wasn't about to die on the vine, like so many British businessmen who seem to lose their drive very early in life by my standards. She expressed the view that I looked pretty robust for a guy of sixty-seven, so I assured her that I was. I suppose it was a bit like buying a second-hand car – she wanted to make sure the engine was OK and kick the tyres. You've got to give her – and Sir Keith – credit. Appointing me was an act of some political courage.

So I went to work. Within a few weeks I got hold of my old friend Roger Morrison from McKinsey's and with him started a reorganization of the management of the business to give people greater opportunity for achievement. The idea was to decentralize the system and to try to make each plant its own profit centre. Over the years I have seen the success of the policy of decentralizing the tactical decision-making, while still keeping a fairly firm grip on the strategic and policy issues. I have found this type of organization format, if properly done and managed from the top, to have an enormous and crucial effect on morale. Most of my life has been spent in trying to make effective management teams out of the best material available.

My first problem was how to deal with Robert Scholey who had been chief executive under Sir Charles Villiers. But naturally this was the role I envisaged playing – as well as chairman. It was, after all, what I had been taken on for. So he and I sat down to discuss the method of operation. It turned out to be a frank heart-to-heart talk and I learned that Bob had for quite some time been 'always the bridesmaid, never the bride' at the top of BSC and it rankled with him. Here it was about to be repeated all over again and I could understand this fine man's frustrations and disappointments. But slowly we got to know and trust each other and Bob took on what I would call in a US organization the president's job as the chief operating officer. He did it without complaint and never looked back.

I needed Scholey as a right-hand man, as a guide to the ways of BSC – virtually to be the window through which I could look into the organization. I didn't have a lifetime career ahead to work my way in slowly and get to know the people and systems – I had just three years. We were in trouble, action was needed. I must have a four-leaf clover somewhere because I had the good luck to find and work with Jimmy Cowan when I went to the NCB.

The long strike and the enthusiastic help from the European steel suppliers left BSC with a fraction of its former share of the home market. Before we could go anywhere we had to get our share of the British market back. Our European competitors were not going to give up easily. This was a crucial fight.

I went to Madrid in October 1980 for my first meeting of the International Iron & Steel Institute, an international body where steel people from all around the world meet to hear reports on the state of the industry. At this meeting I ran into some of the other European producers and prepared for some tough negotiating with the Germans who dominated Europe, as I found little respect or sympathy for BSC. At one stage, talking with journalists, jokingly I threatened to 'bomb' Essen with steel coils to try to get the Germans' attention and to make them realize that we were serious. Unless we could get at least 50 per cent of our market back quickly there was virtually no future for BSC. It would have been better to liquidate it. We served notice on the Europeans that we were quite prepared and well supported by the British government and would try to re-establish a position in the European market for British Steel at whatever the price.

I figured that such a plan might easily add anything up to £100 million to our losses but if we were prepared to do this and signalled our serious intent to recover our market, it was worth the gamble. The idea got around that since I was a new boy I might well be completely unpredictable, so that even the Germans began to feel it was worthwhile trying to humour the British. In the event we all finally agreed to meet at a conference of Eurofer, the organization set up by Brussels, to stabilize the industry and attempt to work out a basis for a more equitable sharing of the market. It was like playing poker, but it was a worthwhile exercise and BSC made some progress in recovering and re-establishing its place in the market. You have to be prepared to lose if you want to win at poker. If we'd lost BSC would have had a long and desperate struggle to survive.

Dealing with the European steel cartel was not a comfortable experience for me. For forty years I had lived in a society which regarded a cartel as antisocial and ultimately detrimental to the interests of the consumer and the populace at large. Cartels provide, as Adam Smith pointed out, the temptation for some businessmen to exploit the larceny in their hearts. As we have seen in the arrogance of some OPEC attitudes, the cartel delays the inevitable impact of the discipline of market forces. It is the 'San Andreas' syndrome again – in the end, when the cartels fall apart, as happened early in 1986 with tin and oil, the explosion of pent-up forces produces far worse chaos in the market in the long run.

At that first meeting of Eurofer I sat quietly but at the end the chairman remarked on my silence and asked me to comment. So I said: 'If this were in the United States we would all be locked up for trying to fix prices and markets – but here we are sitting with the sanction of our governments. I must say I feel a bit uncomfortable but the image that has built up in my mind is one of a fox getting into the chicken coop but he doesn't seem to be able to identify the chickens!' The most humiliating aspect of the entire negotiations came when each participating company was consulted as to the year most representative of that company's production and market share, which could be used as a model or reference year. Naturally each country fought for recognition of its very best year as a basis for any new arrangement. As I looked over BSC's figures I could not find one which had not been crippled at some time or another by strikes or go-slows in our own industry – or by stoppages of our suppliers or in the transport services.

The moment of truth at BSC came towards the end of my first six months in December 1980 when we had to decide what size of business we thought we were going to be able to sustain. We picked an 'Alamein Line' of 14.4 million tons annual capacity and decided to hold capacity at that and fight off the enemy from there. This meant further slim-lining – 20,000 more jobs to go on top of the 50,000 we had already shed in the year. Immediately after the steel strike the number of man hours it took to produce a ton of steel was up to around sixteen. We simply had to get this down closer to the European levels, which averaged less than half that. We also had to re-trench around our five main plants – Llanwern and Port Talbot in Wales, Ravenscraig in Scotland, Teesside and Scunthorpe on the east coast. If we had believed the then current market figures for demand from our customers represented a permanent change we could easily have gone to a lower figure, like 10 million tons. But we believed the recession would most surely bottom out in 1981 and that we should assume some recovery. The continued existence of Ravenscraig, the weakest in terms of market and competitive cost, was the least able to be justified. The Port Talbot installation of continuous casting would not be operating fully until 1983, so prudence dictated that we continue the Ravenscraig plant for the time being.

Predictably the ISTC were not about to admit that one of the major reasons for these cuts was the disastrous strike they had indulged in the year before – a strike which must go down as one of the greatest lemming runs of all time. Bill Sirs, the ISTC leader, publicly postured as Mr Moderate, but was still an old-fashioned and reactionary union boss. He didn't seem to have much understanding of what was happening in the world around us nor of the dramatic decline which had met the steel industry worldwide. He gave me the impression that we should pursue a major protectionist move to ensure that British Steel would have no competition from abroad and that, thus insulated, the UK would be a safe place for socialists. The efficiency or otherwise of the business was not the concern of his union or its members. There still seemed to be this one conviction that the world well and truly owed him and his boys a living. Before I first met him I bought the book he had written on the steel industry. I took it along and referred to it frequently, until he was arguing round and round in circles. The only point at which he seemed pleased was when I said: 'I've been looking at the BSC accounts and I do not see that the labour costs are the problem they have been made out to be.' They weren't a problem. They were a catastrophe.

Here was a classic case of a union's members being the victims of the leadership's policies. I soon realized that British unions are much more authoritarian than American ones and that they are also much more overtly political. This has two disadvantages for the ordinary member – he has less say in the leadership's decisions and those decisions are more likely to be taken on political grounds than in the immediate interests of the members. We have to look no further than Arthur Scargill to see the extremes that these practices can lead to and the damage they can do to the membership.

When the ISTC leadership decided to ballot against our plans, we already knew it was much discredited among its members as a result of the strike. So we decided quickly to save Bill Sirs the trouble and do it for him, especially as the ISTC represented less than 50 per cent of BSC's unionized employees. Sixty-five per cent of the workforce said 'yes' to our proposals – even though, as at British Leyland, they realized it meant that many of them might lose their jobs.

Similarly, the men also accepted a deferred pay award for the sake of getting things right. The union tried to do a sort of 'one horse, one rabbit' deal on this, which showed yet again how little they understood of what was going on around them. They said they would swap no pay rise for no redundancies. Just as you don't trade a horse for a rabbit, there was no trade here. The interesting thing is that the workforce understood – there is no fun in being associated with a business that is regarded as a public disaster – and they could see this as a way of getting the enterprise back on its feet.

Nevertheless, it was a traumatic time for us all. Fortunately, both at BSC and later at Coal, the government understood how important it was that we should give those who had to go the best possible redundancy terms. In some cases we were able to help those who wanted to set up businesses of their own through our enterprise schemes. Both BSC (Industry) and NCB (Enterprise) had the advantage of providing some opportunity for the redundant worker to stay in his community, and to start a new way to create wealth within it.

I remember, near the end of my time at BSC, going to Llanwern and leaning on a rail watching the pouring of a cast with one of the ISTC local men originally opposed to our plans. As we looked down together over this vast works he said: 'You know, there has been a lot of pain and a lot of hardship and I was dead against it all. But it was done. And now it is all over I don't feel quite so bad about it. It was surely the right thing to do. The whole place is better for it and we got rid of a lot of dead wood.' There is indeed a world of difference between the British working man and many of the union leaders who claim to represent him.

We had two further problems which needed urgent attention – improving the quality of the steel we were producing and cutting our energy costs. The Japanese figure largely in any steelmaker's sleepless nights and in these two areas they were giving us a really hard time. Their continuous offerings of higher and higher specification steel had virtually cornered the North Sea market. The Europeans were hard on their heels. But BSC had a long way to catch up and I felt that we would never succeed unless BSC re-established strict disciplines in quality, yield and specifications.

I questioned how effectively we were controlling our use of energy and I also instituted a task force to achieve better management of the use of energy and scheduling of all operations in our mills. At the same time I persuaded my friend Mr Saito, the chairman of Nippon Steel, to send a group of his best engineers to do a report on how effectively we used our equipment. The result was an interesting commentary on our different cultures. The Japanese engineers said that with a few minor exceptions we were quite well equipped to meet most of the steel specifications in bulk steel production. However, they pointed out that we did not seem to get as good yields.

For every ton of liquid hot iron from the blast furnace we ended up with appreciably less shippable product. When I questioned our Japanese friends closely on this they just shrugged and said that in Japan they were used to much tighter discipline and expected every man to do his task in the best possible way. It saves them a lot of waste as a result.

Our efforts were a bit like trying to stop a supertanker going at full speed – you throw it into reverse and three miles later it stops going forward! Slowly, however, we began to stop the headlong decline into disaster and to look forward to the day when we could actually start getting better costs, less waste, and moving towards profits.

But the problem of Ravenscraig continued to get worse, a situation which was highlighted by the secondary recession of 1982. Our financial figures dipped further and we were faced with having to cut back still more on production. So many of our costs were fixed with our huge establishment and capacity that our break-even point was still much too high and eventually became untenable. The crisis was not exclusive to BSC, it was affecting all British industry. When we told the government that whereas we had thought we could keep Ravenscraig open, it now looked impossible, we were surprised to get clear signals from the Department of Industry that this would make them, the new industry minister and his colleagues most unhappy. They had just suffered the reverse of the Hillhead by-election in Glasgow and I think they already had half an eye on the fact that we were less than a year away from a general election and it would be better if they didn't frighten the voters too much.

The setback in our plans, however, got me thinking about what we could do with Ravenscraig. It was losing money hand over fist. We had to find a way of making better use of it – especially with the Port Talbot caster coming on line and Llanwern getting very good quality in their large hot mill too. It occurred to me that Ravenscraig's ability to produce continuous cast slabs was the only thing really going for it. It was a pity that even in the early boom years of North Sea construction in Scotland, local importers had a field day taking over big pieces of the plate market. We had missed the boat on much of the steel for the early North Sea oil ventures. At the same time Scottish heavy industry was in a major decline in the economic upheaval of the world recession and there were few local markets left for Ravenscraig's products.

Quite by accident I learned that US Steel was wrestling with the problem of its Fairless Works in eastern Pennsylvania where the coke ovens, blast furnaces and steelmaking plant of prewar design but postwar installation were really obsolete. US Steel had figured it would cost at least $2 billion to modernize the works. The thought occurred to me that if we put the product of our relatively efficient, up-to-date Ravenscraig slab casters into the Fairless rolling mills and finishing plant, US Steel would be in a better shape to hold on to and service the market on the American east coast. They had a long record of success here but it was now being threatened by imports.

I put this proposition to Dave Roderick of US Steel and he became quite enthusiastic. It made sense for BSC: we could keep the hot-metal end of Ravenscraig open and 60 to 70 per cent of its workforce in jobs, and have the chance to make a profit on the 3 million tons of slabs we would ship to America each year. It made sense for US Steel: they got good slabs, kept the finishing part of their works open and kept their share of the market. Roderick undertook to have preliminary talks with McBride, one of the leaders of the United Steel Workers of America, and soon reported that he had reached a sort of grudging approval. But then events overtook us. McBride had agreed to have talks with his local leaders to get them to agree to the idea. But he was suddenly taken off to hospital with a heart attack (which subsequently proved fatal), before he had had a chance to contact them.

On this side of the ocean I was only too aware that, as head of a nationalized industry, I was not supposed to go around setting up major international deals like this without telling my minister. It wasn't good form to spring surprises on him, so I brought Patrick Jenkin, the industry minister, in on the discussions. He, Roderick and I even had dinner one evening and he was very interested in the plan. Presumably Patrick Jenkin then briefed his civil servants.

One can only speculate on what happened subsequently – whether someone told the Scottish office, who may in turn have passed it on. Whatever the mechanism, the first thing I knew was a press report that our worthies from the ISTC at Ravenscraig were in touch with their counterparts at Fairless Works in New Jersey. Because of McBride's illness the Fairless men knew nothing about the original discussions. They were asked what they knew about the plans afoot for BSC to take half their jobs away. Naturally within days there was a fearful row, cheerfully stoked by the media. Within weeks the plan was, to all intents and purposes, scuppered and it was left to my successor to lay it peacefully to rest a year later.

What I had talked to Mr Roderick about was a ten-year deal which would have provided long-term security for nearly 70 per cent of the jobs at Ravenscraig and made it, despite currency fluctuations, profitable for many years to come. As it was losing a lot of money – money which has to come out of the public's pocket – it was inevitable that unless there was some magic recovery in Scotland's heavy manufacturing it would ultimately be faced with closure. It was disappointing and very difficult to understand how so many people – unions, civil servants and politicians – rejected the economic realities of the situation. It was tragic to see what was almost a conspiracy of resistance at many levels, both in and out of government.

As a postscript it is interesting to note that several years later BSC entered into an agreement to ship continuous cast slabs to a mill in Alabama. That operation still continues and is regarded by BSC as attractive business even though the annual volume is less than 10 per cent of the numbers we talked of for Fairless.

The incident of Ravenscraig and the US connection did raise a question in my mind. I was reasonably sure of security in BSC – so few of the top people knew of the proposals. How the story got around in Scotland will remain a mystery but I wonder whether all parts of the machinery of government are either as secure or as disinterested as they should be. It is perhaps no mere coincidence that we ran into trouble with the Scottish affair.

Indeed, I was reminded very forcibly of the powers within government a few months ago when I switched on my television one night and saw on the news the sad end of an idea I set in train while I was at BSC. There were the prime minister and President Mitterrand signing the agreement to build a Channel tunnel. I thought of a meeting I had had with her on 16 August 1981, when I had put to her my idea for a symbolic 'Queen Mary' gesture – something which could be seen by all to indicate the nation's will towards economic recovery.

The idea arose from recognition of our need to be

able to penetrate the European steel market – indeed all markets in Europe – much more readily. As we were in a deep recession the time was ripe to take advantage of the idle human and productive resources and to restore the country's infrastructure. What better way than with the long-dreamed-about Channel crossing? BSC then owned Redpath, Dorman Long, a huge historic engineering company – builder of some of the world's greatest bridges including the famous one in Sydney Harbour. We began to work on a proposal for a Channel crossing scheme.

Various ideas for a road crossing were examined. At an early stage it became clear that a bridge across the centre, deep-water channel would have posed great problems, not only during construction but also when complete because of the number of supporting towers which would have to be built in the midst of the vessel lanes. Eventually we settled on a bridge and tunnel combination – similar to the one across Chesapeake Bay in America. We proposed to build viaducts out over the relatively shallow, inshore areas, about half the distance to two North-Sea-oil-like platforms in the middle of the Channel. From these platforms the centre crossing in between consisted of two large steel tubes laid on the sea bed. The proposal would have involved no fundamentally new technological innovation, merely copying a successful installation in the USA. Traffic projections were prepared by expert consultants which showed that the whole scheme could be made to finance itself with appropriate tolls, competitive with any ferry cost projections. The scheme would have kept 250,000 people in construction jobs for five years. Because the fabrication of the steel tunnel parts could be done all over Britain and taken to the site in sections, it would also have avoided the concentration of job opportunities in the southeast of England.

The one major problem was ventilation in the under-water tubular section. A large, third tube was required to supply sufficient fresh air to clear the fumes from the two that vehicles would be using. It looked like a great deal of expense just for perfect ventilation, but the experts were adamant – we had to have it.

Eventually we arranged a preliminary meeting at the Department of Transport to discuss the concept. We saw the minister briefly – but were quickly left with the civil servants. They made it quite clear that there was little likelihood of any crossing being approved that did not have a railway line. The railway lobby showed how powerful it was on both sides of the Channel and we were told that a system without railways would 'not be acceptable to the Department of Transport'. This surprised me – in view of the well-known arrogance of the railway unions on both sides of the Channel who have frequently held their countries to ransom. But, realizing we had powerful and entrenched forces to work with, it was obvious we needed an idea which would deal with this difficulty.

Suddenly it became clear that our third tube would have another function as well as ventilation. As the trains would be electric and intermittent there was no reason why this tube could not be used for them as well, to supplement the highway tunnels and earn the added revenues from railway passengers and freight. This, we were told by our engineers, was perfectly feasible and the idea became a permanent feature of our proposal.

At our 16 August meeting with Mrs Thatcher, Ian Gow, her PPS, and the late Sir John Howard of Howard Doris, I explained all the features of the proposal, to which she made two principal comments. When talking about different possible combinations of crossings the subject of a rail-only system came up, and she immediately said: 'I can't see any solution which involves rail only. I am not going to be in favour of that, because it still leaves the whole country in the hands of the rail, docks' or seamen's unions. This country cannot run the risk of being held up by a handful of people. Under no circumstances will I agree to that.'

Then, when I told her what the cost would be, she said: 'That sounds like an awful lot of money to me – you know the government is not going to put any money up.'

'But, Prime Minister,' I said, 'we're not asking you to. It is totally financeable because it will generate the traffic to pay for itself – unlike the rail-only tunnel solution, which will generate a much smaller amount of traffic, and you will end up having to pay in one form or another. Even if the initial estimate of the cost of construction looks much less there will have to be guarantees of revenues from the rail-users and that will involve the government in supporting the financing from the beginning.'

She was mollified at that and said: 'Well, it sounds very interesting, I wish you every success with it.' And that is where it was left.

Her attitude was what I would have expected. She recognized that if there was going to be a crossing then it would be better to get out from under the power of the transport unions. At that time I didn't even suspect that she too might have some difficulty with her own transport department – though in later meetings with them their attitude towards the Euroroute proposal was a bit like that of the legendary Indiana judge: 'Don't bother me with the sordid details – I've already reached the verdict.'

Eventually I moved on from BSC and, because of the need to be totally preoccupied with NCB problems, I decided to withdraw from the project. The scheme continued to achieve wider and wider support on both sides of the Channel under the chairmanship in the UK of Sir

Nigel Broackes and in France of M. Jacques Meyeux, head of Société Générale and formerly my opposite number as chairman of Sacilor, the huge French steel complex. It was only changed in detail in the intervening four and a half years as its financial prospects became clearer to more of the best-qualified observers in both public and political circles.

Then I saw that fateful and incomprehensible bulletin on the television. It announced proudly that we were going to have a rail-only tunnel and, from the details given, it was clear that the government was almost certainly going to have to be involved in the financing of it.

The decision shocked me. It represented a complete victory for the establishment over the prime minister's sound instincts. The policy on the tunnel's operation will now be subject to the usual union vetoes. This will not always be in the interests of the public and their desire to travel when and how they want. I suspect it will not worry those in the Civil Service involved in making the recommendation, because, being administrators of the status quo, they are quite accustomed to union power with all its demonstrable faults. They have grown to accept it as part of the British way of life. To change the status quo is the worst thing to be contemplated, for that could cause the important political equilibrium to be upset. Change is to be avoided at all costs – no matter how much it may undermine the future public interest. That was why it was quite natural to accept the grasp of the rail unions in place of the present grasp of dockers and seamen as preferable to the freedom of a through road system. To change would create a dangerous precedent and the administrator's nightmare of people actually being allowed to do what they want.

Perhaps this reversal of the prime minister's sound instincts was only a temporary phenomenon as a result of cabinet upsets at the time and the run up to the next election. When I watched the announcement on television I suddenly realized the pressure on the prime minister, the problems in working with her cabinet and the strong unseen power of the officials who quietly rule the day.

Not that I needed further demonstration of it, but I was on the receiving end of one more piece of establishment behaviour before I left Steel. I don't know whose idea it was that I should go to the National Coal Board but it was put to me for the first time by Nigel Lawson in November 1982 over dinner at the Garrick Club. I wasn't entirely surprised, since David Prior, my personal assistant, and I had frequently discussed the important challenge of the coal industry. No doubt he had reflected on these discussions with his father, James Prior, who had been employment secretary. Nigel Lawson was then energy secretary. I had had occasional dealings with him on energy and other matters in which I had always found him alert and knowledgeable and aware of the grave problems facing the coal industry. I was flattered by his invitation and pleased that both he and the prime minister clearly thought highly enough of me to offer me the job. However, it only seemed fair to try to persuade him to find someone else much younger, for two reasons. First, I thought they should really check out the field as to available candidates before they came to me and, secondly, quite frankly, I was enjoying the Steel job and was beginning to see a successful outcome ahead. I looked forward to the pleasure of basking in success as a steel man for a while. The figures were coming right: losses were coming down dramatically and it was feasible to contemplate that we could soon go into profit. Productivity had improved quite well as we thinned ranks and the man hours per ton figures overall were down from 13.2 to 7.6. At the Llanwern mill they were gratifyingly down to less than 5. The people in the steel business were beginning to show confidence and the overall performance had begun to gain momentum despite the adverse effects of the strengthening pound, which masked our underlying success.

Nevertheless, three weeks later I was escorted in to Mrs Thatcher at No. 10 where she too told me she wanted me to help with Coal. I said: 'Prime Minister, I will help you all I can, but my advice is to get someone younger on whom you can depend. It's going to be a long haul to turn Coal around, from what I can see. But if you can't get anyone suitable, of course I will help and try to do the job.'

One name I suggested at the time was Gerald Blackmore, a former NCB-trained mining engineer who had gone to Canada where, after a career of progressive successes, he had ended up running one of the major US coal-mining companies. The matter was left like that.

Sir Norman Siddall, the then incumbent, had made it clear he would not continue beyond the summer of 1983. Siddall, a mining engineer and a life-long employee of NCB, had had an impeccable career, slowly climbing the ladder until he was deputy to the worthy chairman Sir Derek (now Lord) Ezra. As I understood it, having had health problems and a severe heart operation, Siddall was glad to occupy the chair after all the years of frustration, but he was not keen to carry on into the years ahead where all the elements of a major confrontation were clearly assembled.

In a matter of weeks Nigel Lawson approached me again and, in early February 1983, I finally agreed to take the job. David Prior, who had joined me initially at Lehman's and had followed me to Lazard Frères and subsequently to BSC, was given the job of sorting out a new contract. This time it was finally agreed there was to be a straight flat fee to Lazard for the three years of my NCB contract. So I started to make plans to ease out of BSC. Subsequently I learned that Gerry Blackmore was found to be 'not acceptable' to 'them' as a prospective chairman at NCB. Who 'they' were escaped me. Whether it was the politicians or the civil servants at the Department of Energy or the hierarchy at NCB headquarters in Hobart House, or some combination of these powers, I was never to know, although I have my suspicions. Neither was I 'suitable', for that matter – but either Nigel Lawson or the PM or both had insisted. It takes a lot of courage to fly in the face of the everlasting and underlying armies of bureaucrats.

I was beginning to get used to those sort of high-handed opinions from people who have no experience of the matter, but what really perturbed me was the manner of my succession at BSC. There is no company in the world I can think of where the board of directors do not have a pretty major say in the appointment of a new chairman and/or chief executive – except apparently in nationalized industries such as BSC. When it became known I was going I talked to the members of the salaries committee of the board and suggested that they, as the key group of non-executive directors, should start to think about who should follow on. They were more or less unanimous that, for all his past alleged poor handling (which he vehemently denied) of the 1979 strike, there was only one man for the job of chief executive and that was Bob Scholey. The thought was that one of the non-executive directors, possibly Albert Frost, should become chairman and help and guide Bob Scholey, who had been a marvellous number two to me, and who should now take over the day-to-day running as chief executive.

As a matter of courtesy a deputation therefore went to

see Patrick Jenkin to let him know how they were thinking. There they got a shock. A decision was being made, but Scholey wasn't going to be the man. A name was mentioned, that of Alistair Frame, of RTZ, and they were told he was a possible. Then, shortly afterwards, on 7 April, Albert Frost was summoned to the minister and told that it was going to be Robert Haslam – a former colleague of his at ICI. It was made clear to him that the decision was the minister's and was final, and that Haslam was on the point of accepting the job. The reason Scholey was not getting it was because both the civil servants and the politicians felt he was not the right man. Albert Frost told Patrick Jenkin: 'I know both these men intimately and I know the job to be done. If you go ahead with this I will have to resign.'

A month later, Bob Haslam's appointment was announced and Albert, true to his principles, resigned on the spot. It was, in his view, too much of an insult to Scholey, if not to him and his fellow board members. His resignation was not even acknowledged until three months later. It was as though he had never ever been there. It was sad. The BSC board thus lost one of the most gifted financial men postwar Britain has seen. I had fifty years' experience in business and I had rarely seen anyone in his league – his financial help to BSC through the crisis years had been invaluable. I shared his unhappiness and was deeply saddened by the totally insensitive way it had all been done. There seems to be an old-boy network system at the top, rather like in France where people from the top rungs of both government and industry are seemingly interchangeable, but not many of these highly qualified candidates were around when the steel job was seen to be a sure loser or the Coal Board was seen to be approaching disaster. It seems to be necessary that the relationships among people who administer the system are maintained. And these are the people who run Britain.

The big policy decisions are made up in this strato-spheric layer, far from the rough and tumble of day-by-day living. There are clearly special people who make these decisions and it takes a very tough and courageous minister, often with the handicap of not being fully informed, to be able to exercise his power and stand up to the system. It is understandable that many ministers opt for a more comfortable existence. Civil servants love the private preserves of the nationalized industries where they can dabble happily in management with anonymity. I suppose if you are recruited as one of the best graduates from the top universities into a peer group with a similar background and a long record of running the British Empire, it is understandable that there should be pride, esprit de corps and perhaps somewhat less humility than in any other group in the community. To want to master-mind a public enterprise would be a natural extension of the basic self-confidence of those chosen to advise.

BSC provided a valuable example of a difficult national-ized industry which required the talents of 'the best and brightest' to turn it round. With a much longer history of public ownership – nearly forty years – the NCB was far more rigidly set in its bureaucratic ways. Indeed, I was to find that a major part of its existence consisted of provid-ing an adequate interface between the political directions at the Department of Energy and its own permanent staff.

My problems in trying to change policies and goals were, I suppose, made harder by the fact that I only had a short three years to achieve major change in each case. I had to be in a hurry, because that was what I was being paid for by my political masters. But you cannot achieve anything unless you can get the troops to accept the same goals. If a general gets too far in front of his army, he will lose touch with them. You have to move them along with you – both management and men, not only with actions but also ideas. In a nationalized industry, you have all sorts of other audiences to play to and keep with you – as well as your own people. There are the politicians – those who are against you, those who are for you and those who would like to be for you. There are your customers. There are members of the public – who after all are your shareholders – and some of them are for you and some against, too. Then there are those who would like to be the arbiters of all that is good and appropriate – the civil servants – they who are constantly vigilant to ensure that nothing controversial is done and no one is upset. You have to play to them all and make sure what you do is broadly acceptable to each of these monitors. But because you are in a hurry you always have to be on that leading edge of turbulence. There were one or two occasions when it was clear that the civil servants felt I had gone over the edge – notably over Ravenscraig and my threats to the Germans. Controversy was clearly too distressing for them.

I had had a warm-up at Steel: now, at Coal, if I was to do the job asked of me, I was really going to be running on the ragged edge of acceptability. Or even into the area of unacceptability.

5

Coal: War Is Declared

By the day I joined the National Coal Board, 1 September 1983, Arthur Scargill had already decided to have his strike. All that remained to be settled was the date. And I was already determined, with the support of the prime minister, that I was going to have as much say as possible in the selection of that day. The government had tried once before, in 1981, to bring some sanity to the economics of the coal industry, but had been forced into humiliating retreat by the National Union of Mineworkers. In my talks with Mrs Thatcher it was clear that she had been very unhappy about this experience and she expressed the hope that, should Mr Scargill continue his headlong charge into combat with the Coal Board, I would not cause her to be embarrassed in such a way again.

The highly combustible mixture in Arthur Scargill of theatrical performer and Marxist autocrat had, in the eighteen months since he took over the presidency of the NUM, led him to attempt a full-scale charge on the NCB and the government three times, only to find on each occasion that a ballot of his members showed they were not prepared to follow him. Now, unable to contemplate that the fault might lie with him, he blamed his members' lack of 'politicization' for their mass failure to see things his way. Nevertheless, he insisted time and again that the conflict was coming – an insistence that was boosted considerably after the June 1983 election, in which the Conservatives scored a 141-seat majority, by the claim that Mrs Thatcher's premiership was 'totally undemocratic'. Only a day or two after her landslide victory he was calling it the 'worst national disaster for a hundred years', predicting that unemployment would soon rise to eight million and calling for 'extra-parliamentary action' against government policies.

It was this last point that he elaborated further into his famous 'declaration of war' in his presidential address to the union at Perth early in July. It seemed clear to me, reading reports of the speech the following day, that the man was obsessed with his antigovernment beliefs, was carried away on rhetoric and that, come hell or high water, he was going to lead the miners to the barricades at some time. In his long ramble through the unfairness and injustice of the world as seen by Arthur Scargill, he also made several other statements, strong on distortion and weak on truth, which I was to hear repeated as a regular litany in the months to come.

The Conservatives and the Coal Board were out to destroy the industry. There was a 'secret hit list' of pits for closure. The bonus incentive scheme set man against man, pit against pit and area against area and had 'set the union back fifty years'. There were not really only three million unemployed – there were nearly five million. The reason why the miners hadn't balloted for a strike was because they were not 'politicized' enough. Miners were being bribed into accepting generous redundancy payments, thereby selling their children's or grandchildren's jobs – which they had no right to do. Miners and their descendants should have jobs in the pits for ever. Not enough money had been invested in the pits. Britain produced the world's cheapest deep-mined coal. All the benefits of new technology should go to the miners, giving

117

them a shorter working week, more holidays and other benefits. The recent inner-city violence was caused by Conservative policies – backed by the 'paramilitary' police. Sixty per cent of the British people voted against Mrs Thatcher, the rise of whose regime was akin to that of the Nazis in Germany. And the working class, led by the miners, must fight, by inference on the streets, to remove her, her government and anyone else, including the Coal Board, who stood in their way. This was a fight which he would conduct, 'to the death if need be'.

It also occurred to me at the time that he must be very confident of the collective power of the NUM to achieve the victory he wanted, for, with three million unemployed, there are not even many union leaders who would contemplate a long strike. It would take an awful lot of money, or an awful lot of fiery talk, to support it.

But then, as the months went by, I began to realize that this was one of the key factors in his personality: all his beliefs – in Marxism, in the might of the NUM, in revolution on the streets – were out of date. For all that he was only forty-two years old, he was 'older' than me. He was living in an earlier age – an age which he himself had never actually experienced, but had only heard about in the romantic mythology of the union movement or in tales of working-class glory at his father's knee. He was in effect Marx, he was Lenin, he was Keir Hardie and he was Arthur Cook, who had led the miners to glorious defeat in the 1926 General Strike.

This idealized perception of a world which no longer, or possibly never had, really existed required that the facts, as they were, be ignored, altered or pressed out of shape until they fitted. Thus there had to be a demon of the boss class. Mrs Thatcher fitted, but she had to be declared undemocratic. There had to be an evil henchman doing her bidding. I fitted, but I had to be labelled some sort of geriatric, jackbooted foreigner. There had to be an heroic, downtrodden working class to become Arthur's army – the miners were presumed to fit, despite many indications, including ballots, that the majority of them were more interested in earning good money than they were in hoisting the red flag over Westminster. And there had to be the revolutionary cause – and the Coal Board's alleged bid to butcher the industry fitted, despite the patent folly involved in insisting, first, that all mines should stay open until the very last scrap of coal was dug and, second, that all miners should have jobs forever.

A man bent on pursuing such a romantic dream of a glorious place in history is, like many a demagogue before him, not going to let the facts get in the way, I thought. He is going to be impossible to deal with, but then he is probably going to be impossible for everyone, including many of his friends, to deal with. He is going to be incapable of seeing reason, but then that in the end might be his downfall. The seeds of his destruction could well lie as much in his inability to see clearly the things to his advantage, as they might in his distorted view of those things he presumed to be to his disadvantage. Thus he was perfectly capable of picking, historically, strategically and tactically, precisely the wrong moment to go on strike. A man who is blind to the facts is not selective in his afflictions. He tends to be blind to all the facts.

And the facts, as I found them the day I started at the NCB's headquarters in Hobart House, opposite the gardens of Buckingham Palace, were as follows.

No matter what criteria you chose, the market for coal in the UK had declined consistently since just after the First World War. Similarly our ability to compete in the export markets had lessened. In 1923, 1,250,000 men had produced 300 million tons of coal. In 1947, when the National Coal Board was set up to run the industry,

700,000 men were producing 200 million tons. By the early 1980s, with billions spent on new technology, we had a workforce of 200,000 and demand for little more than 100 million tons a year. All the histrionics and the calls for revolution in the world could not turn back history to the days when town gasworks consumed 27 million tons of coal a year, when every factory ran on a coal-fired boiler and industry consumed 38 million tons a year, when every hearth was open and householders used 36 million tons a year, when every railway engine in the land puffed out clouds of smoke at the rate of 12 million tons a year. The total loss, or drop, in these markets alone between 1957 and 1983 accounted for more than 100 million tons of output which was no longer needed.

Between the Second World War and the early 1970s the decline of coal had been hastened by the ever cheaper price of oil and gas. Governments, even Labour governments, recognized that coal could not be sheltered totally and that the more expensive pits, where coal was most difficult to win, had to go. Hundreds of pits were shut with very little fuss, particularly in the era of Lord Robens and the stern compulsion of ever-cheaper oil economies. Between 1960 and 1968, 346,000 miners left the industry. The task was, of course, easier for Robens in a world of relatively full employment – some men were actually profoundly grateful to be able to get out of mining and find jobs elsewhere.

Another factor also emerged in this period of sharp reduction in capacity: while hundreds of millions of pounds were spent on modernizing the machinery for gaining coal – no longer were the pick, the shovel and the pit pony the tools of the trade – very little, comparatively, was achieved in productivity. Despite the manifest threat from oil, we managed to remain almost as labour intensive as ever. Output per man-year only went up from 269 to 464 tons between 1947 and 1973, where, incidentally, it stuck more or less for a decade until 1983 – only rising above 500 in the last two years of that period. These were indicators to an outsider of the inefficiency of a nationalized industry which seemed to be dominated by its labour unions.

The formidable power of the NUM was clearly demonstrated in the strikes of 1972 and 1974. But the nature of this power was no longer as a partner in the cosy set-up of the industry but as an adversary against the management of the NCB and the government of the day who set its aims and targets. In the early seventies Joe Gormley, the then president, was coming under increasing pressure from militant left-wingers who were anxious to use the renowned loyalty of the men to test the strength of the union against the board and the government. In 1972 they chose the winter and in seven weeks crippled the country and broke the back of the Heath government's much-vaunted incomes policy.

Incidentally, it was during this strike that a rising young miner from Yorkshire called Arthur Scargill came to national notice as 'the hero of Saltley Gate' – leading 12,000 'flying pickets' into battle with 1000 police to close, by violence and intimidation, the huge West Midlands gasworks. Those glorious days of 'revolution' gave him his first taste of three drugs, the effects of which were enough to addict him forever. They were the glamour of leadership in battle, the power of the revolutionary mob and the magic of performing on television. The young Scargill could have been forgiven, because of the inadequate way the government handled the crisis at the time, for thinking anything could be possible – if only he could harness the power of the whole union to his cause.

In 1974 the NUM went for a re-run, just as oil prices

had started to soar. Again they crippled the country, again they won hands down, and this time they brought the government down too. The miners saw their opportunity – hesitant management and in this case the government – and went for the jugular. Clearly Heath and his people got into the strikes without giving a lot of thought about how long they were going to last or how to get out of them. As I watched from America, it seemed extraordinary that a government could be brought into such disrepute by a labour union. It seemed there were two fundamental questions: how had a trade union been allowed to achieve a position of such power and invulnerability? And why did the government allow itself to challenge the NUM when it had no way of withstanding a long dispute? Managements who get into that position invariably have to capitulate on worse terms than they could have made before the strike started. Governments are no different. Most of Mrs Thatcher's ministers had been around in those two strikes. It is no wonder the experiences haunted them.

The strike in 1974 had one other notable side-effect: that famous Alice-in-Wonderland document – The Plan For Coal. No sooner had they appeased the miners with a settlement – on extremely favourable terms – than the new Labour government set about drawing up a plan for the future of the industry, which, in the light of the rising price of oil, would restore it to its rightful place in British economic life. The document, drawn up with the tripartite agreement of government, NCB and NUM, envisaged a glorious ten years of expansion and prosperity for all up to 1985. By then the total UK demand for energy would be the equivalent of 430 million tonnes of coal. (A tonne is the metric equivalent of the ton and is very nearly the same: 1 tonne = 0.98 tons.) Forty-two million tonnes of new capacity would be created and actual coal output would rise to 135 million tonnes – 120 from deep mines and 15 from open cast. Demand for coal could go as high as 150 million tonnes, in which case output would be raised. The government would invest £4.4 billion at 1983 prices. Productivity – measured in output of coal per man shift worked – would go up by 4 per cent per year and it would, of course, be necessary to close down between 3 and 4 million tonnes of uneconomic capacity each year too, to provide opportunity for the new, more efficient capacity being created by huge investments.

It is worth quoting here just two or three paragraphs of the Plan – since they are relevant to much of the subsequent debate during the strike of 1984–5:

Paragraph 16 says:

> [The industry] will keep production costs . . . down to a minimum and so preserve the competitive margin essential to sustain the greater demand for coal that can now be envisaged.

Paragraph 27 says:

> With the transformed outlook for coal which has been demonstrated throughout our Examination, providing that costs remain competitive overall . . . the need to close pits on economic grounds should be much reduced. But inevitably some pits will have to close as their useful economic reserves of coal are depleted.

And paragraph 78 says:

> We welcome the establishment of a financial framework for the industry, which will give the objective of long-term competitiveness while covering its cost of production and contributing towards financing the new investment programme . . .

This document, revised in 1977 by Labour energy secretary Tony Benn to increase the possible demand by the year 2000 to 200 million tonnes, became the ark of the covenant for Arthur Scargill and great homage was paid to it by all connected with the industry. But unfortunately it was based on a series of assumptions, nearly all of which turned out to be incorrect.

First, it extrapolated the consumption of energy on an ever-upward curve based on pre-oil crisis levels. In fact, the sharp rise in oil prices and the subsequent world trade depression caused energy consumption to fall quite dramatically and it is still falling. Not only are we using less of it – but we are also using it more sparingly. So all the forecasts of demand were out by a very wide margin.

Second, not only was the demand for energy falling, but the proportion of coal used in producing our energy, far from rising as predicted in The Plan For Coal, stayed about the same. Nuclear and oil-burning plants, ironically planned by Tony Benn and his friends in the sixties, were coming on stream on a substantial scale throughout the seventies and eighties.

Third, the assumption that British Steel would continue to take an ever-increasing amount of coking coal was upset both by the decline in its own markets, which I had witnessed only too clearly at first hand, and by the increased world supply of low-sulphur, high-specification coking coals which were available at highly competitive prices. So much so that British Steel, in the late seventies, won government support for a policy that it should not be forced to use less competitive raw materials from the home market and could look elsewhere for its coke supplies. The formula worked out required BSC to use indigenous coking coals if the NCB was able to meet the competitive terms of value taking into account, not only price, but any disadvantages in specification.

Fourth, while all the investment was delivered by successive governments as promised and to an eventual spending of £6.5 billion, very little was delivered by the union in terms of either productivity or cooperation on pit closures to reduce capacity. You have to give Joe Gormley, the then president of the NUM, full credit for the fact that he managed to extract almost every penny out of the shelter that was offered to the coal industry by the rising cost of oil, while conceding next to nothing in return. It was a measure of his domination of both government and management in the NCB that he succeeded so well. As wages soared, much of the money that was supposed to be invested to yield greater productivity actually produced less. In many pits where the quota was not being filled, for example, with two coalfaces being worked, money and men would be thrown in to create a third face to bring production up to the level required. Thus, between 1974 and 1978 productivity actually fell from 2.3 to 2.2 tonnes per man shift. And at no stage did capacity reduction reach anywhere near the level of 4 million tonnes per year envisaged in the Plan. For much of the time the reductions were running at less than 2 million tonnes a year.

If ever an industry suffered from the collection of maladies many had come to associate with the British Problem, it was Coal as it entered the 1980s. Yet far from being modified or amended to enable a new start to be made to devise a future for the industry, The Plan For Coal had been enshrined, not only as Arthur Scargill's tablets of stone – but as the whole industry's too. Everyone genuflected to it, everyone beat the gong for it; every time it was mentioned everyone selected his particular section of it and did a sort of little tribal dance for that particular paragraph. It was quite extraordinary that intelligent adults could pay so much attention to, and take such care never to deviate by one iota from, their own selected parts of a document that was just about 100 per cent wrong in most of its basic assumptions – and that they should continue to do so long after those assumptions had been clearly demonstrated to be false.

There were classic symptoms again of the 'San Andreas' effect. Something had to give – the pressures (and the losses) could not go on building up forever, not even in a nationalized industry. Economic reality would one day have to come to the industry and the longer we waited the greater the upheaval would be in the end. It nearly came in 1981, when, under the first Thatcher administration, the NCB was instructed in the 1980 Coal Industry Act to break even, without any operating subsidy, by the end of the financial year 1983–4. Clearly this could not be achieved at the low levels of productivity and slow rate of closures that had existed since 1974. Major surgery was going to have to be used – not Elastoplast.

Whether it was by accident or design, Marxist blindness or genuine foresight, one action taken by Arthur Scargill at this time was to have a far-reaching effect on the conduct of the miners' strike when it came three years later. He had risen, by dedication to his creed and on his reputation won at Saltley, to president of the Yorkshire miners and was tipped to win the national presidency when Joe Gormley finally retired. Already he had taken the leadership of the left-wing in the NUM, leading the unsuccessful campaign against production bonuses. Like brother Woodcock's automobile workers all those years before, he was virulently anti anything that could lead to one man earning more than another. It had been my experience that, far from setting man against man, as the demagogues would have it, bonuses caused men to work together in the realization that collectively they could earn some of the goodies the twentieth century had on offer: in this case, those well-known enemies of working-class solidarity, the owner-occupied house, the saloon car and the annual two-week holiday abroad.

However, in January 1981 Scargill called a ballot in the Yorkshire NUM on the resolution: 'Are you in favour of giving [YNUM] the authority to take various forms of industrial action, including strike action if necessary, to stop the closure of any pit, unless on the grounds of exhaustion?' The issue at the time was the threatened closure of the pit at Orgreave and 86 per cent of his 66,000 Yorkshire members voted in favour of it. It was one of those notions that was so general and bound the members to do so little that it could not fail to succeed. At the time it had the desired effect. The closure threat was averted and the balloted motion soon forgotten about. However, three years later, it was to achieve enormous significance in the strike.

In the meantime Sir Derek Ezra, who was then NCB chairman, had addressed himself to the task of obeying the government's wishes to bring the industry into line, and on 10 February 1981 he announced to the full executive of the mining unions his plans to take 10 million tonnes of uneconomic capacity out of the system forthwith. He produced a four-point plan, which tried to pay all the right tributes to The Plan For Coal, but pointed out that times had changed and the closures were needed if the industry were to stand on its own two feet. The result was uproar – at the meeting and afterwards. The minutes state that Mr Scargill, in by far the longest speech from the floor, called for: 'the industry to fight for an immediate and complete ban on imports and for subsidization of home coal production'. He described the plans as 'butchery' and ended by threatening: 'I hope that all the union representatives will leave the meeting feeling pledged not to accept the sacrifice of their industry, which has been proposed to them, and that the Board, for their part, and the government would grasp the fact that their present course could lead to one thing only – confrontation.'

I have now heard variations on that theme more times than I care to remember, but it was refreshing to find it there in the minutes in 1981 – a warning even then that, if it came to trying to put the NCB's chaotic finances in order in the interests of the poor taxpayer, then Arthur Scargill, for one, was going to fight and not budge an inch. The next words in those minutes were Joe Gormley's. 'We have heard enough of threats,' he said, slapping down the Young Pretender. But it augured ill for the day, very shortly to come, when his moderating influence would no longer be there at the helm.

I understand that, in the uproar of the next few days during which Gormley was clearly impelled a great deal by Scargill breathing down his neck, the union pressure on Ezra grew until he went back to the civil servants at the Department of Energy, who went to the minister, David Howell, and asked if the government was really ready for a strike, because that now looked as if it was on the cards. We can only speculate that Howell had to react to the cautions from his own department who decided that they could not react positively to this threat. They were prepared to let events happen rather than confronting the unions in an attempt to tighten up the sloppy state of Coal. A symptom of the chaos within came from a steady stream of leaks and disclosures out of Hobart House and the Department at this time. David Howell clearly now had to go to the prime minister with the bad news that their plans looked like being thwarted by a possible full-scale miners' strike.

I think she took exactly the right decision in the circumstances. Bearing in mind that the last Tory prime minister who had faced the NUM had had his legs chopped off at the knees, she looked calmly around the battlefield, examined her forces, recognized that she was outman-oeuvred by the enemy – and wisely withdrew in relatively good order, if somewhat bloodied in the process.

There was very little coal in stocks. A strike called by Gormley was likely to be solid. Attempting to import coal would shut the docks. Even if you could get coal in, the railways would not move it. The TGWU's grip on haulage was still too tight for it to go by road. It was still winter. And so on. The prime minister must have run down the check list of what she would need to win and come up with negatives on every one. So she quietly walked off the battlefield and went off to regroup, with the idea, very much in mind, of living to fight another day.

In the two years before I arrived, production was allowed to run free. Huge stocks were built up – there was more than 60 million tonnes in our hands or at the power stations. After what had happened and with the advent of Scargill, there was a general realization that sooner or later something was going to have to be done to make the industry viable and that any attempt to do so now would, inevitably, lead to an outright confrontation. In the meantime, it was thought to be no bad thing to be ready for that battle when it came by piling up coal all over the place. Ezra's successor, Norman Siddall, backed by his deputy, Jimmy Cowan, did just that and also managed to close some twenty pits – many of which were getting to the end of their useful lives.

Scargill, now the new NUM president, was happy because everyone seemed suitably scared of him and, although he failed twice to get national backing for strikes on closure resolutions very similar to that he had won in Yorkshire, he knew he would not have to wait long before he could lead his men into battle. 'Sooner or later, miners will have to stand and fight,' he was fond of saying. And he regularly asserted that there was in Hobart House a 'secret hit list' of pits due for closure. It was a statement which usefully kept his membership on edge – but, as the House of Commons Energy Committee found in December 1982, it was entirely without evidence. The same committee also found, incidentally, that his claim that coal should be mined, whatever the financial loss, was 'especially perverse'. It added: 'No industry can possibly operate on such a basis. Even a partial concession to this doctrine would involve a massive increase in public subsidies and yet further increases in stocks . . . In sum, to judge by their evidence to us, the NUM appear to believe that, in order to maintain employment in mining, the industry should be encouraged and financed to produce as much coal as it possibly can and that the country somehow has an obligation to find ways of consuming it.'

In these circumstances it was hardly surprising that the miners too were happy. They were earning good money turning out a lot of extra coal that no one wanted. Indeed, on each of the occasions they were asked in a national ballot to follow Arthur Scargill to the barricades they declined. I think many of them too were beginning to be unhappy at the prospect of being used as revolutionary cannon fodder in Arthur's army and were perhaps sensing that the prime minister's economic policies were, in the long run, best for the country. I have a great belief in the ability of the British working man, left alone from some of those demagogues who claim to represent him, to discover for himself the common-sense solution to problems. And I think that many normal working miners were prepared to accept that the world no longer owed them a living and that a day of reckoning was bound to come. After all, if you looked at the figures in the 1983 general election, a large number of them must have voted for that lady, whose 'totally undemocratic' government their leader so much despised.

The administrators in the Department and at Hobart House were happy too, because their lives were quiet and, while all around them money from the public pocket was in full flood, their endless committee meetings and discussions could go on and on. I suspect many of them knew that time was running out – after all, the need for competitiveness in the industry was enshrined in every document and plan for its future from the 1947 National-ization Bill onwards and therefore it could not be long before some government, and probably this government, insisted on it being translated into fact.

It is interesting to note that when the crunch came I got the distinct impression that their resentment of me for bringing it about arose not so much from the fact that I was doing something with which they profoundly disagreed on political grounds – though there were those right up to the highest level in Hobart House who made no secret of this. Nor even did it arise totally from the fact that they thought it wasn't necessary to insist on greater competitiveness – many of them knew it was and said so – but more from their profound distaste for an outsider so clearly bent on bringing about change in the comfortable culture of their well-ordered world.

It did not take me long to discover that the civil servants at the Department and the officials at Hobart House, perhaps more so than in any other nationalized industry, enjoy a happy relationship, and that they have a long history of collectively repelling boarders. It had only been at the insistence of Nigel Lawson and the prime minister that I had been allowed to take the helm at all.

Nevertheless, in all the discussions before I started at the NCB it was made clear to me what was expected of me, and that the government – certainly the prime minister and Nigel Lawson – did not believe that they could any longer avoid Scargill's determination to force the issue. The June election and Scargill's speech in Perth had reinforced that belief.

The election did, however, change one aspect of my task. I had been looking forward to working with Nigel – we both clearly shared the same views on many things. I liked him. He had a clear mind and, although he suffered a little bit from the weight of his responsibilities, he was not at all brash, or overconfident. He knew what the problems were and was not afraid to face up to them. I didn't think he was the sort of fellow who could be pushed around by his civil servants. I was therefore personally quite upset, and felt somewhat cheated, when, after the election, he was moved to the treasury to be chancellor and Peter Walker was made energy secretary. He was a great contrast to Nigel. He was very quick and plausible – all smiles and anxious to help. But I wondered, even at our first meeting, how he would be when the going got rough. Would I be able to count on his support? I didn't see the same opportunity for a warm and intellectual understanding which would encourage me to count on him for an awful lot of help. Indeed, as the strike went on, his need to participate and agonize over details of both strategy and tactics, and his somewhat different political stance, made the relationship quite tense, producing uncertainties in our plans and actions which, in my view, may have prolonged the strike.

My task was made clear to me at that first meeting with Peter Walker when he handed me a single sheet of paper on which were typed the following instructions:

1.   Although coal is one of the United Kingdom's major natural resources, in the government's view the justification for coal production, like that for any other business,

lies in the ability of those engaged in it to earn a satisfactory return on capital while competing in the market place. The basic objective for the NCB, therefore, must be to earn a satisfactory return on its assets in real terms, after payment of social grants; and this return will need to be quantified in due course.

2.   The NCB should aim to maximize its long-term profitability by securing those sales which are profitable on a continuing basis, in competition with other fuels. It should plan its marketing, production and capital investment accordingly and bring productive capacity into line with its continuing share of the market.

3.   The Board's objective should be to ensure that over the next five years its operating costs, including depreciation and capital charges but excluding interest, per tonne of coal produced, are reduced in real terms for deep-mined and for open-cast production separately . . . The objective will be quantified in due course.

4.   Either the Board or the government may propose additional objectives from time to time, and any consequent adjustments to existing objectives would need to be discussed.

There was nothing new in these proposals. They were essentially what the NCB had been set up for in the first place back in 1947. It was the determination to reassert them, after years of neglect and union domination, that was new. They were made even more apposite by the publication, just a couple of months before I took over, of the report of the Monopolies and Mergers Commission inquiry into the state of the industry. If I needed any introduction to the task ahead, then this report did it succinctly for me. Its conclusions give a brisk resumé of the state of play as I took over.

It showed a nationalized industry that needed continuous large sums of money to keep it going – in the last year, 1981–2, the government had provided £575 million including £428 million to cover losses. In addition, finance for new equipment and capacity amounted to £902 million. The External Financing Limit proposed for 1983–4 was £1,130 million – accounting for 40 per cent of all such money given to nationalized industries.

It confirmed that The Plan For Coal had been meticulously adhered to by successive governments, but not by the unions, and it focused very quickly on the nub of the problem: over-capacity and high-cost pits.

On over-capacity the report said: 'The NCB is producing much more coal than it can find a market for, either in the United Kingdom or at acceptable prices abroad. As a result coal stocks have been rising for a number of years and, in the NCB's own view, are now excessive.'

And on high-cost pits: 'Many collieries are being maintained in production although their unit operating costs greatly exceed the proceeds obtainable at the present price levels in this country (at least £10 a tonne higher than current returns from exports), or at any reasonable estimate of future prices.' The report produced the famous Laffer curve, which I had copied and sent to all the areas and the managers. It showed quite graphically that, while we were getting, on average, £35.60 per tonne for our deep-mined coal, fewer than half our pits were capable of producing coal at this price – or under. The rest were turning out coal which, if it were to be sold, would have to be subsidized by the taxpayer.

Just how bad the situation had become was shown in the following example: 'In 1981–2 the 10 per cent of the deep-mined output (10.8 million tonnes) that came from the pits with the highest losses per tonne, involved operating losses of £263 million at average prices.' In other words, if we could shut those pits – accounting for that most expensive 10.8 million tonnes of coal that no one wanted to buy anyway – we could save the taxpayer £263 million in one year.

The reason for the industry being in this state and for these desperate measures being needed was, according to the report, failure to achieve the cutbacks in capacity at a steady rate over the years – the 'San Andreas' fault again. And it added: 'The longer the problems are left the worse they will become. Unless there is a significant reduction in the numbers of high-cost pits, the NCB's finances will deteriorate even further. The industry's ability to invest in modern capacity in the short and medium term will be jeopardized, for, if the problem is not dealt with, there must come a time when it will be quite impossible for any government to justify to the public the large and growing expenditure of public funds that would be needed.'

There you have it. I was 'up to bat' – and I was expected to put things right. I reckoned somebody had to do it – but I didn't think there would be any easy options. And I would need some fairly solid support within the NCB. I found such help in Jimmy Cowan, the deputy chairman, who became the one person I could rely on. Together with a few other people, he understood the situation and had already been attempting to get things in line. Just as I had persuaded Bob Scholey to be my 'window' on the business at BSC, so at the NCB I asked Jimmy to teach me the highways and byways of the organization. Six weeks before I was due to start work we met for dinner at the Caledonian Hotel in Edinburgh – near to his family home on the Firth of Forth and not too far away from my Scottish house in mid-Argyll. Jimmy had been one of the people considered for the job of chairman earlier in the year, but he had had a heart operation and Nigel

Lawson was concerned about whether he was robust enough for the task. I found him, at first, to be a shy man and I can well understand why he was naturally pretty suspicious of me. He no longer had any ambition to take on the job himself, but it is nevertheless a measure of the man how quickly he buried any of those feelings and gave me his total support. It is very easy to say, but it is nevertheless true, that we could never have prevailed in the struggle that was to come without Jimmy.

He too was a graduate. He got a first in mining engineering at Glasgow University at the beginning of the war, and he had worked his way to the top through just about every job there was in the industry. He had been a face worker and had worked underground for three years; he had been a manager, an area director and a director of industrial relations. There was very little Jimmy did not know about the business and very few people of any consequence in it with whom he wasn't on first-name terms. Very quickly we found we had the same attitude to the fundamental issues. But he told me I should have no illusions about the enormity of union resistance to us doing anything to put things right. For years, but particularly since Scargill, the management had been forced more and more on to the defensive. It had to go to enormous lengths to conceal from the union any moves it was about to make, then found, time and again, that its intentions were leaked to the press or to the union, or both, by disaffected parties within Hobart House and in no time its plans would either have to be changed to accommodate the union's demands or be completely abandoned.

At Jimmy's hands my education in the business was rapid and helpful. It was clear from what he told me that the whole situation was building up to some kind of accident – confirming what Nigel had told me and my own impressions. It was clear also that we had a job to do which had to be done and that if Scargill was as hell-bent on a confrontation as it seemed, then a confrontation was indeed inevitable. Therefore the sooner, from everybody's point of view, that we got on with it, the better: from my point of view, because I only had three years to achieve the necessary change; from the management's and men's point of view, because as soon as we could reaffirm our right to manage the sooner we could start to sort things out and get the industry into shape; and from the country's point of view, because the industry would then no longer be an endless drain on its pockets.

Like all nationalized industries, its problems were not solely with its labour force. I found Coal to be different from Steel only by degree. The amount of solid intervention at all levels, day-in and day-out, from the Department of Energy, occupied and preoccupied the management of the enterprise. They were quite simply distracted by an endless flow of paper from their counterparts over the road in Whitehall and were often too heavily engaged to have time to get on with the fundamental function of running the business efficiently.

Not only did the civil servants seem to spend a large part of their time collecting more information than could ever possibly be needed to run the Coal Board had it been a private enterprise, but also large numbers of staff at Hobart House spent a considerable part of their time in consultation with those civil servants about the figures which had been collected. This violated all the principles of management in which I believed and which only recently I had applied successfully at BSC. First and foremost it was a contradiction of the principle of setting goals and reporting on performance against those targets – not on the minute details of every possible variation. I found, for example, that Whitehall kept detailed figures on how much overtime was worked in each pit. I only needed to look at such figures for an area as a whole, and only on a quarterly basis, at accountability meetings when the area director had to discuss his overall performance against our targets. I began to feel that I would have to struggle hard to overcome the influence of people who had no experience at all of running a business but thought nothing of encouraging their Coal Board counterparts to influence the management and to try to have a say in its direction. Maybe after forty years of nationalization they seemed to think it was a government department – not a business.

I remember saying to Peter Walker, quite early on, that one major saving we could both make would be to cut out the number of bureaucrats in the two sets of offices who seemed to be mirroring each other's activities but not actually doing anything to promote the enterprise. He didn't rise to the bait and showed no great desire to alter the system. Indeed he may have found his civil servants congenial and their presence comforting. On another occasion, again very early on in my tenure, I remember asking for some particular thing to be done – only to be met with some resistance and eventually to be told that it should not be done, because 'the Department' would not like it. I was told quite regularly that I would have to do things a certain way, because that was how the Department would like to see them done. It called for a certain amount of self-control to deal with situations like that. I normally did what I wanted anyway, but I could sense it caused considerable concern and unhappiness among the civil servants over the road on the grounds that they felt they were losing their iron grip on the situation.

It cannot have pleased those in Hobart House, either,

when one of my first acts was to bring in my old associate Roger Morrison from McKinsey's to look over the whole structure and see if he could improve management performance. I have preferred a centralized chief executive office – to avoid these endless committees which people seem to love so much – and a high degree of decentralization of management out to the management in the actual producing areas. Roger Morrison prepared a plan which achieved just this, making a clear definition of the responsibilities of the areas and what we were expecting them to achieve. Obviously this meant that much of the work of the many committees which were used to functioning at the centre could be reduced and many people were disturbed at having their participation diminished in this way. Decisions, however, were made very much quicker and we reduced the need for those endless discussion groups. The area directors were happy to be given proper responsibility for their costs and the message soon permeated down to the individual pits that their performance was to be based on their own capabilities and that they weren't going to have a vast army of people in London trying to tell them how to run their business.

I also took steps very early on to streamline the board and bring in some outside non-executive directors, whom I knew would be more in sympathy with the changes that had to be made than were some of the existing members. I could not take the risk of being undermined in these early days – especially since we had to move quickly if things were going to be put right inside three years. I think I shocked the whole system in Hobart House when a stream of decisions started coming out of the chairman's office instead of invitations to sit on countless committees, drink coffee at regular intervals and discuss things. I am sure noses were put out of joint – but what happened would be totally my responsibility. If the government had wanted an Ezra, who I gathered had been a committee man *par excellence* and, therefore, quite understandably, had bucked the 1981 crisis right back up to Downing Street, or a Siddall, who had learned to be concerned about upsetting the union, then they would have appointed someone in the same mould.

In my first three months at the NCB – up to Christmas 1983 – I spent a great deal of time getting to know the people, especially out in the areas and getting to know the nuts and bolts of the industry in this country. I had been chairman for just eight days when I made a point of going to Wearmouth Colliery, near Sunderland, which necessitated crawling the last 250 yards to the face, which was only 42 inches high. I wanted to show the men that although they may have got a seventy-one-year-old as their new boss, he was no geriatric! I understand the word went round the coalfields like wildfire.

The general situation in the areas, as I went round, was that Kent, South Wales, Scotland and the northeast were losing enormous sums of money. The Western Area – after great efforts by its director, John Northard – was struggling towards breakeven. Doncaster and South Yorkshire was a labour relations disaster area. It had some of our best coal measures – yet was doing very badly. The whole of Yorkshire, in fact, was doing very badly – a large number of the pits had a poor record in terms of profitability and there had to be some kind of rationalization. North Yorkshire, which included Selby, was getting going, but the pit was behind schedule and had run into problems. On the credit side: Derbyshire was marginally OK. West Midlands was not too bad. In the south Midlands, Leicestershire had some very old pits getting near the end of their lives – albeit still being reasonably productive – but the rest of the area, with big winning pits like Daw Mill, made it not too bad at all. And the jewel in the crown was Nottinghamshire, which was going along very nicely.

Before I started work Jimmy had been making great efforts to keep morale up in the Midlands, Derbyshire and especially Nottinghamshire. There had been closures in these areas, but they had, by and large, made their sacrifices to get things right. Jimmy could see that the confrontation was coming and had devoted a lot of time to making sure the men knew that when they had suffered the agonies to get their areas straight, no one had stood by them. Now that Scargill was talking about 'no closures', were they going to sacrifice their future for a political issue? All this hard work put in before I arrived, and in the three months up to Christmas, was to pay dividends later.

A few days after my Wearmouth visit I went to Bilston Glen, just south of Edinburgh, where I was able to get my message over in a fairly convincing fashion. The men at the pit itself were a good crowd and put on a bit of a special display of how well they could produce, so I stood them all a drink when the visit was over and told them, 'Produce – and you have a future.' But I was approached during the visit by a shop steward from the nearby Monktonhall pit, which was on strike because the management refused to go back on a bonus agreement the union had signed. I told him, 'You have no future unless you perform.'

I developed quite a fondness for the people of Bilston Glen. It became a sort of token for me. They put up with real hardship, trying to work during the strike, and I helped them all I could. It was very moving, on one occasion during the strike, to be met at Edinburgh airport on my way to London by a group of the men's wives who wanted to talk over their problems – particularly the intimidation they were suffering – but also to thank me for what I was doing.

We still had to make some top-level changes which were accomplished amicably by retirements. But most of our area managements responded quickly to the notion that they were responsible for getting costs in line and shared our enthusiasm for tackling the problems of high-cost production.

I also spent a great deal of time thinking about the confrontation with Scargill and how and when it might come. He and I had our first meeting on 13 September at the regular gathering of the Joint National Consultative Council, one of the many formal groups in the NCB structure which brings unions and management together. There were hands shaken and photographs taken but very little was said between us. I think he still assumed I was some sort of old stumblebum from out of town and I wasn't unhappy for him to go away with that impression for the time being. He and his colleagues made the usual disparaging comments about the management's insensitivity to the legitimate demands of the men. I just sat back and listened, making the minimum of contribution. I likewise got the feeling he was carefully watching me.

There was no way of knowing at that time what he was going to do. All my area directors who knew him – and Jimmy Cowan – said he was spoiling for a fight. Certainly at that meeting the whole NUM attitude was belligerent. There was no willingness to go away and consider points we made; their attitude was all aggression and had the feeling of confrontation about it. I thought the best thing to do was to spend as much time as possible listening and trying to work out what their strategy might be. Alas, at this meeting, I found them no different from some of the other union groups I had met in the UK. Their calibre did not seem to be very high. Scargill seemed quite articulate and very effective in projecting his viewpoint. Even if what he was saying was nonsense, he said it with great conviction. He really belongs on the stage or on a TV show – he is a talent wasted.

For example, he stated at one stage in the meeting that Britain had the cheapest deep-mined coal in the world. Now this was to become one of the great lies of the strike, which nevertheless gained currency over the months on the principle that the bigger the lie and the more often it was told, the more likely people were to believe it. The claim was then, and is now, fraudulent. Our costs vary over a massive range from £20 a tonne at some pits to more than £100 at others. We have some that is the most expensive in Europe and some that is reasonably competitive. But North American, South African and Australian coal dominates the world markets and we can only get near to the price of that coal with what we produce at Selby – and only then when currency fluctuations help us. American deep-mined coal at the pit head would cost about $24 a tonne at the moment – but because of the strength of the pound Selby's would cost $45 a tonne. In Europe, we are among the lowest-cost coal producers overall – but the rest of Europe has almost ceased producing coal, except for Germany, where it is subsidized heavily in order to maintain the dominance of their steel industry at home and in EEC markets.

Since it seemed certain that Arthur Scargill was looking for any excuse to call a strike, I felt we had to tread carefully, and not provoke it at a time unsuitable to us. He had already tried and failed in his earlier efforts to get the men out through the balloting process, on either pay, pit closures or a combination of the two. It would have caught us unprepared if he had managed to start a strike as the winter of 1983 came on. Thus, all this time, Jimmy Cowan, Merrick Spanton, our IR director, and the area directors were probing – trying to find out what the mood was in the coalfields.

A great deal of thought therefore went into the pay offer we were due to make the NUM at the end of September. The government had set pay guidelines of 3 to 5 per cent for public sector workers. But Scargill was already on record as wanting a much higher sum than this – up to 25 per cent for some men. He also wanted the bonus incentive schemes consolidated into basic wages and, predictably, a shorter working week and no pit closures.

Jimmy and I figured out that a 5.2 per cent pay offer was just about enough to prevent the NUM using it as an excuse to walk out on the grounds that it was too small. It was, after all, in excess of the limits the government had laid down, so they were unlikely to turn it down flat. We felt we could head off a mid-winter confrontation and a snap strike call. If, on the other hand, they did seek a strike ballot on it, it was highly unlikely the men would down tools in support. We were right; our 'first and final offer' was not so small that the NUM leader felt impelled to call a ballot. He chose instead that well-known tactic of the left, the delegate conference.

Whereas nearly all unions require a ballot for any form of national industrial action, from go-slows to overtime bans to selective or all-out strikes, some, particularly where the leadership is much more militant than the men, get around this by mandating 'delegate conferences' to vote on actions – especially those short of actual all-out strikes. The idea is that local branches are by and large 'officered' by the more left-wing members, who tend to choose from their numbers the most keen and left-wing as delegates to national meetings. Therefore, while pretending he is speaking to the whole membership, the union leader who addresses such a conference is, in fact, preaching very largely to the converted. Without having to go through the process of possible rejection in an overall membership ballot, the leader can thus get his policies – short of total strikes – through an 'inner council' of 'the faithful' at a delegate conference.

Arthur Scargill was no stranger to this process and chose it, on 21 October, to get a national overtime ban – to start from the last day of the month. At last I began to get an impression of what he was up to. The technique was clearly going to be to run the ban through the winter, attempt progressively to slow production and try to whittle down the coal stocks – then, if all went well, to continue to hold down production and eat into the stocks through the next summer and hit us with the big strike in the autumn of 1984. The whole plan may not yet have coalesced in his mind, but certainly at that stage it looked to us as if he felt unready to launch an all-out assault until he had made an important dent in the stocks.

In July he had declared war. Now in November the first skirmishing began. Stanley Baldwin once said: 'A wise man would never take on the Pope or the National Union of Mineworkers.' Presumably he saw the two as the principal sources of power in the spiritual and temporal worlds respectively. In time I was to have some leading representatives of the former ranged against me, but for the time being I was now irrevocably committed to struggling with the more worldly might of the latter.

6

The First Skirmishes

To our astonishment, we heard just before Christmas 1983 that Arthur Scargill was planning to start the strike in March. I could not believe it at first when Jimmy Cowan told me of an extraordinary meeting he had had with Mick McGahey, who was vice president of the NUM, at which McGahey, a lifelong communist, had sought to alert him to both the date and the nature of the impending battle.

Surely, I thought, Scargill must wait in the bushes until at least August next year before he tries to do anything? He couldn't be so convinced of victory, so carried away by the rhetoric and the glamour of it all, that he is prepared to risk going on strike at the time of year when he can have least effect and when he knows we have more than 50 million tonnes of coal in stock? Or could he?

Jimmy's evidence was quite startling. He had met McGahey, whom he had known for years. Through being adversaries − at both a local level in Scotland, where Jimmy had been area director, and nationally when he had been in charge of industrial relations − there had developed a great deal of mutual respect. This meeting had started off with them chatting about the state of play between the two sides and Jimmy ventured the opinion that he did not think that a strike was inevitable − even though he found Scargill almost completely irrational. He felt sure that there were still forces within the NUM executive which were powerful enough to exert a calming influence on its president and make it possible to get through this necessary transition without a lengthy and damaging strike.

At this point the conversation apparently took a different tack. McGahey suddenly reminded Jimmy of his ill-health and spoke sympathetically of a family tragedy which had recently devastated him and his wife Harriet. Then he said: 'If I were you, Jimmy, for your sake and for the sake of Harriet, I would get out now, because it's going to be very unpleasant. The die is cast – it's too late. The strike will take place. It will start in March with the Yorkshire area led by Jack Taylor – and Henry Richardson will look after Nottingham and make sure they join in.'

Jimmy got very angry with McGahey. He accused him of doing nothing to stop Scargill. 'How can you support a leader who so clearly exploits his members?' he demanded. 'I am not going to stand by and let it happen. I will fight you to the end, even if I do leave you with a broken union. That man will not be allowed to destroy the industry I have worked all my life for.'

Jimmy came back and reported the essence of the encounter to us. On reflection he thought McGahey was perhaps salving his conscience for what was to come – by giving Jimmy a warning just in case he did feel like giving up. He believed McGahey had an innate sense of humanity which might encourage him to do this – though others on the team thought it could be a ruse to try to remove one of our key men. If this was so then it had the opposite effect; from that moment on, Jimmy never wavered once in his determination to see the thing through.

By that time anyway, Jimmy and our IR people were

beginning to see other, more traditional signs of preparations for war from the union side. The number of spontaneous walk-outs was rising. Tempers were getting frayed and the number of fights was also going up. The men were dividing into those who were getting their heads down and earning as much as they could before it happened and those who were contributing to the rising temperature – led by the opinion-formers in each pit, who were in turn more voluble than usual. They all had one thing in common – they knew it was coming. The belief was being put about that a short, sharp strike, backed by the steel, transport and rail unions, was all that was needed to see the government back down and get rid of this new chairman. Scargill was convinced by now that everyone felt as violently anti-Thatcher as he did and that all the other unions would therefore be only too pleased to follow his banner into battle.

They had already started to orchestrate the attack on me – through the media and through their own poodles in parliament. People were beginning to make speeches and write articles about how the industrial relations climate had been all right until I had come along, but now it had been destroyed by my intransigence, the idea being, presumably, that once they went on strike, the government would be so embarrassed they would have to sack me, abandon their plans and everything would return to normal again.

I was thankful that we had been so careful over the pay offer, because Scargill was now clearly in no mood for peace. But none of us could yet work out how he was going to get his strike without a ballot. As we went over the many imponderables again and again we could not see how, for all his raising the temperature, he would get a sufficient majority to order a national strike.

I had been impressed with the oft-repeated conventional wisdom about the tremendous loyalty of the NUM membership, but the overtime ban which had started with a great flurry in November was revealing cracks in the hitherto united façade. As it came up to Christmas we were hearing more and more about discontent with the Scargill style of leadership, which, in the words of the complainants, had so far 'achieved a lot of aggro but very few results'.

The principal purpose of the ban was to stop mainten-ance work being done at weekends, traditionally done at this time so that the men could start work straightaway on Monday mornings instead of having to wait. But we found that there were a surprising number of people willing to breach the ban unofficially, to keep their fel-lows' wages up. Obviously not everyone was sold on Scargill's message.

Nor was the ban having a good effect on the morale of the troops generally. They could see losses in wages of up to £40 a week going out of their pockets – but they could not see the amount of coal at the pit heads and the power stations disappearing. By Christmas we were only 4 million tonnes down – we still had 57.8 million in stock at the pits and at the power stations. Also, in the past a device like an overtime ban would normally have caused great meetings to have taken place between unions and management, endless hand-wringing and constant nego-tiations until the NCB made some concession and the action would be called off. It had got to the stage, I sometimes felt in those first few months at the Board, when the attitude was that the NCB was not meant to do anything at all without asking the NUM's permission.

There were joint committees for this and for that, con-sultative machinery, conciliation machinery and negotiat-ing machinery – all set in place by the extraordinary legislation which had been enacted at the time of nationalization. But I saw no need to use any of it now. There was no need to talk to the NUM. The pay offer was on the table. The overtime ban was their decision. It was their move. The men were affected by this attitude too. They could see nothing very much happening – an almost complete lack of concern about their overtime ban – and I think it may have disconcerted them a bit and caused some to lose heart.

But as the ban went on through January and February it began to have a cumulative effect. The maintenance time began to eat into production time and we started to lose output. Nevertheless, the stocks remained high as consumption by the CEGB was below expectation – a combination of milder weather and pretty slow industrial production. That is why I could not understand Scargill's rush to go now. If he had waited until the autumn and got a proper ballot, he could well have prevailed. Certainly life would have been much more difficult for us.

During this period I had a lot of learning to do – as well as a lot of teaching. Not only was I learning, through Jimmy Cowan's 'window', about the complexities of the areas and the mining unions, but also about the people around me at Hobart House. As my learning about the areas progressed, it slowly became possible to predict how things might go in a dispute. Scotland, South Wales, Durham, Kent, Barnsley, Doncaster and South Yorkshire would almost certainly act with total solidarity, but the rest were obviously open to varying amounts of persuasion. Jimmy's propaganda campaign in the Midlands and Nottingham seemed as though it might be bearing fruit. Nottingham had a history of not following the national direction of the union – the men were still held to have 'scabbed' in the 1926 General Strike, despite the fact that there were few alive who could remember it. Although its area leaders, Ray Chadburn and Henry

Richardson, were firmly in Arthur's militant camp, the indications were that the men would be reluctant to follow. Nor was the NUM entirely united by sections: the Power Group, led by Roy Ottey, who was subsequently to resign from the executive because of the way the strike was conducted, were demanding a ballot on the overtime ban itself.

In addition to the NUM, there were two other unions – NACODS and BACMS. The National Association of Colliery Overmen Deputies and Shotfirers was responsible for front-line supervision and safety in the pits under the very strict, but somewhat outdated, mining laws. The union had not traditionally been very militant: its members were nearly all ex-NUM, but regarded themselves as being on the first rungs of management. However, their role and duties in providing 'safety cover' at pits where there was a dispute was, to say the least, ambiguous. It was this issue, coupled with the election early in 1984 of a new left-wing general secretary, Peter McNestry, and his desire to strut a wider stage – a desire which was amply encouraged by others in all quarters with malice in their hearts – that was to project NACODS into the forefront of the dispute at a crucial time.

The British Association of Colliery Management was a very British institution in that it seemed to have the freedom both to run with the fox and hunt with the hounds. It was, exactly as it says, the union of pit managers, but also, as I learned to my utter surprise, of most of the people who worked in Hobart House. Even the area directors were members of it. Although it never really joined in the dispute when it came, it took some getting used to a situation in which people who clearly laid full claim to being representatives of 'management' could, and did, through their union, criticize that management.

But freedom to criticize and to undermine seemed to be par for the course at Hobart House. I have always found that where the morale of the management is low, an enterprise tends to 'leak' like a sieve and the NCB headquarters was no exception. Sadly, it became my experience very quickly that, if more than two or three people knew about any decision that had been taken, then so, very quickly, did Arthur Scargill or the media or both. Such disloyalty seemed to be accepted with resignation by those around me. It was a fact of life in the fantasy world of Hobart House. My task was clear – there was no secret about that – but in terms of day-to-day decisions Jimmy and I began to keep our cards very close to our chests.

I think it came as a surprise to some of them and a shock to others that I was not going to continue the way of my predecessors and that, having had a good look around, I was going to start cutting out the dead wood. I also needed to be sure that I knew exactly where those who were going to stay and work closely with me stood on the issues and methodology I had in mind. It was for this reason – to test the water – that, in the early months, I threw a few stones down the well. To draw them out, I suggested on one occasion that we might have a ballot of the NUM membership to find out if they wanted the overtime ban. After all, I had used this tactic before to great effect at BSC. Later I suggested that I might put the 5.2 per cent pay award in the men's pay packets anyway for Christmas, thus going over the head of the union. The storm these two suggestions provoked within Hobart House taught me a lot about some of the people there. Ned Smith, in industrial relations, was appalled and told me to my face that I could not do these things. I'm afraid he resented my whole style of management. The idea that the chairman should simply say what was going to happen was clearly alien to his and many other people's culture.

By the end of February I think the way I liked to do things was becoming clear to people, particularly in the areas where most of them jumped at the chance to 'manage' for themselves, without interference all the time from Hobart House.

My efforts to encourage the education of Arthur Scargill, however, had not been so successful. I had never tried to conceal from him what my aims were for the industry, nor the very rosy future I saw for it, if we could but get its costs right. My predecessors, forced on to the defensive by the sheer scale of the resistance to change inside and outside Hobart House, had become ultra-cautious and secretive about their plans. I saw little point in being so. Everybody knew I was there to put things right. I could only presume that Mr Scargill did too. Thus, from day one, I put my cards very much on the table with regard to my views on the long-term resolution of the coal industry's problems.

Right through the winter, at the various preordained meetings arranged between us and the unions in the regular industry calendar, I tried to make him progressively aware of my thinking, in the short, medium and long term, as it evolved.

In the short term we had to shed that uneconomic tail which was turning out coal we didn't need at costs we couldn't afford. Market prospects seemed to settle around an output of 90 million tonnes a year of deep-mined coal and 15 million of open cast to start with. So, depending on the circumstances in the spring when the time came to giving the areas their targets for production, we would need to reduce capacity initially by a few million tonnes.

In the early days, before Christmas, I was purposefully vague about the amount of capacity we would have to shed and when – since we were still looking at the situation ourselves – but already I was indicating that, in time, between 6 and 8 million tonnes would have to go. When we put this broad outline to a meeting in November, there was a great deal of rolling of eyes and shaking of heads from the other side. Scargill chose the word 'catastrophic' to describe our plans. I thought the word would apply to the situation if we didn't go ahead with the plans we had formulated. In December, when we met again, he raised the temperature a little more by claiming we had admitted that our plans would mean the loss of 70 pits and 70,000 jobs. We had said no such thing.

In the medium term, the CEGB was by far our biggest customer, taking three-quarters of all the coal mined in the UK at well above the world market price. Electricity generated from coal accounted for 80 per cent of the CEGB output and purchasing it amounted to nearly half of their costs. We pointed out to the NUM that this comfortable arrangement would clearly not go on forever and, unless we did something about our costs, other sources of electric power – nuclear and even oil and gas – would have a growing impact. One really misleading aspect of The Plan For Coal, which the NUM refused to acknowledge, was that the Plan had anticipated a vast growth in energy demand in the UK which had simply not materialized. However, in order to meet that fanciful projected demand, a large number of nuclear and oil-fired stations had been planned and had now actually materialized. Much of this was the brainchild of Arthur Scargill's close friend, Tony Benn. The net result was that the older coal-fired generating stations were now in a vulnerable position.

We were even more vulnerable with our second largest customer, Steel, as I knew only too well. At one time the NCB provided as much as 10 million tonnes of coking coal a year for the manufacture of British steel. But

BSC was becoming increasingly unhappy with the high sulphur content of much of our deep-mined coal, which added cost and increased the problems the corporation had in producing the high-specification steels which were becoming more and more necessary in the highly competitive steel markets. Also, it was, as we have seen, a matter of time rather than debate before BSC was forced to close one of its five main plants – probably Ravenscraig – thereby reducing further the need for NCB coal.

I made it clear that neither of these problems was insurmountable, if we could get rid of our high-cost capacity – which was dragging the rest of the industry down – and that in the long term I had great hopes. In fact when at BSC, working closely with Bob Scholey and Frank Fitzgerald, I encouraged the introduction of a system known as coal injection. Coal additions could be made in the blast furnace or steel converter with various regular bituminous coals, all of which could be produced in the UK at competitive cost. These ideas have now been expanded and will progressively lead to the steel industry using more and more NCB coal.

However, in our union meetings I kept plugging away, trying to get the message over – if not to Scargill then to the moderates on his executive and to the other unions – that there *was* a future. I made a point of visiting our research laboratories at Stoke Orchard and subsequently announced a plan to build a pilot plant to test a new process for coal liquification in a small plant next to the Point of Ayr pit in north Wales. It was this sort of pilot project – to enlarge the markets for coal and to prepare for the inevitable time when petroleum liquids would be too scarce and expensive to remain as our source of liquid, or 'portable', energy as in petrol or jet fuel – that I felt showed the way to the future. I was able to tell the NUM that, as opposed to British Leyland and British Steel, which were dependent on converting raw materials and manufacturing for a living, and therefore had no particular comparative advantage other than their ability to be more cost competitive, the coal industry did have basic resources. The task of survival, therefore, was much easier than it had been at either of the other two. The big proviso was, as always, that we *had* to get our costs right.

To show them that I meant business I started banging the drum for coal exports, especially as the pound was weak against the dollar at the time. We had discussions with the Tampa Electric Company of Florida, where some of the directors were friends of mine. They expressed interest in buying coal from us for some of their waterfront power stations. But in the end it was the cost that beat us, a lesson I made sure to pass on.

I had the very strong feeling, which the recent fall in oil prices has not dispelled, that the world coal market was going to expand fairly rapidly in the next two decades and that therefore, while we might not yet be able to compete in the world markets on a major basis, there was no reason why we should not look to Europe. During this period there was an energy meeting in Sweden, where the government was reacting anxiously to the antinuclear lobby and looking at alternative sources including coal. Jimmy and I knew that the questions we were going to be asked over and over again would be about our costs and our reliability. Could we get our costs in line? Could we guarantee supply would not be interrupted by strikes? There was only one man who could answer those questions, we decided. Besides, it might open his eyes as to what our real task was. So Arthur Scargill was approached and asked to go, but he turned us down. It was a pity because he might have found out something more about the real world: that British coal was not necessarily the cheapest, that strikes can do permanent harm to the enterprise and that if you want to make a living, you have to earn it. We didn't give up, though. Eventually we managed to persuade Jack Jones, the NUM's Leicestershire man, to go, and Jimmy came back and said he had done a great job as a salesman for British Coal.

I was trying all the time to get the NUM to look at the far horizon. I had a saying: 'Petrochemicals originated from coal in the nineteenth century and will again be produced from coal in the twenty-first century.' In the last century the generation of town gas from coal had led to many by-products, such as tars and benzine compounds, which were the building blocks of the early plastics. In this century, particularly since the Second World War, cheaper oil and natural gas provided these building blocks and the fantastic expansion of petrochemicals and plastics that we have seen was based on them. However, I would say that before the end of this century the availability of liquid petroleum and natural gas will be declining and the process will start to reverse. Once again coal will become the principal source of petrochemicals and plastics. Within the next fifteen years we will be moving clearly in that direction and there will be a vast new market opportunity for coal, if it is at the right price. We will still have to compete with the rest of the world.

I told Scargill all this. I told him that was why I got into the business in the first place in America. Coal has a potentially better future than any other business I have ever been associated with. I think he understood in a vague sort of way but felt that it just was not relevant to the argument. He liked the bits about coal being a valuable resource, but not the bits about its cost. His argument was that, since coal was a valuable resource, all pits should be kept open until the last ounce had been dug out of them. My argument was that coal was only valuable if somebody wanted to buy it and therefore it was only valuable if the cost was right. I used the analogy that since there are a few parts per million of gold in all sea water, there are probably hundreds of tonnes of the precious metal in the Firth of Clyde – but nobody would want to buy it at the price it would cost you to extract it. But I don't think he wanted to understand it. It interfered with his rosy perception of the world, in which miners should be kept in jobs and pits kept open for them at whatever the cost to the taxpayer. One might say in his defence that he probably had some justification in holding that view, on the grounds that the history of the submissive policies of successive governments seemed to indicate a general acceptance of these ideas, judging by what had actually happened.

We would be subjected to long lectures at these meetings warning us of the grave consequences of trying to disturb the status quo. Scargill's brain was clearly locked and bolted against the concept of any pit closing for any reason other than safety or total exhaustion. While it was fascinating to watch him wriggle and squirm his way through the facts, I was also coming to realize what a dangerous man I was up against.

His arguments rarely changed. They ran the usual gamut from butchering the industry to pit closures. It seemed sometimes as though we were using totally different dictionaries. He talked about the 'right to work', for example, as though the job somehow belonged to the employee and his union, no matter what the cost to the customer, employer or taxpayer. My idea of the 'right to work' was to emerge a few months later: it was the entitlement of a man to be able to go to his place of work and do a day's work and earn his living there without being subjected to violence and intimidation against either himself or his family.

He was never prepared to accept the idea that most

times we were doing his members a favour by shutting the most uneconomic pits. These were often the pits that were the most difficult and dangerous in which to work, frequently with very thin and irregular coal seams. I had been quite happy to prove a point by crawling underground all that way to the face a few days after I started in the job. I have always been careful never to ask people to do anything I would not do myself. When I see people working in bad conditions I want to change things and get them out of there. The working conditions of many of these old pits were, quite frankly, intolerable, and my instinct, from day one, was to close them and get those men who wanted to stay on into decent pits while giving those who wanted to leave as handsome a sum of money as possible.

I remember many years ago the Thunderbird coal mine in Indiana. Shortly after Amax took it over I found out what the underground conditions were. As I said at the time, I wouldn't want any human being to work in that mine. I was told by the managers that they could still get half a million tons out of the pit. I remember my rather heated response: 'To hell with that. Shut it.' We do not need coal so badly that we have to expose people to that sort of danger. I still have that strong conviction about working conditions anywhere, but particularly underground.

Recent analysis of the safety records of our industry over the years has made it clear that our newer, more modern and most efficient pits have by far the best safety records. So much for the canard put about by Scargill and friends that pressure for production has reduced the safety standards.

Men working in bad conditions also helped prove his point that we were anti-working class. I came to the conclusion that Scargill wanted to scrap the bonus system

– not because it set man against man, as he claimed, but because the men earned good money from it and men who are earning good money are, quite rightly, more interested in two weeks in the sun than they are in fighting his political battles. I also concluded that the reason why he wouldn't take our pay offer was not because it was derisory, as he claimed. We had the feeling that if he had put it to his men they would have accepted it.

Scargill's attitude demonstrated, to my mind, that hidden facet of the militant left-wing in the unions. It was probably only matched by his attitude towards the long-suffering taxpayer, who was supposed to subsidize these jobs forever, who was supposed to pay for coal to be dug out, whatever the cost and whether there was a marekt for it or not. The brunt of his oft-stated claim that the miners should be kept in work because it would be cheaper than having them go on the dole (the claim, you notice, presumes automatically that all miners who leave the industry stay on the dole forever more) would, of course, be borne by the taxpayer.

After Christmas 1983 there was very little pretence. Every word, every action indicated preparation for a campaign running at us head-on. There was no sign in the leadership of the NUM; there was no sign of any willingness whatsoever to sit down and discuss the problems, and the timing of what we had to do, in order that we could work out an agreed and phased restructuring of the industry with the minimum of personal disruption for the union members involved. The claims got wilder and wilder. Enormous efforts were made to turn the screw on the overtime ban. There was a steady increase in outbreaks of trouble at pits – particularly in the militant areas.

We knew there were dissenting voices within the NUM

executive – Trevor Bell, who had stood against Scargill for the presidency eighteen months before, Ken Toon, who would go on to lead the Union of Democratic Miners, Jack Jones from Leicestershire, Ted McKay form North Wales, whose staunch supporters at the Point of Ayr pit had given me such a good welcome, and Roy Ottey of the Power Group – but increasingly all debate was being subordinated to the left-wing faction who saw vindication of their policies in the election of Peter Heathfield to the post of general secretary on 20 January.

Heathfield's success at the polls – as Scargill's nominee – was not quite the triumph the left-wing element claimed it to be. His majority – only 3516 out of 191,000 members – might have warned a more sensitive miners' leader that not everyone agreed with his conduct of the NUM's affairs. His challenger, John Walsh, was able to make great issue of the lack of a national ballot on the overtime ban and the need which he, too, stated for 'less aggro and more results'.

The election brought together the three men at the top of the union hierarchy who were to be my principal opponents for the next fifteen months – Scargill, McGahey and Heathfield – and I spent some time wondering how long their apparently united front would last. McGahey, the vice president, was a tough hard-line communist dedicated to the party. Since Scargill's accession to office McGahey seemed more or less to defer to him totally. Whatever revolutionary fire there still was in him seemed to have been transferred to Arthur Scargill. It was as if he was reconciled to living vicariously through Scargill. He didn't demonstrate in my presence much independence of spirit. Even if he disagreed with Arthur, he never gave us any sign in the meetings we had that he was prepared to say so. He was going along with it all, but letting his president make the running.

I knew nothing about Heathfield, beyond the fact that he had apparently been a fairly important NUM figure in Derbyshire and that Merrick Spanton held the view that his record would lead them to expect him to be somewhat easier to get on with and more pragmatic than Scargill. I took that with a grain of salt. I suspected Arthur would not have picked him as a running mate unless he was satisfied about two things. First, that his left-wing credentials were impeccable and, second, that he would do as he was told. In a union run by a publicity-seeking Marxist there would only be room for one star – the rest would be strictly supporting cast. I came to the conclusion that if we were to try to drive a wedge between them, it would be unlikely to have much success.

So we were going to have to deal with Scargill across the table: not a task I looked forward to with any enthusiasm. He had emerged over the months as a skilful performer who could think quickly, but was not really a negotiator. He postured, but never seemed to be able to enter into the usual trading that characterizes a good negotiator. He could only accept victory for his side. There was no grey, only black or white. Jimmy put both Heathfield and McGahey streets ahead of Scargill in terms of ability to analyse a problem and to negotiate a deal.

Heathfield's election, incidentally, revealed one other aspect of Scargill's use of the rules for his own ends. Was it a coincidence, we asked ourselves, that just as Joe Gormley and his executive had waited until Mick McGahey was a few days too old, at fifty-five, to stand for the presidency – thus clearing the way, perhaps inadvertently, for Scargill – so now Lawrence Daly, a lifelong communist, but no great ally of Scargill's, was persuaded to step down early so that Heathfield could be elected just a few days before he also would have been too old to qualify for election to the post? We nevertheless took some encouragement from the narrowness of the result: it seemed further evidence that Scargill would be crazy to try to start a national strike now. Yet that seemed more and more to be precisely his aim. The temperature was rising rapidly as he worked his supporters up into a frenzy.

In early February flour and eggs were thrown at me when I was on a pit visit to Brodsworth Colliery in Doncaster. Three weeks later there was a large and well-led 'spontaneous' demonstration against me on a visit to Ellington Colliery in Northumberland. The men surrounded the manager's office shouting, 'Let's go in and get the old bastard out!' The police were unable to control the mob, but it was decided that, as they were being wound up by the inflammatory efforts of their militant leaders, we should try to get out. The police said they would drive a corridor from the back door to the car park. As I emerged the mob lunged forward, broke through the police line and one hefty lout grabbed me by my duffle coat lapels and shouted to his frenzied friends, 'I've got him!' At this point the press of the mob pushing towards the office broke down the supports of the solid wooden retaining fence and wall. The front of the mob, policemen and all, collapsed in a heap with my hefty collier falling on top of me. I had the wind knocked out of me so I just lay there. The crowd suddenly became quiet, and the TV cameramen now had no trouble in moving in to take their classic shots of how the coal board chairman had 'stumbled and fallen' at Ellington. Some stumble!

It was strictly a put-up job. The idea was to frighten this old man so that he would quit, so that he would be too scared to go anywhere. Then they could go to the government and demand he be got rid of. The line would be: 'All you have to do is send him home and all will be peace and quiet and everybody will be back in business.'

The trouble was I had seen it all a dozen times before and I had been frightened by better men than Scargill.

Jimmy Cowan, Ned Smith and Merrick Spanton were all now reporting to me early each morning on the build-up of tension in the coalfields. I spent most of my time listening, trying to feel the mood and going over each of the area reports with them to try to assess what was going on. We were now convinced that Scargill was planning it all to coincide with the announcement we were to make at the beginning of March of the first 4 million tonne cut in capacity. We were getting messages that they had got their final plans under way – the movement of money, the booking of transport and instructions to their 'field commanders'. Many men, apprehensive of what they knew was coming, were asking about what the redundancy plans would be. They wanted out; if possible, before it started.

It had been clear since Christmas, if not before, that as soon as we tabled our plans for 1984–5 as required at the next industry consultative council there would be an immediate reaction. I was not there to delay, or to ask the union when it was they would most like to have their strike. If, as seemed certain, Arthur Scargill was spoiling to get a strike as soon as we announced our plans, I decided there was no point in holding back – even if it might postpone the inevitable for a while.

By March we had decided on what we had to do in the year ahead. If Scargill's only reaction to the announcement of our plans was to go for a confrontation, then, in the absence of any evidence that there was a willingness on his part to negotiate, I decided we would have to place those plans firmly on the table. If we were to be faced with strike action then so be it. I just felt so sorry for his members and the sacrifices they were going to have to make on his revolutionary altar in the months ahead.

In facing the imminent probability of a strike with no apparent escape road being left by the union other than total NCB capitulation, I had to take careful stock of the disposition of the forces. If the country were to face a prolonged coal strike starting in March, the impact on our customers would be less than if it were to start in October. I could not understand Scargill's strategy. He was choosing the beginning of that part of the year when coal consumption usually starts to decline dramatically. Thus, if the NUM insisted the strike had to come, it would be less harmful from our point of view for it to start now.

I presumed it was still the least inconvenient time for the prime minister – though I had not seen her since just before Christmas, when I had been invited to lunch at Chequers. Contrary to the popularly held belief on the left, I did not have to report to her every five minutes about what I was doing. I did not get a string of orders from her either. We had discussed my job. I had told her what I thought would happen. She accepted that and left me to get on with it. I had only briefly updated her at that lunch in December.

Peter Walker, in the meantime, had expressed some anxieties about the continuation of the overtime ban. I presume that, prompted by his civil servants, he could not understand why we were not having all-day negotiating sessions and making the usual concessions to try to end it. But when, early in the New Year, it became obvious that there was going to be a strike, he took it very calmly. I think he too realized it was inevitable. I think he realized that I had been hired to get the industry right and that that could not be done without a clash, so he was content not to interfere for the time being and to let events take their course. I could easily imagine him feeling that if I was digging my own grave he wanted to be seen neither hindering me, nor handing me the shovel. Similarly, his civil servants were prepared to lie low and did not seem to be keen to get closely involved. A fair reflection of their attitude would be that they were content to be working on other energy problems.

Towards the end of February I called all the twelve area directors to London and Jimmy and I together saw each of them in turn through the day. I decided to see them individually, because the message we had for each one was personal and varied according to the area he came from. First we gave them the next year's targets for the reductions in capacity in each of their areas and the budgets they were to meet. Then we went through an assessment of the likelihood of trouble in their area and whether the men might be persuaded, or might even decide, to continue to work. Obviously we would have to handle with kid gloves those areas where there was any chance of the men working on, whereas there was very little point in being anything other than straightforward and blunt in the more militant coalfields. Nottingham would therefore be handled very differently to Doncaster. Bert Wheeler's task in Scotland was going to be very different from Michael Eaton's in North Yorkshire.

But I also had a message common to them all: that in the coming months they would have the total support of Jimmy and me. Life was going to be very difficult for them. They were the field commanders and they were going to be faced with some horrendous decisions, but I wanted each one to know that we were with them all the way. One of my earliest lessons in management made it clear that one can always delegate authority but never responsibility – only top management can share responsibility. That was why we said we were with our men. The second lieutenant must always lead the charge personally if he is to enjoy the authority of being the leader.

Our interview with George Hayes, the South Yorkshire area director, was the same as the others in all but one respect. We gave him his target, which was to cut 500,000 tonnes out of his 7.6 million annual capacity. He then pointed out to Jimmy that, if he moved quickly now, he could achieve this cut by shutting just one pit, whereas if he waited he would almost certainly have to shut two. We both felt he should get on with it. After all, what he was planning was in the best long-term interests of the men. He made the announcement locally on 1 March that he intended to shut Cortonwood pit as soon as possible. There is no doubt that he was right to shut Cortonwood. It had lost £4 million in the previous year. Its coal, costing £64 a tonne at the pit head, could only be sold at enormous loss – a testament to this fact being that half a year's output was still lying in the colliery yard. But the outcry that followed the announcement was only partly due to the fact that Hayes had not technically followed the accepted procedure for announcing closures. The whole South Yorkshire coalfield was in a ferment, whipped up by months of Scargill's speeches and rallies, and it was looking for just such a 'grievance' to finally ignite. The fact that it did so, with a decision to strike from 9 March, taken without a ballot by the NUM area council – on the day before we were due to announce our plans for the whole industry in London – was, we felt at the time, almost the inevitable sequence of events.

Thus on 6 March at the meeting of the Coal Industry National Consultative Council we gave the unions our plans. Jimmy did the presentation – his mastery of the detail and the history was much better than mine. The meeting took place in Room 16 of Hobart House, a large, artificially lit room, where the two 'sides' sat opposite each other at tables formed into an oblong with a sort of empty 'no-man's-land' in between. The military analogy was particularly pertinent that day because the atmosphere was, frankly, hostile.

First we covered the ground, again, of the future of the industry – always with the proviso that we could get our costs right. Then, as the temperature dropped, Jimmy began to go into detail of what would be required to bring about this high-volume, low-cost industry. I think you could safely say that the strike started the moment Scargill asked if the requirement to take 4 million tonnes out of capacity would involve a 'similar programme of rundown' to that experienced the previous year and Jimmy answered that it would be of 'broadly the same order'.

Scargill never could and never did accept that there was no longer a market for all the coal that some of these pits were producing and that therefore, whatever words were used, they had to close.

I had an opportunity to watch as this was going on. I could see McGahey rolling his eyes and mouthing the word 'disaster' and I could sense Scargill winding himself up for one of his speeches, which duly came. He gets into a sort of groove, almost a trance, as he recites the same litany over and over again – a sort of mantra of Coal Board mismanagement – and when you tell him what nonsense it is, he doesn't hear you, because it interferes with his train of thought. Then some of the rest made their set-piece speeches, pointing out the wicked ways of the Coal Board, how it wouldn't work and the men would never go for it. There was no evidence they even heard the NCB statement that no one would be forced to lose his job and that we fully expected to achieve all the cuts by transferring men and voluntary redundancies. As I listened to Jimmy Cowan's moderate and modest plans for a start on restructuring in what was at last a logical programme, I became increasingly pessimistic as to whether there was any chance of achieving them peaceably.

In South Yorkshire, men in a handful of pits had decided not to wait until 9 March to strike and that morning, even as we met in London, they had started to picket out the rest of the pits in their area. The following morning an angry and bewildered Robert Taylor, a face-worker at the Manton colliery at the other end of the coalfield, on the Nottinghamshire border, was advised – for his own safety – not to try to go to work through the picket lines. His emotions were aroused by the fact that only a few days earlier his pit had decided not to back strikes in support of other pits and now he was being undemocratically robbed of the right to work. His anger was subsequently to sustain him all the way to the High Court and, in the end, to tie the NUM up in knots.

Arthur Scargill left the meeting and predictably gave a whole series of press conferences and statements with all the usual accusations. By that night the Scottish area NUM executive, where pits faced a 750,000-tonne cutback in capacity from 5.9 million, had voted to call for a strike too.

None of us was prepared for what happened in the next few days. I think it took a while for it to sink in, at all levels, that any semblance of democracy in the National Union of Mineworkers had been kicked out of the window and that mob rule had taken over.

I was surprised by the speed and the extent of it – but not by the fact that it happened. I knew we were dealing with someone who was prepared to use numbers of his men as cannon fodder for his assault on the NCB and the government. If anybody had any illusions, then they should have listened the following night as Mick McGahey told radio and television interviewers: 'We are not dealing with the niceties here. We shall not be constitutionalized out of a defence of our jobs. Area by area will decide . . . it will have a domino effect.'

The rule of the bully boy, the hooligan and the threatening thug had come to the coal industry. Arthur's army was on the march. And no one – not me, not the police and particularly not Margaret Thatcher – was going to be allowed to stand in his way. It *was* civil war.

7

Battle Commences

Surprisingly the violence of the following week – and after – didn't seem to shock the public very much. Perhaps it was because television has inured us to violence. We have grown used to it and there is a degree of acceptance of it in situations like strikes as a means of achieving objectives. I was struck most forcibly, in the early days, by the fact that those people whose clear intention it was to smash not only the democratic institutions of their own union, but also of the country itself, were given the same – if not more – air time and credibility as those who were seeking in one way or another to defend our way of life.

On many occasions the hostility of certain sections of the media was such that I got the distinct impression it was considered entirely wrong to stand in the way of the president of the National Union of Mineworkers and his mob as they went about their 'legitimate' business of bringing the country to its knees. I felt particularly sorry for the police, who, far from being the agents of a neo-Nazi state as Arthur Scargill could be heard declaring night after night, were trying, to their personal discomfort, to uphold some of the most fundamental laws of the land. It was with great sadness that I saw, time and again, their hours of restraint under a constant barrage of missiles and abuse left unrecorded and a day of humiliation and danger on the picket line reduced to a thirty-second clip of film. This showed only the dramatic bits of 'good television' in which the police found it necessary, in order to do their job, to move forward into contact with the pickets and were therefore seen to be attacking them.

There was an air of unreality about the whole situation – as though people found it impossible to believe the evidence that their eyes and ears presented to them – and were further hampered in giving that evidence any credibility by the fact that large sections of the media treated it all as being perfectly normal. I can remember the shocked headlines and astonishment of political commentators when the prime minister, some weeks later, described these attempts to bring down our democratic way of life as the work of 'the enemy within' (as opposed to 'the enemy without' whom she had faced so bravely the year before in the Falklands crisis). Those of us who had been through the first few weeks of the strike knew precisely what she was talking about and found the generally negative reaction to her words a symptom of dangerous apathy or, even more serious, the sign of a naive public.

Arthur Scargill was indeed one of the enemies within. Of all the many, many fundamentally antidemocratic sentiments expressed by him and those around him at the time, let me just quote one which sums up how terrifyingly near we were to the rule of the mob in those days. After the long and bitter battle within the NUM executive over the failure of the union to hold a national ballot on the strike – a battle in which the moderates were outmanoeuvred, ignored, intimidated and finally, in my view, cheated of the vote – Scargill grabbed a loudhailer and told the 7000-strong massed ranks of 'Arthur's army' outside:

I am the custodian of the rule book, and I want to
say to my colleagues in the union that there is one
rule, above all the rules in the book, and that is that
when workers are involved in action you do not cross
picket lines in any circumstances.

That simple statement finally made it absolutely clear
that he was not interested in democracy or in the views
of the mass of his members. The only rule he recognized
was the rule of the mob at his command. Wherever two
or three pickets were gathered together, there thousands
shall not work: that was Scargill's Law. It led to some
ludicrous situations. On one occasion a group of miners
hung a flag on a bridge over a railway line and deemed
that to be a picket line. As we shall see, the actions that
resulted from that gesture nearly paralysed the entire
country. On another occasion workers at power stations
were asked by letter to consider themselves picketed and
therefore to walk out. Fortunately they had the sense to
say no.

Scargill's words also showed that the events of the
previous few weeks had been entirely premeditated, as
we found out later when we saw how much of the union's
funds had been transferred out of the country. There
never had been any real intention of holding a ballot. He
believed the legendary loyalty of the NUM membership
to the leadership was such that, while at most only 10
per cent of the members would follow him willingly into
battle, the vast majority of the rest would not actively
hinder him. It was on this calculation, coupled with the
belief I shared with him that if he were to go for a ballot
he would not get the 55 per cent majority required, that
he decided to force the issue and go into battle.

And it was on this basis also that I came to believe we
were now probably in for a three- to six-month-long

dispute. I did not see him winning. I could see it lasting through the summer, sustained largely by his revolutionary rhetoric and the constantly reiterated promise that the NCB was about to collapse. But when we failed to lie down in front of his mighty army and the winter set in and there were still no power cuts, I could see him having considerable difficulties. As I had indicated to both the prime minister and to Peter Walker, they should have no illusions that it was going to be over quickly. Once Scargill charged it would be a long and bloody battle; for the NUM were not accustomed to backing off and historically had very good reason to believe that any time they exercised their muscle the Coal Board – and the government – would retreat. At least, that was what had always happened in the past. In fact, I thought, the best way to get it over quickly would probably be to plan on it going on for a long time.

I shared Scargill's scepticism of the proliferating public opinion polls at the time – all of which showed majorities of more than 60 per cent of miners in favour of striking. It was one thing for a total stranger to approach a miner in a street, in his village, or even knock on his door in a row of miners' houses and ask him, in effect, whether or not he was a good union man. Quite another to ask him, after due consideration of all the factors involved, in total secrecy to put a mark on a piece of paper which would commit him and his family to ever-increasing hardship for weeks, if not months ahead. I believed then and I still do now that Scargill would not have got a 'yes' vote to strike, even at the reduced 50 per cent level he later instituted.

Faced with this prospect, I believe he chose many months before to embark on the other route – the mob rule way to a strike – which was, after all, in many ways more appealing to the performing side of his personality than the more orderly, circumspect processes of traditional union democracy. Leading 'Arthur's army' was essentially more exciting, more dramatic and certainly more televisual than standing on the steps of his union headquarters announcing to a few assembled reporters the results of a duly held vote.

My impression from events of those first few days was that Scargill and his cronies had been preparing for a strike for about a year. They were formidably well organized and clearly had a cohesive 'battle plan' long before it started. From day one they were out in large numbers, moving with well-coordinated instructions and in constant communication with their area headquarters. They didn't look to me like people who had suddenly found themselves out on strike and were looking around and wondering what to do. They knew exactly what to do and where to go. Their tactics in the field were laid down by local command centres, using CB radios, and buses to organize troop movements.

The overall strategic plan was clearly based on the militancy of Yorkshire, South Wales, Durham and Scotland, and aimed to bring the whole industry to a halt as quickly as possible. Long before I joined the NCB, stories and rumours had been filtering back to the upper reaches of Hobart House that movements were afoot, and dispositions being made. The technique, we presumed, would be based on the Battle of Saltley Gate twelve years before, where, as I have already mentioned, Scargill had had his first whiff of revolutionary triumph. This time he was not one lone commander out in the battlefield, he was the field-marshal who had gathered round him an impressive coterie of advisers, including academics, whose counsel he was regularly seeking on how to arrange all aspects of the coming conflict, from getting round the union rules to finding legal loopholes and handling public relations.

It quickly became clear that the whispers we had heard had been correct – not only on the ground, with the buses and the cars and the communications systems, but in contingency terms too. Plans were ready, the moment the strike started, to remove the union's funds from the reaches of the government's industrial relations laws, and arrangements had already been approved not to give the men strike pay from union funds – the traditional method of ameliorating hardship in cases of official union disputes – but to pay the men instead for serving on picket duty. You only got Scargill's shilling when you signed on in Arthur's army.

His first offensive was swift and sudden. Our meeting with the NUM executive had been held on Tuesday, 6 March. Yorkshire had already decided to strike – ordered out by their area council as from 9 March – over the proposed closure of Cortonwood. But many pits had already come to a halt and by the weekend the stoppage was total in the county. On the evening of 6 March the Scottish area council also met and ordered its 12,000 men out on strike – this time to protest at the 'provocative and bullying' tactics of the NCB. At nearly all the Scottish pits the men called for a vote. At nearly all of them they were reluctantly allowed to do so on a show of hands – and at nearly all of them they voted overwhelmingly *not* to strike. Bilston Glen voted 80 per cent in favour of working. They were not allowed a ballot. By Friday, 9 March most of them had been picketed out by the minority of militants – never more than 10 per cent – and on the Monday afternoon, with considerable intimidation, the task was completed when the shift at Bilston Glen gave up the unequal struggle. Scotland, as they say in the proud terminology of the trade union movement, was thus rendered 'solid for the strike'.

These two preliminary moves in Yorkshire and Scotland

were essential for what was about to follow. On Thursday, 8 March the NUM executives met and, after the preliminaries had been dealt with, Arthur Scargill announced that letters had been received from both the Yorkshire and the Scottish areas requesting that their strike calls be recognized under Rule 41 – and urging general support from the other areas.

On the surface they were simple, spontaneous and innocuous requests under a clause of the rule book of a type which is normally used in the trade union lexicon to get a spot of help with a little local difficulty. But all the evidence points to the action having been completely premeditated as Scargill's way of forcing the men out on strike without a ballot. In any event the effect of it was to be the months of violence and intimidation which were to rend the union asunder. It is one of the principal ironies of the strike that it was this move – not anything the NCB did – which, in Scargill's own favourite phrase, 'set man against man, pit against pit and area against area'.

There are two methods by which a strike can be declared official in the NUM rule book – Rules 41 and 43. Rule 43, which had been used in all previous major industrial actions of the NUM, states that 'a national strike shall *only* be entered on as the result of a ballot vote of the members'. Rule 41 covers local area strikes, which can go ahead (i.e., be declared official) only after approval has been sought and granted at national level.

Rule 41 had never been used for anything other than local disputes before. The moment Scargill mentioned it at the meeting one or two members of his own executive smelled a rat. Roy Ottey, of the union's Power Group, who later resigned in protest at Scargill's flouting of the law, says of that moment: 'I realized this could mean a national strike without a ballot. It was obvious that Britain's miners were in danger of being brought out through mass picketing and intimidation. The sickening part was that it was all so predictable. The alarm bells had already sounded when I had heard Mick McGahey saying on television that we would not be constitutionalized out of action. Though I have often admired Mick as a statesman, this sort of behaviour I found difficult to accept.'

Ottey's eye-witness report of the subsequent debate among the 24 members of the executive, plus Heathfield and Scargill, makes depressing reading for anyone with an interest in democracy. The moderates were outmanoeuvred. It was not deemed necessary to have a ballot. Indeed, as one member pointed out, there was danger in asking the men to vote because too many of them were either earning too much money, or wanting to take the generous redundancy terms, to be trusted to come up with the properly militant response. Two proposals were put on the table: the original Rule 41 request and one, from the moderates, under Rule 43. Scargill took the vote on the first, which went 21–3 in favour, and never put the second one at all. He said on television that night that the vote 'was unanimous by virtue of a substantive motion'.

Since the rule above all rules is 'Thou shalt not cross a picket line', all he had to do now was picket the rest of the nation's pits and he had his strike. In this, of course, he was dependent on two things, each a side of the same coin: the men's loyalty to the union and their fear of going against its leader's command.

The extraordinary loyalty of the men, which surprises many outsiders, is common to miners all over the world. Men who work underground rely heavily on each other every day of their lives for their protection and safety. There is a sense of common cause among miners and mining management right up to a high level, because to be a manager you must first have been a miner. At grass roots this loyalty of man to man is expressed in a great camaraderie. In union terms it is expressed in an almost blind faith in the leadership to see the men right in wages and conditions. It is this unquestioning loyalty that Arthur Scargill was banking on to tip the balance in area after area and to pitch the miners, without a vote, into direct conflict with the government. And those who didn't show sufficient loyalty would be frightened out of their place of work.

Before the strike I believed that Arthur Scargill would be forced by the traditions and disciplines of his union to hold a ballot. The NUM had a long history of democratic procedures. I was surprised therefore, to say the least, by the speed and sureness with which he hijacked democracy from the grasp of his members.

The preparations for this had been made, as we have seen, well in advance. The Yorkshire motion of 1981, allowing for any action deemed necessary in support of an individual pit, was now used to substantiate and legitimize the Cortonwood strike – on which in turn the whole fabric of the strike was now built.

The use of the special delegate conference as a policy-making body superior to the national executive had also been carefully phased into common NUM practice. It is a well-known tactic of the left to hold branch meetings at times inconvenient to the average family man who makes up the mass of workers. Few but the most committed – and therefore, nearly always, the most left-wing – will turn up on Saturday mornings or Sunday afternoons to argue their way through the minutiae of union politics. As we have seen, delegates chosen from among their ranks are therefore likely to be the *crème de la crème* of the left. This applies to many unions which have tilted leftwards in the last decade or so, and the NUM is no exception.

It had become clear before the strike, but now it was clearer still, that not only was Scargill anxious not to confront his members in the traditional way with the decision about a strike, but that he was also not going to let his national executive approach the matter either. If push came to shove the matter would be carefully removed from their grasp and put in the hands of such left-wing-dominated delegate conferences. There, surrounded by mobs of thousands of loyal marching men, baying for the blood of anyone who suggested anything less than the most militant of action, the 'delegates' could come to the task with a clear view of how the membership felt and act accordingly.

Thus democracy had gone from the NUM long before it ever came to the strike and I suppose we should not have been surprised by what happened. In its place had come a terrifying form of authoritarianism in which the price of dissent, if you were lucky, was the threat that you might never be allowed to work in a pit again. If you were unlucky, you might be beaten senseless, your home wrecked, your wife and family frightened silly, *and* you still might never be allowed to work in a pit again.

It is really a very shattering thing that, at this stage in the twentieth century, in one of the world's most civilized countries, so few people, with such little right to it, should have so much power over others. Literally the power of life or death.

Fanning out from Yorkshire and the other militant areas, the bully boys of Arthur's army sought in the few days after the 8 March executive meeting to impose his will on the rest of the miners in Britain. As we have seen, Scotland was swiftly smashed into submission and, by Monday, all pits except one in Yorkshire were also out. Durham – keen to be in the militant vanguard – struck immediately, as did the three pits in Kent. In South Wales

19 pits voted to work and 11 to strike. The area union officials told the men that the recommendation to strike still stood and 11 of the 19 were picketed out on the Monday morning. Six more went in the afternoon and they had all succumbed by the following day.

It was the same story nearly everywhere. In north Derbyshire, for example, Ken Moses, the area director, saw the local police to try to warn them that heavy and violent picketing was expected on Tuesday, 13 March. He watched thousands of pickets from Yorkshire duly preventing, at pit after pit, his Derbyshire men from going to work. The police seemed either unable or unwilling to intervene, only threatening to do so when he told them his men were going to form up like a phalanx at Shire-brook Colliery and force their way in. He was then warned that such action would constitute, and would be treated as, a potential breach of the peace in exactly the same way as any of the picketing. He begged them to do something to stop the intimidation but, for whatever reason, nothing happened.

In frustration and desperation he called Jimmy and me and, quite rightly, vented his feelings on us. His was one of a number of anguished calls we were getting from our area directors all over the country.

On Friday, 16 March, with still no pit in the north Derbyshire area working fully, the men held a ballot. The result, announced next day, showed 4307 for striking and 4323 against – a majority of 16 against strike action. At this time it still required a 55 per cent majority to strike so the vote was well short of the required majority in support of the strike. On the Saturday night the NUM area secretary declared 'no strike' in north Derbyshire.

But on Monday morning the area executive council of the NUM met – along with the pit delegates, naturally – and disqualified the votes of the people in a small non-

NCB mine and at an NCB laboratory, presuming them to be against striking. Thus they overturned the ballot result and declared the strike in Derbyshire official.

By Tuesday, 20 March, Moses was left with seven men at Shirebrook and half the men at Bolsover fighting their way through the picket lines to work. He was on the point of giving in and sending the Shirebrook men home because of all the trouble their action might cause when the strike was over, which, from where he was watching, must have looked like being soon.

Similar assaults on democracy took place in nearly every area where any reluctance was shown to falling in line. In the days immediately after the NUM executive meeting Lancashire and Nottinghamshire were overrun by flying pickets, mostly from the militant Doncaster branches in Yorkshire. On several occasions in the home villages, where men had gone to work, pickets rampaged, smashing windows and terrifying women and children as a warning to their husbands not to work.

The word 'ballot' ceased to be a symbol of the democratic way of life and became instead a signal for abuse, a tag to be hung on faint hearts who didn't have the courage for the glorious war that was being waged. Yet in every area where ballots were held at the insistence of the men they showed majorities against striking. Nottingham and the Midlands, notably, each polled 73 per cent against, and south Derbyshire 84 per cent.

The moderates made one more attempt to force Scargill to hold a national vote. They met towards the end of March to plan their tactics for the NUM executive meeting on 12 April – working out that they could win the day, with those who were unhappy about the way things had gone, by 13 votes to 11. When they arrived in Sheffield, however, they had to fight their way through a chanting mob, who kicked and spat at any of them they recognized.

Again Roy Ottey's eye-witness account dramatically highlights the way the atmosphere inside the meeting was affected by the mob outside. One member even asked if the venue could be changed on the grounds that someone could get killed. From the start Scargill warned that the idea of a ballot vote, which he claimed had already been rejected by the executive even though it had never been put to the vote, was not going to succeed. He generously allowed a wide-ranging discussion in which those who wanted democracy were accused by the left of betraying the union and those who wanted nothing to do with a ballot were portrayed as the true democrats!

All pleas for a ballot fell on deaf ears. Even Henry Richardson, the militant Scargillite from Nottingham, who complained that the violence in the villages had destroyed all the area's support for Scargill, was moved to ask: 'If we lose a ballot – are we in any different position to now?' Jim Colgan of the Midlands area produced an incredible piece of topsy-turvy logic when he said that, even though 73 per cent of his men had voted against the strike, he and his area council had overturned the vote and ordered the men out on strike – 'to protect them from the violence of the picket lines'.

It was left to Peter Heathfield to put the final nail in the ballot coffin. 'It is important that we listen to the lads at a special delegate conference,' he said. 'We don't want a ballot vote. Democracy is not about voting another man out of a job. We should not be going up that path.' The argument raged on, but Scargill eventually ruled that the motion for a ballot was out of order, on the grounds that such a proposal had already been made and rejected at the previous month's meeting. But, as if to show democracy was still alive, he said the issue could be aired at a delegate conference – where the union could at last achieve unity on the issue.

As Roy Ottey says: 'We [the moderates] had been routed. No adjective can describe my feelings at that moment. I certainly felt exhausted and, to a great degree, bewildered that so many would go to what seemed any length to make sure the individual miner did not express his opinion.'

Predictably, to the roar of 7000 'lobbyists' outside, the special delegate conference on 19 April threw out the idea of the ballot and sanctioned strike action in all areas under Rule 41.

It had become clear, even in the first days of the strike, that there were a considerable number of miners who were not at all happy with what was being done in their name. In fact it rapidly emerged that the union membership was divided into three broad groups. First, those who believed implicitly in the militant stance, who saw it as their role to bring the NCB to its knees and, beyond that, if it failed to capitulate, the government too. Second, those people who saw no reason why the union should interfere with their right to work on account of an openly political cause. And third, in between, was the great mass who were torn – loyal to the union but also dominated by fear of reprisals. Many of them had no great conviction either way. They looked at the balance of power and they worked out for the time being that the union could do them more harm if they worked than if they didn't. Whatever their loyalties and fear for the future, they were trapped in a sort of balance of terror – if they didn't work, they had one form of economic privation, if they did work, then they had ample reason to fear another.

The anti-Scargill sentiment was strongest in Nottingham and the Midlands, where the attitude among the men was that they had already been through a lot of closures – and what had Scargill ever done to help them?

Jimmy Cowan had been working on the area since before I arrived, trying to create a special atmosphere and get the message over that it was not in their interests to be part of a political strike such as Scargill had in mind. They had a tradition of not being pushed around and a respect for democracy which was totally alien to the Scargill creed. Jimmy also accurately predicted that Chadburn and Richardson, the two Nottingham area officials, would not be able to carry their men with them into a strike. It was on this basis, and from this area, that we were subsequently able to mount our counteroffensive.

But not before we had hastily organized ourselves. We put together a sort of war cabinet which met every morning in my office. At the centre of this were Jimmy and me. We would both get in before eight o'clock to discuss our strategy and tactics. We then had discussions with our group and assigned people tasks, or asked for information very much on a need-to-know basis – as opposed to the Coal Board tradition which had been very much on a 'need-to-gossip' basis. Jimmy is naturally a fairly secretive person and I have always played my cards close to my chest so, while we trusted each other, it was second nature to both of us not to want to confide in too many others.

Merrick Spanton and sometimes Ned Smith from industrial relations would join Jimmy and me before nine o'clock. We would go through the daily reports from each of the area offices and discuss any measures that needed to be taken. It was a sort of *ad hoc* group, but I found that if it got to more than half a dozen then we might as well have held the meeting live in a television studio, so quickly would our discussions get leaked.

From the beginning I had always been uncomfortable with Ned Smith. We were, I suppose, polar opposites. His general deportment worried me. I am sure he would never have thought of letting down the Coal Board – it had been his whole life – but I am equally sure that this sense of loyalty did not extend to me personally. Indeed I suppose my general approach to this type of labour anarchy was alien to his previous experience and must have generated conflicts within him from time to time.

Smith had a rather supercilious attitude, and I had the feeling that many of his speeches to me were based on an unconscious condescension – the feeling that if you hadn't been with the NCB for umpteen years then you couldn't really understand the ins and outs of the details. This naturally upset me. He was probably right that I could not understand many of the intricate points – but that was not what I was there for and, realizing that, I think he resented me. He thought many of the things I suggested would cause trouble, and his naturally establishment mind had been developed in a culture trained to avoid aggressive confrontation.

He gave me the impression that the traditional school in Hobart House believed that we should not do anything which might upset the NUM. At its most extreme this view was expressed in the opinion – held by many of the younger people in the building – that far from upsetting the NUM, we should always seek ways to reach an accommodation. They were not at all convinced of our aim to make the NCB economically viable. They felt we had an obligation to conduct ourselves as a sort of glorified social service, and, if politic, at the beck and call of Arthur Scargill.

As I had done earlier over the overtime ban, one of the suggestions I made in the early days of the strike, to test them out and find out where many of them stood, was that if the NUM was not going to have a ballot, then we should do it for them. It was a kite flying expedition – though it was immediately taken as serious. In fact, the ballot would have been far too difficult to carry out in practice; but it produced a level of hysteria in Hobart House which was quite surprising. I learned that not many people were ready for that kind of intervention and realized that when and if we did decide to mount a counteroffensive, a major part of the job would be selling the idea to our own people.

Many of the area directors – apart from those who had many of their pits working, like Ken Harris in the Midlands and Jack Wood and Harold Taylor in north and south Nottinghamshire – were frankly disbelieving that a back-to-work movement could ever be launched. The suggestion further identified those who preferred a low profile and those who were willing to fight back and would be looking to us for support. In this last camp were John Northard of Western Area, Albert Tuke in hard-line Doncaster, Bert Wheeler from Scotland and Ken Moses from north Derbyshire, while others, like Michael Eaton from North Yorkshire, were rather relaxed about the strike and gave the impression that they preferred to avoid controversy at this stage.

There was one other reason for suggesting we should ballot the men ourselves: it helped Arthur Scargill to make up his mind not to. There was a great feeling at the time in the upper reaches of the NUM that if Ian MacGregor wanted a ballot and Margaret Thatcher wanted a ballot – then they were damned if they were going to have one. That was fine by me, as we shall see.

One member of our inner circle, the NCB secretary, David Brandrick, also gave the impression of being 'on side', but I felt that, true to his long training as a quasi-civil servant, he would remain as totally inscrutable as all good mandarins. He was Oxford educated and, though an officer of the NCB, was really an archetypal administrator. He was very much more at home with his contemporaries over the road at the Department of Energy than with me and some of his colleagues in Hobart House. I felt that when the crunch came he would find his loyalties very severely strained. For the time being, I felt that it would be better for him to run the liaison between us and Peter Walker's parallel group of strike-watchers at the Department of Energy. My group was essentially dealing with the realities of the situation; his with the politics and, as I was to discover, the public relations aspects. I saw Peter Walker quite frequently – at this stage. He was still acting the role of the interested observer as the government's posture in the House of Commons was one of 'hands off'. Brandrick kept the Department team in touch with the details of what we were doing so that nothing came up that surprised them in any way. The system seemed to work quite well – there were not too many anxious phone calls querying why we had done things or why they had not been told something.

I am sure, also, that Peter Walker was not keen to get involved in anything I was doing, as it was, of course, the stated government policy not to interfere. I suspect he felt that he had inherited me on sufferance from Nigel Lawson, who had been poorly advised in hiring me, and that he might as well make the best of a bad job. I got no strong feeling that he had any particular regard for me.

Our industrial relations department – along with Jimmy Cowan – put together very quickly an accurate information service as to what was going on in the areas. In the first couple of months Jimmy travelled thousands of miles by car alone – as well as countless plane journeys – seeing as many pit managers and area management people as possible. Some colliery managers were, like their counterparts in junior management at Hobart House, somewhat upset with what we were doing. After all, many of them had been loyal members of the NUM.

However, we soon found a progressively favourable change of attitude after the strike started, and a growing revulsion against the arrogance of Scargill's aims and methods, on which Jimmy's great efforts were able to capitalize.

Information did not only flow upwards through the area offices to us from the managers who were very close to the grass roots. It also emerged that several of our senior people had 'moles' deep within the NUM, and they too helped us piece together a picture of what the union hierarchy was up to. Just as in a war misinformation is deliberately fed to the enemy, so both sides fed each other false stories from time to time during the strike, though I suspect we became somewhat better at recognizing theirs than they did ours. In any case, time and again we received remarkably accurate information on the thinking and activities at the top of the NUM.

We also started to receive a number of phone calls from miners seeking or offering help. Their information too was added to the mass of facts and impressions from elsewhere and sifted and placed in the general picture. Those men who rang were amazed to get straight through to me, or my secretary Sheila Mann, who fielded hundreds of calls and became expert at sensing the ones that were potentially important enough to put through to me. Just one such call, from a Nottingham faceworker called Rudolph 'Randy' Florence, was perhaps the most important single call I received in the entire twelve months of the dispute. What he told me was to electrify and change my whole thinking about the strike and bring an entirely new area of possible action into sharp focus.

Much of our time in the early weeks was also spent taking stock of the situation – assessing the strengths and weaknesses of the enemy – constantly asking ourselves questions such as: how strong was the NUM's position?

What were the reactions emerging from the other unions? How much support was the NUM going to get from them? Would there be a total blockade on the movement of coal? Would other industries be dragged into the dispute to the extent that there might be a total collapse? How could we avoid this happening? And how could we go on the offensive?

Jimmy's travels – and mine too – helped raise morale and show many of our people that they had, for the first time, a management that was going to fight for its right to manage. In Jimmy's words, our message to them was that we, the Coal Board, would deal with the humanities of the situation, if the NUM would only deal with the realities. In other words, the men whose jobs were to go would get the best and the most sympathetic treatment possible – with generous redundancy – or help to move to a new pit. We were not trying to duck out of any of our responsibilities in that area. But on the other hand we could only do this once the NUM recognized that we also had responsibilities to manage the industry and make it economically viable. It was a two-way street and, over the months, I think many of them came to see it as such.

We were helped by the fact that many of the miners themselves had been profoundly shocked by the scale of the onslaught from the pickets in the first few days. It was a tidal wave of intimidation and thuggery which had taken us all by surprise – none more so than the police. Between Scargill's executive meeting on 8 March and Tuesday, 13 March, all but about 30 of the 171 pits were picketed into submission – and only 11 would be left working normally 48 hours later.

Scargill clearly found his successes on the picket lines heady stuff. He was acting like a successful field commander. I imagine he felt a bit like Rommel must have done as he swept across the desert – he was knocking them down like ninepins. He began to believe in his own invincibility, yet a further reason why he did not need a ballot. He could win without it.

But it was the ill-equipped and tactically disadvantaged local police forces who were thrown into complete disarray that caused me most concern. It was clear that here was the law being broken on a massive scale – not only the government's industrial relations law, but ordinary day-to-day laws to do with violence and intimidation, both at work and in their homes, and the right of a man to go to his work peaceably. The police at a local level seemed incapable, often understandably, of handling the situation. In some cases they were frankly unwilling to get involved in a fight they did not see as being theirs. I was particularly concerned by reports I got that some local left-wing police committees were putting heavy pressure on their chief constables not to get involved, with the implication that the financial future of their forces could be made quite unpleasant if they were seen to be adopting the role of strike-breakers.

Something clearly had to be done, and soon. That is why I sought, and was quickly granted, an appointment to see the prime minister and the then home secretary, Leon Brittan, at 3 p.m. on Wednesday, 14 March. I was boiling with a righteous indignation.

8

The Second Front

Once again, I suppose, the prime minister must have sat there wondering what kind of man it was she had brought in to run the Coal Board. It is never easy for Britons to admit that the policing of their country might be anything less than perfect – certainly a thousand times preferable to the stereotype image of the typical American cop I was now invoking to help us. But my indignation at what was happening in the coalfields the length of the country had not dissipated overnight, nor did it evaporate in her presence.

I put it as vehemently as I could. All over the country men were being deprived of their freedoms and liberties, they were being threatened and intimidated – as were their families. 'Prime Minister,' I said, 'I am sorry to have to say this, but I never thought I would be sitting here in the UK, wishing I had a bunch of good untidy American cops out there. Because, whatever else you can say about them, if someone points out to them a law is being broken, then they go and *do* something about it.

'Unhappily, I must tell you that our British police don't seem to have the same conviction about their job. This aspect of the fight is not between the NCB and the NUM. It is between men who want to work and a bunch of thugs who are trying to deprive them of that right – yet

The 'geriatric American butcher'! – Sir Ian MacGregor. (NCB)

Wearmouth Colliery, 9 September 1983. The new NCB chairman inspects the face after a long crawl to get there. (NCB)

The tension in the coalfields mounts. Ian MacGregor (right) was greeted with bags of flour at Brodsworth Colliery, Doncaster, 2 February 1984. (NCB)

Three weeks later he was grappled by a miner (whose face is hidden behind a policeman) in a 'spontaneous' demonstration at Ellington Colliery, Northumberland. (NCB)

12 April, and the last hope for a ballot vanishes at the NEC meeting. Arthur Scargill, flanked by Mick McGahey, gives the news to the chanting mobs outside. (Press Association)

The 'right to work' movement fights back, 1 May 1984. Nottinghamshire working miners demonstrate outside their own area headquarters in Mansfield. (Press Association)

'Here we go … Here we go …' Scargill surrounded by pickets at Ollerton, 28 April 1984. (John Sturrock, Network)

Police under attack at Orgreave, 18 June 1984. Often the barrages of missiles would go on for hours before the pickets were driven back. (John Sturrock, Network)

Harassed by the press. A photographer bursts into the negotiating room at the Rubens Hotel to snatch this picture of the NCB and NUM teams at work. (*Daily Express*)

The writ is finally served. Scargill's amazement is evident as the process-server does his work at the Labour Party Conference in Blackpool, 3 October 1984. (*Daily Express*)

Back to work, July 1984. Pickets face to face with police at Bilston Glen Colliery, near Edinburgh, as the numbers of men returning to work increase. (John Sturrock, Network)

Left: 'Can't you see I'm not here?' The joke that backfired on the NCB chairman as he arrives for a secret meeting in Edinburgh, 9 September 1984. (*Daily Express*)

Police and dogs guard Kellingly Colliery, near Pontefract, where 120 men were back at work by 20 January 1985. (John Sturrock, Network)

It's all over now. Scargill and McGahey face the media
to announce the decision of the special delegate conference, 3 March 1985.
(John Sturrock, Network)

One year on and David Jones has been raised to status of NUM 'martyr'.
A commemorative march at South Kirkby, West Yorkshire, 16 March 1985.
(John Sturrock, Network)

the law-enforcement machinery seems to want to keep out of it.'

To my delight I found I was preaching to the converted. She too was concerned about the mayhem of the last few days and had already been wondering what to do about it. I suggested that, were this America, the authorities would have called out the National Guard by now. She reminded me rather sharply that it wasn't America and such a move would be political dynamite. 'Well,' I said, 'you've got to do something, because you are dealing with a well-rehearsed and organized rebellion here. You know, from what Scargill has said, that he is out to topple the government. If it goes on, I fear he will succeed.'

The discussion among the group, which included Peter Walker and Leon Brittan, ranged among the options open to them in the light of my conviction that the numbers of miners at work were not decreasing sharply as a result of any change of heart on their part, but because of their failure to get protection. Later surveys confirmed that there were a surprising number of men who were unwilling strikers, but the vast majority of them simply feared the consequences to them and their families of returning to work.

The picketing and its attendant violence were particularly strong in Nottinghamshire, which was vital to us. Indeed, as we talked the problem over, the events that were to lead to the first death of the dispute were already unfolding. That night David Jones, a young Yorkshire miner, who had cheerfully signed on in Arthur's army and gone off to 'invade' Nottingham, collapsed and died near Ollerton pit. He was not the martyr the NUM and the whole Labour movement tried to make him in subsequent months, with wicked insinuations that his death was somehow caused by actions of the police – allegations which were not substantiated by one shred of evidence.

The injuries which led to Jones's death were in fact sustained in the crush of a mob of his fellow pickets. I find it frankly hypocritical that Arthur Scargill should contemplate putting a plaque on the wall of the NUM headquarters to commemorate this 'martyr' of the working-class movement.

After that session in the prime minister's study – and very quickly indeed – the National Reporting Centre at Scotland Yard was brought to life. Leon Brittan's promise of action changed the situation within hours, as he told the House of Commons the following day: 'Any attempt to intimidate those who wish to go to work is a breach of the criminal law. The mere presence of large numbers of pickets can be intimidating. The police have a duty to prevent obstruction and intimidation.' Overnight David Hall, the chief constable of Humberside, had set up the NRC and the first units of police from outside the coalfield areas – which were later to number up to 7500 men – were on their way to Nottingham. The national organization of squads of riot-trained police had never been required on this scale before and there were many predictable left-wing expressions of alarm about it. But all their protests begged the question: what was the country supposed to do? Lie down and let Scargill walk all over it?

I have nothing but admiration for the many thousands of police from all over the country who had to live for long periods of time in uncomfortable, makeshift accommodation and spend their long working days and nights under tirades of abuse and regular attacks with rocks and other more lethal missiles. The fact that only a tiny, and regrettably well-publicized, minority of them broke ranks and retaliated to this endless provocation is a measure of their fundamental good sense and discipline. Nor do I stint on my praise of the chief constables of some of the pit areas, whose equal bravery under different

forms of harassment and provocation was also a prominent feature of the struggle. I have never met Charles
McLaughlin, chief constable of Nottinghamshire, but his
contribution was outstanding. This battle of fundamental
rights was not only the NCB's battle – it was crucial for
the country that it be won.

Thus the siege of Nottingham, which was to last all
summer, started. At first, the police efforts were concentrated on stopping the pickets closing the area's pits; then
they had to do something about the appalling intimidation
going on in the villages, where often groups of pickets
from outside the county would, like terrorists, hide up in
'safe houses' offered by striking miners during the day –
and go out at night to attack the families, homes and
property of men who had chosen to work. We gave the
police, locally and nationally, all the assistance we could
in terms of useful information picked up from our networks as well as handing over any evidence we acquired
– such as video films – of criminal acts carried out on and
around NCB property.

Indeed the key to the whole strike was Nottinghamshire
and its 31,000 miners. If we could keep this vast and
prosperous coalfield going, then I was convinced, however long it took, we could succeed.

At root it was as much a question of money as principle
on all sides. It was remarkable that our surveys done
throughout the strike showed very little variation on the
fundamental issues. Most keen strikers, under Scargill's
persistent propaganda, had come to believe that I was
about to 'butcher' the industry, but they also expected to
come out of it better off. The promised land being offered
to them by Scargill was not only an illusion of job security,
but also of more money. Not for nothing had he kept them
poor by resisting incentive bonus schemes and putting the
ban on overtime. It is a standard operating practice of

the left to keep the troops as hungry as possible, while promising them a big meal on the spoils of victory.

On the other hand most non-strikers – particularly those in Nottingham – wanted nothing to do with Scargill's blatantly political ends, and the other side of the same coin was that they neither felt particularly threatened in their jobs, nor did they see any reason for sacrificing good wages for a holy war in which they had no interest.

In addition, if we could keep Nottingham going, we could keep the lights on in Britain. The chain of massive coal-fired power stations on the Trent were fed from its 25 pits, which could produce a quarter of the NCB's total output. Keep these going, and we could build out from this prosperous central region into those areas where men had also been reluctant to strike or were still working on in small numbers – the Midlands, Derbyshire and the Western Area – and form a solid belt of coal production which could in turn keep all the central belt of coal-fired power stations going.

There were other reasons why it was essential to keep Nottingham going – not just the fact that every tonne of coal produced meant we could hold out that much longer against Scargill. While the men there were working, their presence would act as a beacon to encourage those elsewhere to come back too. It would show that it was possible to defy the NUM and live. It would show that there was an alternative argument – a legitimate one, which thousands of men clearly believed in – to that being relayed by Scargill day after day in the media.

Much of our time in the first two months of the strike was spent making sure that the men had every reason to want to work and no reason at all, that we could avoid, not to want to. It was a tightrope exercise, for the men were by no means united or totally convinced from the outset that the strike was necessarily wrong. The 73 per cent who voted against striking included many, I believe, who did so because they didn't like the way Scargill was going about things. We had to tread very carefully not to give them reason for joining in. We also had to bolster every possible feeling that what they were doing was right. With those who were not at work, but would like to have been, we had to try hard to reduce the balance of fear that was keeping them away.

Success in holding on to the area was, in the end, the key to the successful solution of the dispute. From it everything else flowed. Conversely Scargill's failure to force Nottinghamshire into submission led to his downfall.

In union terms, what happened after the Nottingham men voted not to support the Yorkshire strike call was a series of efforts by their own officials and by national officials to persuade, or force, them to change their minds. All the time this was going on the pickets were doing their best to avoid contact with the police – often succeeding – while keeping up their barrages of missiles and abuse at pit gates and intimidation in the villages.

It is a testament to the Nottingham men that, apart from a few days at the beginning, nearly 25,000 of them braved the mobs and worked on right through the strike. But, as we shall see later, this did not prevent them from feeling isolated, alone and very unsure of themselves as the pressure on them mounted. The problem was exacerbated by the disappearance to the 'other side' of many of their most trusted union officials. Men whom they had voted into office to represent them were now giving them alien orders to obey. Working miners found themselves being treated like the private slaves of Scargill and their own union masters. The idea of service to the membership had gone out of the window. From Scargill downwards it was made clear to them that their job was to do as they were told. This authoritarian approach to things was offensive to many of them; but for a while they were confused by the fact that it was coming from their own officials. This further strengthened their sense of isolation and doubt as to whether what they were doing was right.

Matters came to a head for many of the men who were working on May Day, when 11,000 of them went to lobby their own NUM area executive in Mansfield, only to find that 4000 strikers – many from outside the county – had taken over the union building and the public address system. With Nottingham leaders Richardson and Chadburn, they were pouring endless abuse on them for having the temerity to work when they had been ordered not to. It was the last straw for a number of them who, individually, and later collectively, decided the time had come for them to do something.

The time had also come for us to do something. The pressure of the picketing was relentless. Our reports on the situation contained incidents of violence in Nottingham every day. The 'Sheffield militia', as Scargill's men also became known, would some days number more than 10,000, with the vast majority concentrated on Nottingham and anything up to 3000 at one pit or rampaging through the villages around. Our intelligence gathered at the time showed that rarely more than 10 per cent of the men on strike were willing to picket. The vast majority of them would rather have done without the money and stayed at home than get involved in the mayhem that was going on.

It is difficult to imagine now how it was. But it was civil war. Figures compiled later showed that in the first seven months of the dispute more than 7000 people were arrested for offences connected with the dispute – most of these on the picket lines or for attacks on property – 790 police officers were injured, 65 of them seriously, two working miners committed suicide, two died as a result of picket line violence and 255 were injured. Such was the price of opposing Arthur's army.

You didn't have to be a miner to join up. Sensing anarchy and chaos, the whole ragtag mob of the militant left was soon on the bandwaggon. They were quick to see it for what it was: a chance to coerce and perhaps bring down the government. For them it was class warfare, even though the kind of working class they were representing had long since disappeared. The Militant-dominated council in Liverpool gave both financial and physical help to the picketing – particularly in the Western Area, where John Northard, the director, made great efforts to keep half a dozen or so of his pits open throughout the strike and to encourage the back-to-work movement. Right across the central coalfield the pickets' numbers were swelled by hundreds who had nothing to do with the dispute beyond wanting to cause further trouble. A sinister mob of almost-uniformed anarchists – led by a woman – appeared at one stage and caused a great deal of damage in Yorkshire. But at the core of most of the trouble was a hardened group of miners who had obviously been trained well in advance in the techniques required to force dissenters into line. We had had reports of these cadres, mainly of young miners based in the Doncaster area, being created and trained – but we did not realize how effective they could be until the battle for Nottingham was on in earnest.

I suppose none of this should have surprised us, for it was all part of Scargill's heroic vision of himself in the vanguard of the red army leading the way to the revolution. He had given us plenty of warning of both the strategy and the tactics in an interview he gave to *New*

Left Review in 1975, in which he had talked of his first use of flying pickets in 1969:

> We launched from the coalfield here squads of cars, minibuses and buses, all directed on to predetermined targets, with five, six, seven hundred miners at a time. Of course the police were going to come, but they couldn't cover forty points at a time, without bringing the British armed forces in . . . I believe in a class war you have to fight with the tools at your disposal.

Later he related how he perfected the technique in the Battle of Saltley Gate: 'We had to declare war on them and the only way you could declare war was to attack the vulnerable points.' The shutting of the depot by a combined mob of miners and other militants was 'living proof that the working class had only to flex its muscles and it could bring governments, employers – society – to a total standstill.' And of a group of lorry drivers who dared to stand in his way, because they said they had contracts with the firms involved: 'My retort was that they had a contractual arrangement far above that, they had a contractual arrangement with the working class and if they didn't honour that contractual arrangement we'd make sure physically that they did. For we would have thrown their lorries and everything else into the dyke.'

A man who saw life in these terms was clearly not going to be bothered about his political bedfellows – as we were to see later when striking miners turned up alongside known IRA men in Ireland and Arthur, himself, sought money from the archetypal terrorist Colonel Gadhafi of Libya to keep his army on the march.

Despite the valiant efforts of the police and the effective use of the National Reporting Centre, Scargill's saturation attack on Nottingham was having some effect. Since we had a war on our hands, Jimmy Cowan and I began to think increasingly in military terms and we came to the conclusion that what we needed was a 'second front'. It was obvious that Scargill was able to concentrate his fire power on Nottingham, so we began to look at ways of dispersing that fire. What if we started to try to get people back to work in Derbyshire, Scotland, the northeast and in the rest of the Western Area – all the areas where there had been a demonstrable reluctance to strike in the first place? Even if they only came in small numbers at first, Scargill would surely have to mass his pickets at any pit where a return to work was even threatened – which would stretch his resources and take the pressure off Nottingham.

The travelling that Jimmy and I had done now paid dividends; for, not only had we got our message across, but we began to sense a very genuine revulsion among our managers at what Scargill was doing. Many of them had started out in the dispute viewing themselves as neither on one side nor the other – they saw the scrap as one between me and the NUM, with their role being to look after the pits in the meantime and make sure they were safe and in good condition when work started again. Now, however, their attitude had changed: Scargill *had* to be beaten and there was a growing enthusiasm for getting the men back to work. I wish the same could have been said for all the area directors – for there were some, unfortunately, who could not see the strategic thinking behind the move and dismissed the whole idea as impossible. They sat back and did nothing.

Ken Moses in north Derbyshire, however, was one who needed no prompting. On the day I had gone to see Mrs Thatcher, the area voted not to strike but the decision had been overturned and the men forced out by picketing.

All he had left were seven men working at Shirebrook Colliery. His remaining nine pits were out of action. Some men were working at the Bolsover pit – but that was because of a situation which had existed since the General Strike of 1926. While the pit was in the north Derbyshire NCB area for administration, it was in Nottingham for union matters. Moses actually thought of sending home the seven men at Shirebrook – on the grounds that he knew their continued presence would only cause him and his management trouble when the strike was over.

But he resisted the temptation for the easy life; he had watched the rise of Scargill at first hand during a spell in Yorkshire management and came to the conclusion – even at that stage – that there was no way the man was going to negotiate a settlement. In his view the only way to beat him was by getting the men to do it. His area officials – and many of his managers – were frankly disbelieving when he outlined his plans, principally on the grounds of the men's well-known loyalty to the NUM. But, nothing daunted, he pressed on – at first slowly on his own – then, with our encouragement, more adventurously.

His first problem was to keep Bolsover pit working – as ours on a larger scale was to keep Nottingham working – for if one pit could be shown to be in operation with men working, then that raised big question marks in the men's minds about the whole strike. Bolsover's manager, Arnold Healey, was one of the heroes of the strike: for nine months he personally attended every shift change – three times a day, five days a week – to see that the men were all right. He was there from five in the morning till midnight, with only two short breaks at home, every day. Many of those days he faced hundreds of pickets, sometimes thousands. They tried to intimidate him and his family, but he is not the sort you can frighten: his courage kept that pit open.

Next Moses began working on Shirebrook. He evolved a plan to 'roll the strike back from the edges'. He and the pit manager studied maps and painstakingly plotted exactly where each of the men lived and, starting with those away from the villages and hence away from the intimidation, the manager and his team visited every man at home. They talked to him about coming back to work and how he would be looked after if he decided to. It was a trickle at first, but slowly the men began to return. From a low of 10 at the end of March and 19 at the end of April, the numbers for each week in May were 26, 29, 31 and, at the end of the month, after the police moved into Shirebrook village to stop the intimidation, they went up to 52. The same operation at the other pits in the area had got the numbers of NUM men back at work by the end of May up to 343. Slight progress, but it was also tying up hundreds, if not thousands of Scargill's pickets every day.

Nor did Bert Wheeler need much encouragement in Scotland. All the time when we were looking for groups of men who might return to work we had to avoid those people who were doing it for the wrong reasons – those who perhaps wanted to glory in the publicity of it. We looked for areas and pits where it appeared the men had some genuine conviction about working and in Scotland, Bilston Glen was a classic. The men had voted not to strike and nearly every day in the first few weeks of the strike a few of them had tried to fight their way through the lines to get to work, but in the end they had been beaten back. The video records we made of those early days do not make pleasant viewing, but show the vicious behaviour of some of the pickets.

We knew the belief in the right to work was there, so

Bert set about making the most of it. By the time the pit's annual holidays came up at the end of June he had 33 men back at work and a handful at Barony pit. We calculated that no more than 10 per cent of Scotland's 12,000 workforce had taken part in the regular picketing, but it had, nevertheless, been particularly violent. Scargill had clearly hoped to use a detachment of Scottish troops to bolster his efforts in the Midlands, but now, not only were the Scottish militants unable to contain what was happening in their own country, but reinforcements had to be sent up from the northeast too. At 4 a.m. on the eve of Bilston Glen's holiday on 28 June, 80 pickets from Durham, including several women, attempted to break into the pit and take it over. Bert Wheeler's smile after that day was not because the police had moved promptly to arrest some and clear the rest out – but because the pickets had been shouting, 'Scottish miners have no heart for the struggle'. They could not have done a better job for the back-to-work movement and, when they threatened to return after the holidays, he knew that would set the seal on it.

Those pickets who had come from the northeast were very soon called back there because of trouble on their home ground. The men in Northumberland had shown some reluctance to strike and, working on this, David Archibald, our area director, was able to persuade a handful back. This number grew in the summer to 19 and that small number was as valuable to us as a thousand in other places, because they took the northeast mobs back to base and kept them there.

Jimmy Cowan was a marvel at organizing and pushing all this. Once you started a scheme you could see the effect of it almost overnight. All you had to do was make it known that you were going to get men back at a particular pit and all the pickets from that area would disappear from Nottingham or the other areas to cope with it. If we managed to get men back in one area, then often the coachloads from Yorkshire, or the northeast or south Wales would not be long in arriving. We began to see a steady attenuation of the NUM's lines of supply, along with which there must have been a vast increase in their operating costs, having to be in so many places at the same time. It had a further bonus: every time we pulled the pickets away from one area it meant that we could get more men back there too.

Of all these efforts to divert Arthur Scargill's fire power, the biggest, the most spectacular and the most successful was the famous month-long battle of Orgreave coke works. On many days between 23 May and 18 June the number of pickets all told in Nottinghamshire could be measured in the low hundreds, simply because of the thousands needed by Scargill to fight in the massed set-piece battle of the South Yorkshire plant. It became a *cause célèbre* for Scargill, a fight he had to win. We were quite encouraged that he thought it so important and did everything we could to help him continue to think so, but the truth was it mattered hardly a jot to us – beyond the fact that it kept him away from Nottingham.

Scargill made great efforts, throughout the strike, to invoke the support of other unions – particularly to block supplies going to our two biggest customers, the Central Electricity Generating Board and the British Steel Corporation. It must have been a great disappointment to him that, in the end, so few other unions shared his enthusiasm for the great working class revolution he envisaged mounting on the backs of his own poor members. But in many cases, they had their own jobs to worry about and were not going to go into battle for a man who seemed to want them to sacrifice those jobs on his revolutionary altar.

The principal point of contact between the miners and

other unions was over steel. While the edict from the top of the NUM remained that all supplies of coal to BSC should be banned, many local deals were done to allow just the minimum through to stop the catastrophic close-down of the furnaces at the five main steel sites in the country. Even if Scargill was not prepared to recognize the dangers inherent in closing down a steelworks – the principal one being that because of the continuing knife-edge state of the market for British Steel, it might never open up again – the men at the local level were only too aware that Scargill was demanding a sacrifice from them that might mean their own jobs vanishing. The point was also constantly reiterated to them by BSC management as it struggled to produce as much steel as possible and to fight off European producers who were happily eyeing the British market again.

Orgreave works, where NCB coal was 'coked' in huge ovens ready for use in the blast furnaces at Scunthorpe, forty miles away, was fed with its coal by a number of pits in the South Yorkshire area – including, ironically, Cortonwood. But like Cortonwood itself, Orgreave's days were numbered. Scunthorpe was developing its own self-sufficiency in coke production using more foreign coal, which had a lower sulphur content and improved the quality of the end product. Indeed at the outset of the strike, Scunthorpe hardly planned on getting any supplies at all from Orgreave, which BSC correctly anticipated would be heavily picketed. However, an accident in one of the furnaces at Scunthorpe in mid-May changed all that, and, in order to save the furnace, a large tonnage of Orgreave's coke was needed in a hurry.

From the NCB's point of view we had been forced by competition from foreign sources for some years to sell the coal from Cortonwood and the other pits at a price far lower than it cost us to produce. So when Arthur

Scargill decided that this was to be the Battle of Saltley 1984 – it wasn't really in the long run a critical matter to us whether he won or lost. If he won, and Orgreave and Scunthorpe were shut, then all the NCB would have lost would have been the obligation to supply some high-cost production from a pit which we would now have an even better reason for shutting down. If he lost, then clearly, since he chose the site, the day and the weapons for the pitched battle, it would be an enormous blow to his confidence and his credibility. Either way, it would keep his army out of Nottingham.

It mattered more to BSC – for the few days until it could organize the movement of a consignment of Polish coal through the terminal at Flixborough on the Trent – but after that, while it was handy for them to have the prospect of coke from Orgreave in reserve, it was no longer essential. BSC, however, continued to stress the importance of Orgreave because it diverted attention away from the lorries delivering the Polish coal from Flixborough docks.

Thus Scargill's militia got the battle he had been looking for. It started with one rock, thrown through a lorry windscreen by one of 25 pickets on 23 May, and escalated over the Bank Holiday weekend into a full-scale confrontation with thousands of pickets and police. Scargill, no doubt seeing himself in the role of Wellington – standing on the hill directing his troops by loud hailer – arrived on Sunday, 27 May confidently predicting that no force in the land could stop a well-organized picket from shutting a factory gate. The police stopped him and his men that day – and every day afterwards, with one or two tricky moments, until 18 June. The biggest clashes were on 29 May and finally on 18 June when, after impassioned pleas that all it needed was determination and numbers, Scargill amassed an army of 10,000 from all over the country and, disposing them with 'secret' orders issued in brown envelopes, prepared for the 'big push' against Orgreave, which was to be defended that day by just over 4000 police. All morning the clashes went on – 89 people were injured, 37 of them policemen, and there were 93 arrests. Scargill himself was one of the 'injured'. According to South Yorkshire's assistant chief constable Tony Clement, who was the policeman nearest to him, he suddenly tipped backwards over some fencing, hitting his head. Scargill claimed otherwise, but the incident occurred as things were going badly for the miners, and who knows if it wasn't time for a 'dive in the area' to see if the referee would give a penalty?

That was the end of the battle of Orgreave. Unnoticed by the pickets as the fighting raged, lorries had moved the last of the coke from the plant anyway. The battle had, I think, brought it home to the public at large that we were dealing here with a man who had declared war on the system. It is only unfortunate, once again, that much of the stoning, catapulting, missile-throwing and abuse hurled at the police went unrecorded by the media. On the other hand, the one or two incidents of over-reaction were faithfully played over and over on the news bulletins here and throughout the world. It gives one cause to wonder whether the power of the cameraman to edit simply by pointing the camera here and not there, perhaps the most potent tool in the world of television, had been used dispassionately or whether it was in sympathy with Scargill when he complained that the perfectly legitimate and restrained tactics of the police in the face of his 10,000-strong mob were reminiscent of Chile or Bolivia?

The battle also proved that Scargill was not infallible. The Cecil B. De Mille treatment of these encounters was designed to show him as the ultimate revolutionary leader. Unfortunately it revealed him merely as a bit of a clown, if a dangerous one. In order to explain his defeat he had to resort to more and more extreme flights of fancy about the fascist, Gestapo police – claims which were, in the end, to become so extreme that they turned an increasing number of the public away from his rantings. The simple fact was that he had set out to destroy a section of the economy. His aim had been to close down the Scunthorpe steel furnaces, but what he didn't know at the time was that the objective was unattainable. The forces of law and order had prevented him doing so. For all his, and the media's, ambiguous projection of the issues, I believe the public were steadily beginning to understand.

As the hysterical reaction against the police built up over the months – based as it was on the premise that they had no right to stand in the way of the NUM's efforts to smash the working miners into submission – it became obvious to us at Hobart House that a more subtle campaign was also being waged against many of the senior police involved. After that meeting with the prime minister and Leon Brittan the general attitude of the police changed, in that they then saw it as their role to stop the prevention and intimidation of men who wished to work. We only heard of isolated incidents after this of forces not wishing to be involved in such duties. In Scotland, for example, Bert Wheeler was told by one senior policeman whom he rang to arrange cover for a handful of men who wanted to return to work: 'Tell them not to bother.' From time to time I would pass on what you might call complaints about 'soft' spots in the police coverage to the Department of Energy committee for them to pass on to the appropriate authorities – but there were not many.

However, it was not unusual to hear about chief constables being threatened by their own politically orientated police committees with all sorts of financial penalties if they continued to 'attack the miners'. There was even one case where the hounding of a senior policeman out of office on a disconnected accusation was strangely coincidental and provided an excuse for a politically motivated attack on the man for his activities on the side of law and order in the strike. It was no surprise that the attack was led by the chairman of the local police committee who was well known to be in total sympathy with the miners.

It was not only Labour-controlled police committees all over the country who attacked the use of their men in policing the strike. Local councils in mining areas also did all they could to make life uncomfortable for visiting forces. Derbyshire County Council, for example, banned the police using council property for billeting incoming men – even the health authority would not let them sleep in a disused hospital. Local councils also gave hundreds of thousands of pounds to miners' funds which, while they may not have gone directly to finance the violence, must have had the effect of releasing other funds to be used by those who wished to organize violence and intimidation.

Very slowly that violence and intimidation began to rebound on Scargill. Not only were many ordinary decent men, who had joined the strike because they could not contemplate the thought of disloyalty to the union, sickened by what they saw on the picket lines, not only were many of the working miners made more determined to go on by every threat aimed at them and their families, but we also began to see among the forty or fifty thousand 'reluctant' strikers a greater willingness to consider facing the opprobrium of their colleagues and come back. The second front, hard work though it was, had a great effect in those early days. Nottingham kept going and eventually we were able to build on the foundations laid in the areas.

It also began to be obvious that the more Scargill talked about victory being just around the corner, the more he was doing it not because he believed triumph was in sight, but to stop men returning to work. I began to see that, in a matter of time, the pressure to go back could be so great that all his assurances of victory would not be enough to stop the trickle turning to a flood. This seemed to us to be an opportunity, which we had to seize upon – but it also presented us with many difficulties.

Increasingly I found myself addressing my efforts to many different audiences – and the need to reconcile one against another was sometimes very difficult. For example, every time we reopened negotiations with the NUM, the numbers of people coming back to work would dry up. What point was there in coming back to work and risking the opprobrium of fellow miners if it was soon perhaps to be over? Yet we were sure the public would not be very tolerant of a situation where we, the NCB, were seen to be refusing to negotiate. The politicians of each shade had their own pressures and points of view, as did the people in Hobart House. These had to be taken into consideration before each move, let alone how such moves would look to those working, or those we hoped to get back there soon.

It was very difficult for people to understand at the time that we were not running around as puppets of the politicians throughout the strike. I had my overall instructions for the industry from Mrs Thatcher – I felt she was there if I needed to consult with her – but the conduct of the conflict in those early months was left very much to me. I saw Peter Walker quite regularly to report progress – he exhibited the somewhat detached stance required by government policy at the time. But I began to feel that he was now thinking we should be doing more to settle the dispute. Beyond that there was no great governmental pressure on me. Due to the lack of contact, problems developed in almost exactly the opposite direction. Far from acting daily on a stream of orders issuing from Downing Street, my 'distance' from current thinking at the top, and theirs from me, led to occasions when senior members of the Conservative Party said things that actually worked against the conduct of the strike. On one occasion, in the midst of our battle, Norman Tebbit called for the privatization of the industry. I am sure he held those views very sincerely, but his expression of them could not have come at a worse time. Such remarks were used with glee by Arthur Scargill to help tip the balance of doubting miners back towards him and to damage our case. The struggle for Nottingham was by no means over.

9

Economic Warfare

Rudolph (Randy) Florence is a machine driver at Mansfield pit in Nottinghamshire. On Friday, 25 May, I travelled, in great secrecy and by a roundabout route, to meet him and two of his colleagues. What they had to tell me that day was to change and crystallize much of my thinking about the conduct of the strike. It is all too easy, as chairman of a large enterprise like the NCB, to fail to catch the mood of the men at the grass roots. Both Jimmy Cowan and I had done our best to travel round and support the Nottingham men who wished to work. Even though we were aware of many of the problems of those men, I had not really understood the exact extent or nature of those problems until I met Randy and his associates.

In desperation he had telephoned my office several days earlier and had been rather surprised that I had taken the call. 'My mates thought it was a million to one chance, but they felt it was worth trying,' he said. It transpired that he and many of his colleagues were at the end of their tethers. They felt completely alone and isolated. Some of them would be terrified for their lives and for their families if they tried to work. It was not so much the harassment on the picket lines – they could all cope with that – it was the intimidation in the villages that really threatened them. Recognizing the agony of my caller I quickly decided that it might be a good idea for us to meet so that I could hear the full story – but I said that we would have to be careful, since I didn't want to jeopardize his safety further (and there was always the chance, though remote, that this was a trap).

Hence my trip, first by rail to Leicester, then in a car belonging to a colleague's wife, across country to the home of a trusted local businessman in Mansfield where Florence and two of his colleagues, Cook and Taylor, were waiting to meet me.

It was one of the most moving experiences of my life as, for two hours, they poured out their troubles. The poor fellows were pleading with me to do something to help protect them and their homes so that they could work. It shone through that they were simply straightforward honest men – fundamentally typical of so many of our workers – probably Labour voters to a man and certainly staunch trade unionists. But they felt there was no reason for them to be on strike – pits had always closed for a variety of reasons and Scargill knew that, but he was trying to make a political issue out of it. They were insistent that I should not take it that Scargill represented anyone but himself in Nottinghamshire.

They spelled out what was really happening. There were some very ugly scenes taking place, which they reported to me at first hand – terrorizing of families and brutal beatings of men. The resolve of the men going to work depended on the amount of protection they felt they were going to get. I left them promising I would do what I could to help.

As soon as I got back to London I started banging on any door I could think of in government, and meeting senior politicians whom I knew, like Lord Whitelaw, David Young and Ian Gow, to get something done about the policing of the villages. There was a speedy response and the effect was dramatic, as we saw at Shirebrook in north Derbyshire, for example.

But the session with the three miners set me thinking about a much wider scene. I could not help but be very moved by their plight and the way they were being put upon by their union. They had assured me that word of my encouragement and support would go around the coalfield grapevine like wildfire and that there were thousands more like them out there. That led me to the most important idea to come out of that meeting: the notion that there had to be some protection for these individuals under the common law of this law-abiding country.

I found myself thinking over and over again about the long history of British law and the individual and his rights. What was the Magna Carta for? Why did all those people gather at Runnymede if it were not to help the vulnerable individual victim of injustice? These people were victims of the barons all right – barons of the NUM. Surely there must be a way in law to help them. It was not a matter for any new industrial relations legislation. It was more fundamental than that. These people were having their civil rights violated and therefore we should attack Scargill on that basis.

Although Nigel Lawson was very busy at the treasury at that time, he was kind enough to give a few minutes of his time to talk it over – not as a specific minister, but more as someone I knew would listen and offer good advice. After all, it was he who had talked me into this job! I outlined the problem to him, adding: 'You know, I have to go back to my American experience and the recent US preoccupation with civil rights. If I was there I would be looking round for some public interest group who would take up the legal cudgels, so to speak, on behalf of these men and help fight for their rights in court.' He agreed, but neither of us could think of one group which was not so left-wing dominated that it would be useless asking them. We agreed that perhaps he might ask among his colleagues or in his constituency, which was in the Midlands, to see if anyone there knew of some bright young lawyers who might be interested in helping in such a cause.

In the meantime I started thinking how I too could assist in supporting the men with their legal actions without being directly involved. Any NCB action would be counterproductive in the extreme and would probably repel as many working miners as it would attract. The whole concept of the operation would be like the wartime Department of Economic Warfare. In parallel with our Department of Strategic Warfare we would try to stimulate actions which would cost Scargill so much money that it would reduce his ability to finance flying pickets. It was the success of this area of operations which was to progressively tie the NUM up in knots and ultimately may well have been the single most important factor in bringing about an end to the strike. And it was my meeting with Florence which sparked it all off.

In the early days we had, tentatively, gone down the route of using the government's industrial relations legislation against the miners' picketing. Indeed on Tuesday, 20 March Mr Justice Nolan had granted an injunction in our favour banning flying pickets. But we never pursued the matter as far as taking contempt proceedings – for the simple reason that, having started down this path, we debated at great length the impact of our action on other unions and decided it could do more harm than good. It is ironical to note that pressure to use the IR laws came originally from people in the government who, as soon as they understood the upset it could potentially cause, were quick to 'leak' their disquiet about invoking this form of legal action.

Our reasons for not going ahead with it were simple – and, though I hate to disappoint the conspiracy theorists, nothing to do with the government. We were, of course, asked what we planned to do – but I explained our position and felt no pressure to change it. Having dropped the stone in the well, I could listen to and gauge the likely reaction if we were to go ahead with the injunction and it was on the basis of that, not government pressure, that we decided not to.

The two best reasons for abandoning the injunction came out in our debates and from Jimmy Cowan's soundings. The first and most important one, which I had begun to sense already, was that this was the one action which was likely to coalesce the whole trade union and Labour movements behind the miners. We gleaned from rumours that there were quite a number of far-left politicians who couldn't wait for us to go to court to try to enforce the injunction. Jimmy volunteered that it wasn't just the politicians. Arthur Scargill was hopping from foot to foot in his eager anticipation of the event. If we did pursue it many trade union leaders, whom we knew, and he knew, to be less than keen on Scargill's private war with the government, would feel bound to join in, because of their need to be seen to be totally opposed to the legislation and its use.

We looked at Scargill's support in the union movement and to us it seemed to be pretty thin. If we abandoned the injunction then his support was likely to remain thin on the ground. Some of the railwaymen might help him; the seamen and the dockers – if they were given an issue – could be drawn in, as could a few of the TGWU sectors. But not the lorry drivers, since there were too many freelance individual operators for them to be effective. That was about the limit of it. Neither the steelworkers (ISTC) nor the electricity supply unions had so far shown much sign of enthusiasm. In fact, if anything, the very opposite. I was impressed by the inaction or impotence of the Triple Alliance of miners, railwaymen and steel-workers which Bill Sirs had threatened from time to time to invoke. So why raise the hornets nest of the entire TUC, when it would almost certainly do more harm than good?

The second reason was to do with the men who were still working, principally in Nottingham. A move like this could well drive many of them back into Scargill's arms and we knew we had to hang on to that area at all costs. We also had TGWU men continuing to dig coal at our open-cast sites (which yielded over 12 million tonnes a year) and while, as yet, we had no means of moving the coal that was being dug, it seemed a shame to risk losing this further production, as we almost certainly would if we started to press the injunction.

In abandoning our own action, however, we did not wish to discourage private companies from using the legislation, and several did, to useful effect, during the strike. I also had several sessions with both Bob Reid at British Rail and Bob Scholey at BSC, in which I counselled them against also trying to use the IR laws. My feeling was that the more the TUC, specifically, and the trade union movement in general, were kept out of this conflict, the better our chances would be. We should give none of them a reason to start sympathizing with Scargill or wanting to help him.

It was a fine judgement to make at the time in those hectic early days of the strike – but Jimmy was convinced that the violence in Nottingham, unchecked by an injunction, would work more in our favour than it would cow the workforce into submission. Indeed it turned out to be so, and when the shameful scenes took place at the NUM's Berry Hill Lane offices in Mansfield on 1 May, when the majority of working miners were barred access by a minority of strikers, several men there were at last galvanized into action by the total failure of their union to pay the slightest heed to their wishes.

Among those men was Chris Butcher, a thirty-three-year-old blacksmith at Bevercotes Colliery, who was to win national recognition as the mysterious 'Silver Birch'. He went round the mining areas talking to groups of men who wanted to work, raising their morale, and showing them they were not alone. He confined his activities that day to handing out slips of paper among the men, asking them to phone him if they too didn't like what was being done.

Colin Clarke, a long-time branch official, could also clearly understand Scargill's strategy and did not like being used as a pawn in so blatant a political strike. At one point he tried to get to the microphone, which was in the hands of the strikers, to address the vast majority who wished to work, but he was pushed back. Later he met an old friend, John Liptrott, also a branch official, at Sherwood Colliery, who felt the same way as he did and the two of them decided to press ahead with a legal action Clarke had already discussed with his family solicitor, David Negus.

Roy Lynk, the number three in the Nottingham NUM after Chadburn and Richardson, was the fourth man to be stirred into action that day. He had already crossed swords with his two superiors and with Scargill in private, for which he had been virtually ostracized in the union offices where he worked every day. But now he decided enough was enough, and he broke his silence. He managed to get to the microphone and tell the working majority in the crowd to stick to their guns and he would support them, before he was dragged off under a hail of missiles and spit.

Out of the actions of those four men that day came the Nottingham Working Miners' Committee, the National Working Miners' Committee and eventually the split with the NUM and the Union of Democratic Miners. It was men like these, who were already taking the first steps to defend their democratic rights, that I asked David Hart to go out to find and help when he volunteered to be my 'Indian scout' for our Department of Economic Warfare a few weeks after my encounter with Randy Florence.

David is a curious character. He is forty-two years old; an old Etonian who had made and lost a fortune in the 1970s property boom. He is a novelist and a writer of occasional articles for *The Times*. He could, and did, circulate just as easily among the miners of Nottinghamshire as he did in the highest political circles. When I first met him at an Institute of Economic Affairs lunch on 2 July he had already spent a considerable amount of time in Nottingham, reporting for *The Times*, with a mounting sense of frustration and anger at what was happening to the men who wanted to work. I had worked with his brother, Tim, at Lehman Bros in New York and, as we chatted, I began to realize that he was the man I had been looking for.

He too had had an experience like mine with Florence. He had been in Shirebrook village talking to the people there about the intimidation and had been directed to one house where bricks had been thrown through the window. He knocked on the door and the working miner's wife invited him in and offered him a cup of tea. She picked up the kettle and walked to the sink and suddenly he saw that her hand was shaking so much that she couldn't hold the kettle under the tap. She looked on the verge of having a nervous breakdown. So he filled the kettle and made the tea for them and they sat down and her story came pouring out. Her husband was working; her son by a previous marriage was on strike. The family was torn apart. The house had been daubed with paint, bricks had been thrown through the window and, in the middle of the previous night, when she had been alone, the front door had been kicked in. Her whole world had collapsed – all because of the evil of Scargill's operations. Out of David's anger at that moment came his determination to help bring about the defeat of Scargill in any way he could.

What he told me about his experiences confirmed my feelings that there must be numbers of men out there who would respond to any help, guidance or encouragement we could give. Someone like David could assist them in launching campaigns to go after the NUM on legal grounds. Clarke and Liptrott had already started the ball rolling with judgements given in their favour in May which, in effect, forced the Nottingham NUM to hold elections and declared the strike in the area unofficial. In the next few days 2000 men returned to work and in the subsequent elections only three of the 31 seats on the area council of the NUM and only four of the 310 seats at branch level stayed in the strikers' hands. The election was marked, predictably, by great violence against those who were actually daring to stand up and be counted.

So David set off to find the men who wanted to fight and to help organize them. Many of them were extremely nervous and suspicious of him at first – and rightly so. But he won their trust and slowly began to bring them together into a more united force. There was a very fundamental emotion waiting to be tapped. At its simplest it was a feeling that the union should serve its members, not the other way round. Their democratic rights had been purloined and they were now ready to fight for them.

But their morale had been sapped by the events of the

previous few months and they felt very insecure and isolated. By talking to them and bringing them together – as Chris Butcher was also doing – David was able to show them that they were not alone. He was able to raise their spirits and convince them that they could win – if they stuck to their guns. He too began a series of travels which took him more than 35,000 miles in three months, with secret meetings in pubs and hotels all over the Midlands. Slowly he put together about 25 cells of men who would act as the basis and the rallying point for local back-to-work movements.

He and Tim Bell, who was then with Saatchi & Saatchi and in whose direction I had been pointed by David Young, then head of the Manpower Services Commission, worked on an advertisement together. Its headline was 'Come Off It, Arthur' and it appeared in the *Daily Express*. Not only did it bring many miners to the cause, but it also raised £86,000. The advertisement launched the National Working Miners' Committee, which was to be the springboard for many of the legal actions against the NUM. David gave them considerable help in getting properly organized, with a proper charter and accountants. Eventually, when they were up and running, he slowly withdrew, only helping when asked to because he felt it could have been counterproductive for an outsider with his obvious connections to have been too visible in the organization.

Inevitably, I suppose, there was some falling out among the men who had inspired the fight, but that should not detract from the contribution each made. Chris Butcher had generously financed the first Clarke and Liptrott action from funds he had raised, and, though they later drew away from him, they continued to credit his early inspiration. They were all criticized as being the 'tools of the Tories' – but that was inevitable too. What the critics never saw was that these were men of tremendous individuality and character. They would not have done what they did if they had not had guts and conviction. They were nobody's patsy. They were perfectly happy to work with David, or to accept help indirectly from any source – if, and only if, it helped their cause. It was not for any intrinsic love they had for the management of the Coal Board itself. I met Clarke, who was a very distinguished and thoughtful fellow, and Liptrott on several occasions. They were both impressive men.

It was indeed a special type of person who would brave taking his own union to court. You needed to be very, very strong and, alas, some were not strong enough. David Hart sat down one day with one of the men who had started an action and he began to cry. He said: 'I don't think I can go on. Nobody will talk to me. My wife can't even go shopping, she is so nervous about the abuse. The pressure is too much for me. I never thought it would be as bad as this.' It is almost impossible for us to understand the pressure those men were under every hour of every day. They were normal working people until this happened. What is more they had been brought up to believe that the union was more important in their lives than almost anything else. It was their job, their security and their safety and it demanded absolute loyalty. But now they had to turn round and fight it. That required real strength and guts and fantastic moral courage – especially since the moment their names appeared on a writ, they were singled out for special attention from the thugs. They got the real works: the cars driven off the road, the death threats to the children, the spitting in the wife's face – and the subtle drip, drip, drip of intimidation.

I admired them and I can offer them no greater tribute than to reiterate that their actions collectively were the single most important factor in resolving the dispute.

Where Scargill made his mistake – and he probably does not know it to this day – was that his demand of loyalty from these men to their union was couched in terms which were absolutely alien and abhorrent to the vision of the world with which they had grown up. The majority of decent working people – however they vote – don't like violence, they don't like corruption, they don't like threats or intimidation. But they do like to make up their own minds and be free to express their convictions through the democratic system their union proudly and painstakingly built up over the years. These men were just such extraordinary, ordinary men.

The first wave of legal actions – most of them spontaneously embarked upon by individuals across the country – was mainly defensive: to get the strike locally declared unofficial. Such actions succeeded in North Wales, Lancashire, north Derbyshire and the Midlands.

The second wave, which started as David got busy in July, went on to the attack with the aim of tying up the NUM with its own rules and limiting the power of Scargill and his like-minded officials to take action. David called the tactics behind the second wave of actions the Gulliver Concept and the Insect Concept – Gulliver, because each one of the many actions tied another tiny legal rope around the NUM until it woke up one day and couldn't move; and Insect because the NUM was just that: with Scargill as the head, the national executive as the thorax and the miners the body. The aim of the actions was to apply pressure to the thin connections between each part.

Of all the legal cases brought in the next few months, one was dramatically responsible in the end for crippling Scargill's power to continue the strike. Robert Taylor, the man who had been stopped from working at Manton Colliery in Yorkshire on that second day of the strike, had linked up with another angry colleague, Ken Foulstone, and together they had spent four months carefully digging into the history of the Yorkshire NUM's deliberations leading up to the strike call. Their researches went right back to the 1981 vote on the issue of Orgreave pit, which the union seemed to think gave them the right to order any action at any time, even three years later. They collected a mountain of minutes and copies of the national and area rule books – which are like gold dust and very jealously guarded by the leadership. The normal member rarely gets a chance to see one, let alone read it. They acquired a disaffected 'mole' within the area offices who fed them information and documents, sometimes by the sackful. Foulstone spent hours at night, unable to sleep, walking up and down his garden path trying to work out, in his head, what it was that was legally wrong. Finally, they believed they had put their finger on the key, and were ready.

On 25 July they met David Payne and Andrew Fearn of Hodgkinson & Tallents, a Newark firm of solicitors, and that lunchtime went with Fearn to the Happy Eater restaurant on the A1 near Retford. There they met their 'mole', who gave them yet more papers. Fearn can still remember his sense of excitement that day as he read through the papers and realized there was a chance for justice to be done. On 8 August they went to the High Court with a case, similar to the original Nottingham action of Clarke and Liptrott, but which also sought injunctions against Yorkshire because its local rules clearly stated that there could be no strike in Yorkshire without a local ballot. They also wanted an order for a national ballot.

Andrew Fearn, though not working with Clarke's solicitor, David Negus, had talked to him and had acquired the services of Michael Burton, QC, the same barrister Negus had used for the Clarke and Liptrott actions. The action was heard between 24 and 28 September, when Mr Justice Nichols granted interim injunctions which, in effect, declared the Yorkshire strike unlawful and unofficial – and therefore the national strike too. Inside two hours Arthur Scargill was giving the first of a number of interviews that evening in which he stated that no judge was going to take away his right to call a strike and that he did not accept the ruling. Fearn worked all weekend and was back in court on Monday morning, this time seeking an order for contempt of court which he was told could be heard on Thursday if the writ could be served on Scargill that day.

There then began an exciting scramble to get the court paper and process-server from London to Blackpool and into the Labour party conference, where Scargill was sitting surrounded by his men. He looked very pleased with himself, having just persuaded his brothers in the movement to give uncritical support to the miners' struggle. David Hart eventually flew himself from Battersea to Blackpool in a borrowed helicopter and, having persuaded a *Daily Express* photographer to part with his pass in exchange for the picture of the moment, they located the miners' leader, then, with minutes to spare, the writ was served.

It was that fine for contempt of the court – £1000 for Scargill and £200,000 for the union – imposed on 10 October, which was to lead to the appointment of the receiver to run the union and the sequestration of its funds. In imposing the fine on Scargill and the NUM, Mr Justice Nichols said that the men who took the decision to commit the contempt would be personally liable to the NUM members for reimbursing the loss. Hart then got 16 members of the National Working Miners' Committee to start actions to make members of the executive repay the money.

Thus Scargill and his colleagues, in the end, lost control of their union's finances, and found their power to finance picketing and many of their other strike activities severely curbed. They became embroiled inextricably in a war with the courts, which was a war they could not win by any of their usual tactics. What is more Scargill's 'enemy' – the courts – was not one that would go away. The legal wheels, once set in motion, grind exceeding small. The consequences of his actions – particularly in the matter of the receiver – are still being felt in the NUM as I write this.

There was one dramatic footnote to Scargill's performance at Blackpool. The day after the writ was served, the NUM put out a statement which said at the end:

> Following discussion, the NEC *unanimously* [my italics] agreed to fully endorse and support the view expressed by the National President during an interview on Channel 4 television news last Friday, 28 September 1984: that no high court judge will take away the democratic right of our union to deal with internal affairs, such as crossing a picket line or urging others to cross a picket line in defiance of our union's instructions, and to reaffirm as *official* strike action in the coalfields sanctioned in accordance with National Rule 41 as determined by the special delegate conference on 19 April 1984, the extraordinary annual conference and the NEC.

The NEC meeting, at which all this was alleged to have been agreed, was attended by Roy Ottey. He felt they had been deprived of any of the information needed for it to reach a proper decision. When it came to it he found himself unable blindly to follow Scargill and the rest into breaking the law and he resigned. Thus the NUM lost one more of its moderating voices.

The thugs and bullies kept up the pressure on the men who dared to take the union to court. Two days after the writ was served at Blackpool two striking miners were charged with threatening to kill Taylor and his family after an accident in which a car tried to run them off the road on the way home from a shopping trip. Both he and Foulstone had to have 24-hour police guards on their houses. It had not been an easy decision for either of them to pursue the matter to sequestration once they had won the first judgement. It was only Scargill's insistence that his actions were 'official' that caused them to take it further; they had no wish to deprive the members of funds. In the end the continuing harassment forced Taylor to decide that he and his family could not go on taking the punishment. After the strike was over he accepted redundancy and left the industry. Foulstone too had his troubles; his family was torn apart by his stand and he became the target of an organized campaign with union men, even journalists, and others enthusiastically participating in dredging up every possible infraction of the law with which he could in any way have been connected in the past. With his divided family providing evidence against him, some of which turned out to be false, he was finally convicted of a crime in which he was alleged to have participated. Such were the lengths people were prepared to go to bring these men down.

Nevertheless, the cumulative effect of the court actions was to give a tremendous boost to the back-to-work movement. Every time a case was won it gave a few more uncertain strikers pause for thought: maybe working was not disloyal, maybe Scargill was not right, maybe it was not letting your colleagues down. When the clamp went on the union money and there were no longer the funds for mass picketing, then, at last, men no longer feared they would be intimidated and threatened by the mob and began to flood back.

The rift between the working miners – particularly those in Nottingham – and the NUM continued to widen with every month that passed and every court case that was won. In July, at the NUM's extraordinary annual conference, they passed a new Rule 51, which set up new disciplinary committees – with little pretence that it was for any reason other than to punish 'scabs'. Obviously, come the end of the strike, the working men of Nottingham were going to be the targets of this new 'star chamber court' – especially Roy Lynk, who had eclipsed Chadburn and Richardson in the area. Lynk is an ex-Royal Navy man, a patriot and a democrat – not at all a Scargill type. Sure enough, after the strike, when it became clear that the Nottingham men could no longer stay in the NUM, it was Roy who led them out and helped form the Union of Democratic Mineworkers. It was the logical conclusion of the working miners' movement.

Throughout the autumn and into the winter, David Hart's group also kept up a barrage of propaganda, which was useful in contradicting, at grass roots level, several of the Scargill fantasies. For example, the NUM leader proclaimed long and loud throughout the strike that all the violence on the picket lines was caused by the police. The Working Miners produced a booklet called simply 'A Catalogue of Violence' which detailed hundreds of documented instances of thuggery at the hands of the strikers and their supporters. It had a great impact.

None of these efforts, particularly not the lawsuits, could have taken place without the aid of considerable sums of money. David estimates that altogether about half a million pounds was raised and spent during the campaign. Much of that came in small contributions from ordinary citizens in response to pleas from people like

Chris Butcher or to advertisements, sometimes given cheaply by sympathetic newspapers. When David gave me a sample roll call of people prepared to contribute, it made me realize that there was a vast groundswell of concern across the whole of the nation about what Scargill was up to.

The National Working Miners' Committee also received contributions from business groups, and several well-known businessmen expressed great enthusiasm and support for the idea right from the start and willingly passed the hat round. I could obviously not be involved directly in either the raising or the spending of the money. I never even knew how much was spent on the lawsuits. However, there was one exception to this: an occasion when I did feel it absolutely right to go fund-raising for the working miners – and for it I have to thank Mr and Mrs Scargill.

On 28 November I read, to my considerable surprise, that Mr John Paul Getty II, the multimillionaire son of the legendary oil magnate, had donated £100,000 to the striking miners' Christmas appeal, which had been launched the previous week by Mrs Anne Scargill. This item in the paper intrigued me, so I asked David Hart to arrange a meeting with Mr Getty at the London Clinic, where he was more or less permanently in residence. To my surprise it was quickly fixed for the following Tuesday. Mr Getty greeted us warmly and asked what he could do for us. He confirmed that it was true he had donated the money, which gave me my cue: 'Have you really thought about what you have done?' I asked him.

'Why?' he said.

'Well,' I said, 'Mr Scargill is no doubt delighted with the money and it will no doubt help their cause. But you do realize, don't you, that if their cause is successful and the miners triumph in this struggle – which is not only against the NCB but the government as well – if they win, then you are going to be right at the top of the list they will draw up of people to be got rid of. He is already on record as saying that the Queen would be put to work in Woolworth's come his revolution, so who knows what sort of nasty fate he would have in store for the likes of you?'

'You really think so?' he said, reaching for his cheque book.

'I do,' I said as adamantly as I could. He reached for his pen and wrote out a cheque for £100,000 to the National Working Miners, which I handed to David. Thank you, Mrs Scargill, I thought as we left.

David's enthusiasm and interest never flagged throughout the strike. He was not only useful for the enormous amount of work he did in helping with and coordinating all these efforts, but he also gave me another, vital perspective on the whole dispute. He gave me a non-NCB dimension on the issue. The NCB view of things tended, for obvious reasons, to be biased, limited and, in some of the local areas, sadly passive. The attitude in some cases was that there was nothing we could do, therefore there was nothing we should do. David was a great antidote to all that pessimism. Without Florence and without him my vision would have been blinkered and we might never have seen the value of those good old fundamental principles of British law.

Foulstone's and Taylor's action was thus the key to the solution of the strike and it showed us all that ultimately the British legal system will defend the rights of the individual against the mightiest of powers. Not for nothing did those people meet long ago at Runnymede.

But it also shattered one of the great myths of postwar British life – that the unions were somehow above and insulated from the common law, that they could treat their members like serfs without any regard to their fundamental rights. The 1984–5 coal strike may well go down in history as a very important turning point, in that it raised the following questions: how valid are the immunities from the law that the unions take so much for granted? How far do they now consider themselves to be beyond the reach of parliament and above the interests of the people? What the strike showed is that they are neither above the law, nor are they immune from it, when they trample on the fundamental human rights of their members.

10

Peace Moves

Considering the scale and importance to the nation of the strike, it will surprise many people to learn that the prime minister and I had so little contact with each other during it. It was one of Scargill's constant refrains that I was a puppet with the strings being pulled from Downing Street. But this was simply not the case. Naturally, when we did meet in those twelve months – which was on no more than half a dozen occasions on business – we did so with a measure of secrecy, lest any of the many events of the time be blown out of all proportion and given a significance it simply did not have by the mere fact that we were known to have met. This desire to be discreet about our meetings will, of course, give great fuel to the fantasies of those who see a conspiracy round every corner. However, I have to disappoint them, since for the most part our encounters were for the purpose of bringing her up to date on the situation. We had some fairly wide-ranging discussions: but I recollect her giving me a specific order on only one occasion in the entire year of the dispute.

Nevertheless, I did get the impression at a number of points during our various conversations – particularly later in the strike – that my views, my intentions, my motives and sometimes my actions were not always being fairly reported to her. I had the feeling, on more than one occasion, that she wished to see me so that she could check up herself on what was actually happening, rather than believe the reports she was getting. Within the British system of government there are a number of routes through which information on what is going on in one corner, such as the Coal Board, can be communicated to Downing Street, and there can be no guarantees that either the originator of the message or the carrier of it has everyone's best interests at heart.

One such occasion, when I felt she wanted principally to check out what was going on for herself, was at lunch on Sunday, 3 June at Sir Hector Laing's house, which was conveniently close to Chequers for a discreet meeting. There were only five of us present: Hector and Lady Laing, Mrs Thatcher and her husband Denis and myself. Before we sat down to eat, she and I went off to one side so that we could talk.

The NCB was between two sets of negotiations with the NUM and I had indicated to Scargill through various channels that we might be willing to 'trade' to get a deal. He, as was his way, had taken this as a sign that we were about to cave in and lie down in front of him and was crowing about 'imminent victory' to his men. I got the impression that reports of this had reached the prime minister, and the version she had been given of our position stressed more the things we were prepared to give away than those we were going to demand in return.

I explained to her that I felt we must be seen to be trying to negotiate a solution to the dispute and that we had some room for manoeuvre – provided that we re-establish the right to run the business. I was quite happy to offer trading material, as long as our strategic and key position was accepted by Scargill. I was prepared to offer some tactical ground, but unfortunately, in these matters, it is always assumed that the management are expected to provide the compromises.

We were already getting the feeling that Scargill was going to be a difficult man to move from his position of total victory. She asked me how long I thought it would last. Would it go on through the winter? I said: 'Prime Minister, I have no way of knowing – but if we want a successful solution to it, then I think we should work on the assumption that it is going on indefinitely.' There was at this time no sign of Scargill's men running out of money, or their picketing activities lessening and he still seemed to be holding them together with his rhetoric.

I asked her about the electricity situation. She replied that the people responsible were now more confident we could get through the winter with no power cuts and that the CEGB had been able to do a lot with oil-burning stations. 'Well, Prime Minister,' I said, 'at least we have the bonus of the working miners in Nottingham and we are hoping to do all we can to keep them at work and build on that base.'

I told her of my moving encounter a few days earlier with Randy Florence and outlined my preliminary thoughts on possible legal action. Then I added: 'There is a long history of the NCB lying down in front of the NUM. It may take a while before they realize that we are not going to give in on the central issue here and that they are going to have to pay some heed to what we have in mind.'

Before we went in to lunch, Mrs Thatcher thanked me for the briefing and said: 'It's up to you. You are going to have to see this thing right through. You are going to have to come up with the answers to your problems.' I assured her we would and we joined the others. Throughout the conversation there was no sign of any change in her thinking, no sign of shaken resolve at the turn of events – and certainly no attempt to interfere in what I was doing or make me change course. But she has a grasp of events and way of showing concern which makes you feel your problems are fully appreciated.

There had been, and were still going to be, many occasions during this set of negotiations when the accusation was flung that Downing Street was interfering in the strike and preventing a settlement being made. Many of the people who made these allegations were still living in the era of 'beer and sandwich' negotiations at No. 10 – the days when prime ministers paid homage to the union barons and personally offered them compromises and appeasement on a plate. We were no longer in that era. It was, for the time being at least, as the prime minister had said, up to me.

I don't know if her confidence in me was shared by Peter Walker; I suspect not. He always seemed much more concerned about political 'appearances' than she did and therefore expressed far greater anxieties than her – and did so more publicly. I had established that it was my responsibility to keep him informed on the strike and the negotiations, and one of my staff attended his daily briefing meeting in the Department. I believe he recognized that it was much better for him and his colleagues to be able to say truthfully that what was happening at the Coal Board was a matter for the NCB management. Of course the other side of that coin was that they could also dissociate themselves from anything which went wrong.

There were three organized attempts to negotiate a settlement with the NUM in May, June and July. The issue, whichever way it was dressed up in words, was the Right to Manage the Industry. When it came down to it – whatever other items there were in the solution to the dispute – it *had* to contain an element that recognized the

NCB's authority and indeed responsibility for making the final decision about which pits we closed, why and when.

Over the years the consultative machinery at Hobart House had become distorted and diluted to the point where it was no longer a question of management outlining and consulting on the best way of carrying out its policies. These discussions seemed to be dedicated to finding some way to get the union to permit the management to take any action at all. Often this took the form of trying to sell to the union something to appease them. There was little give and take. From the mid-1970s the NUM's interpretation of the consultation process was translated into the idea that nothing could be done without their prior agreement and approval. Scargill had even attempted to escalate that strange concept and we had reached a position where there was such a phobia within Hobart House about the power of the NUM that the NCB had to go to absurd lengths to disguise even its gentlest of intentions. So great was the risk of 'leaking' from sympathetic elements within the management that any plan to do anything had to be elaborately disguised, encoded and hidden away lest it be transmitted at once to the NUM. Indeed the NUM leader would frequently turn up at meetings – or make thundering speeches – waving sheafs of confidential Board documents. As we have seen, I thought it was time to put a stop to all this nonsense and to reassert the NCB responsibility to manage the enterprise effectively.

My other problem with Scargill, when it came to negotiations, was getting him safely through all the tribal dances his position as a revolutionary Marxist leader required, and to the table. Thus in May, well before the first session could start, I had to establish whether the NUM were serious about talking. I couldn't just ring them up and ask them round, because that would immediately be interpreted as a sign that I wanted to sue for peace – that I was caving in. Thence I had to lay out some bait – to let slip a remark to someone that I knew would be passed on. Therefore on 17 April at one of the regular consultative meetings between the unions and the management at Hobart House, I casually said that I might be ready to reconsider the phasing of the proposed pit closures – if there were some give on the other side, conceding my right to do so. Since the start of the strike Scargill had boycotted most of these get-togethers – but NACODS and BACMS still attended, and I thought one or the other would be almost certain to tell the NUM.

We had already lost a considerable tonnage of production in the strike, so I had in mind using the leeway this gave us as a bargaining counter and to show the NUM we were not entirely unwilling to move. I thought, correctly as it turned out, that it would bring Scargill to the table and negotiations could begin.

But before we started I was glad to be able to demonstrate to him – by the example of Nottingham – that he was not having it all his own way in this dispute. I wanted to show him that we were in business mining coal and were happy to talk if he wanted to – but we were not lying down in front of him and rolling over. He was the one out on the limb. He had talked himself, like so many other union leaders, into a position from which retreat might cause him to lose face. I was quite happy to come along with a ladder and help him down – but there was a price. Until that was clear, I was happy for him to stay up there.

Nevertheless from the beginning Scargill chose to portray every one of these delicate moves as a sign that we were suing for peace and that he was on the verge of a great victory. As the dispute went on, however, and the prospect of victory receded, he became trapped by these flights of fancy in his speeches and lost a good deal of credibility. Unfortunately this did not render him any more willing to help in the framing of compromises on his side. In fact, the very opposite was the case. He became even more intransigent. In the end his intractable insistence on total victory and no compromise whatsoever became completely predictable and, hence, useful to me.

But it caused enormous pain and hardship to his members. Most of them, while they feared the idea of it, understood that uneconomic pits had to close. Normal workmen realize that if an enterprise cannot be made profitable – or at least sensibly viable – then, like the corner shop, it has to go. In the middle of the strike Ken Sampey of NACODS said to Jimmy Cowan that, if the NUM were to settle and the NCB to offer redundancy to anyone who wanted it, it would be like running out on to the M1 and trying to stop the traffic – so many of the men were disillusioned with Scargill's constant confrontations and wanted to leave the industry. All those months he was insisting that no pit should close, he was condemning his men to further misery: not for anything they would gain, just for his vision of death or glory.

When he and I had last met in March and the NCB had outlined the plans to take 4 million tonnes out of production, I had regarded this as the first pull on the reins of the runaway horse. It was a gentle tug to tighten them up a bit and to indicate that we were making plans to make sure the enterprise functioned once more as a business rather than a social welfare institution. We had to do something to stop the vast and expensive accumulation of coal and bring production into line with the sort of market we could realistically achieve.

My negotiating technique is to lead the union through the problems and tell them what we plan to do – then to try to set down, stage by stage, all the things we can agree on. We agreed that the NCB's job was to manage the industry. We agreed that the NUM didn't intend to interfere with that task. We agreed on how much coal had to be produced. We agreed that we could not go on losing money hand over fist. We agreed that pits had to close for safety, or if they were exhausted. We agreed that pits had had to close in the past because they were no longer economically viable. I found we could agree on all that. But then we would come to the logical conclusion of all this – that we have to be able to shut pits for purely economic reasons – and we would grind to a halt. So I would start all over again and try it another way round.

This was the technique I used when we finally met, for the first time since the strike had started, on 23 May. The hint I had dropped to the other unions a month earlier had worked and, after several hiccups – while Scargill made his ritual moves for the militants – we got around the table at Hobart House. One of the problems was that Scargill was constitutionally incapable of bringing himself to cross a picket line and, since Hobart House from day one had had an NUM picket outside, he could not come to meet us. However, I believe that, after pressure from Neil Kinnock among others, he agreed to come and the picket was removed for the day so that he could enter the building without betraying his *capo di capi* of trade union rules.

However, the meeting was hardly a success. It only lasted just over an hour. I took him through the negotiating process, but he hardly seemed to listen. I indicated that I might be prepared to reconsider the timing of the package, if I could get the agreement I wanted. I even indicated that I would get him off the hook on his absolute demands that five specific pits, which were up for closure, should not be shut. If we could establish our right to shut them, then we would be happy to sit down and go through the review procedures all over again and talk to the NUM about what to do with them in the long term. But we kept going round and round in circles. His position on uneconomic pits was absolute.

The five pits, Polmaise, Cortonwood, Snowdown, Herrington and Bullcliffe Wood, had been incorporated into Scargill mythology in the previous three months as a sort of Maginot line, beyond which the NCB should not pass. The closure or 'development' (exploration underground to see if they had any more mineable coal) of the first three had been announced in the weeks prior to the strike. But none of us could work out where he got the other two from. Nevertheless he had cleverly put the five of them up as a 'front' issue before any discussion of the main body of closures that our plans would certainly entail.

We were further hampered on that first day of proper negotiating by having the whole NUM executive and their hangers-on sitting in the room with us. All told there were 51 people in there – a crowd definitely not conducive to hard negotiating. At one stage Scargill turned to one of his own people and told him to 'Shut up'. I got the feeling that, having come to the meeting under some sufferance, he was only interested in the propaganda he could get from it outside afterwards among his supporters and the militant left generally.

Certainly, throughout the meeting he kept up the same litany of accusation and complaint, and when he left he immediately went on television and said the government were stopping the NCB settling. It seems to be symptomatic of the high-profile, militant-left union leaders that they have to be seen to be achieving, or at least on the brink of, great victories all the time. So his reason for us not lying down in front of him that day was that the government had stopped us! That would keep the troops happy. I supposed it had escaped his notice that the reason why we were not suing for peace was that by then we already had less need to.

There was another reason for him blaming the government. It was, after all, his real enemy. His audience was only partly the striking miners, who were sacrificing all for him. They were the cannon fodder foot soldiers – there to win the battle for him. But he was also talking to the wider public of the revolutionary left, as their leader, who had set himself the glorious task of bringing down the 'unrepresentative' Thatcher.

I had the feeling during and after that meeting that – apart from the picketing – he was faintly disappointed in the strike so far. We had deliberately kept it as low key as we could. There were no great statements of panic, from us or from the government. Not one minister had made a major speech about the dispute. On past form he must have been expecting an immediate rush to man the pumps; all hands piped on deck to try to find some way to prevent the ship sinking. Instead he was surrounded by a great lack of concern – even from the other unions – and I think he must have felt let down at not being as totally centre stage as he had anticipated. He was in the spotlight as far as his own fans were concerned – night after night he was enthralling great rallies of supporters all over the country – but somehow he was aware that things were not going according to plan. The government was not yet on its knees.

I had noticed one other thing during that brief encounter in May: Scargill's absolute insistence that nowhere in The Plan For Coal was there any reference to the closure of pits on economic grounds. It was to be a major stumbling block between us. It was clear, from the paragraphs I quoted earlier (page 123), that the closure of pits for reasons other than safety or exhaustion *was* contemplated in the Plan – but just never spelled out as such. Many, many hours were to be spent arguing about this point and searching for a form of words which would satisfy both our insistence on the right to close pits for economic reasons, and his insistence that we had no such right.

Just two weeks later, on 8 June – a few days after my meeting with Mrs Thatcher at Hector Laing's house – we were back negotiating again. This time the whole arrangement was more sensible. There was only Scargill, Heathfield and McGahey on one side, and me, Jimmy Cowan and Ned Smith on the other. Jimmy had set the meeting up after we had received a number of frantic signals from the NACODS and the BACMS people asking for some kind of discussion. We did not know whether these messages were coming from the NUM, or whether they were just part of the other unions' desire to see things sorted out. Anyway, Jimmy went to see Scargill, McGahey and Heathfield to see whether there was really any point in talking.

Once again we had to be very careful not to undermine the whole operation, nor to jeopardize our back-to-work movement, by giving Scargill the chance to claim he was on the verge of victory. We arranged for the meeting to be in secret, well away from any of the known 'haunts' of either side. It took place at Monk Fryston in the North Yorkshire area and Jimmy took them over the ground steadily, including what we might be prepared to trade and what we would expect in return. He came back and reported that it would be worthwhile for us all to meet – on the grounds that they seemed to want to talk.

That night, 31 May, Scargill addressed a rally in London and claimed that 'victory' was on the way and the NCB were preparing to climb down on everything, including his Maginot line of the five pits. There was little we could do except deny it and be patient. I remember shaking my head when I heard the news and using what had become the miners' refrain: 'Here we go. Here we go.'

My general thought had been that there was not a great deal of importance attached to these five pits and most of them were very near the end of their reserves anyway, so if they were so important to Scargill, I might be able to use them as a trade also – in exchange for a clear agreement on the NCB's right to manage. However, Scargill's outburst caused a great deal of consternation at the Department of Energy and Peter Walker spent a large part of that weekend denying we were about to climb down and demanding to know what was going on. I can understand that with little previous exposure to tough labour negotiations like this, he found these ploys and counterploys difficult to follow. I am sure that he was concerned and nervous, and that his feelings were somehow communicated to the prime minister by the time I met her on Sunday. I was relieved to find, therefore, that she had a complete grasp of the situation.

The meeting with Scargill actually took place in Edinburgh on 8 June. We started out by saying that we were going to close pits and that in our view there were three reasons for closure. Safety and exhaustion, we could all agree on; but historically there had always been a third category of pits that fitted into neither of the first two pigeon holes. All I wanted to do was to find a way of spelling out in black and white a mutually agreeable system for the third category. I took them through the Colliery Review Procedure, a longstanding process which has to be used before any pit is closed. I pointed out that over the years this system had been used in the closing of a number of pits for reasons other than the first two categories. So why were they being resistant to setting this procedure down and agreeing on the machinery?

It was a much more reasonable discussion than before. We even got to first-name terms. But we still kept going round and round in circles. I finally said: 'Look, all I am asking you to do is to find a way to regularize what you have already agreed to many times before. Spell it out so we both understand it.'

Slowly the search for those elusive words began to concentrate around alternatives for the word 'uneconomic' which Arthur made absolutely clear he could in no circumstances accept. We started talking about pits where the reserves could no longer be 'beneficially' developed. That was Jimmy's word – though at one stage McGahey sent out for a thesaurus, to see if there was any other phrase we could use. We went on all day, but I was confident we were getting somewhere. Finally we agreed to break and resume the following week.

Throughout the entire session Arthur's attitude was somewhat difficult to plumb. He seemed on edge. He didn't seem to want to settle anything and he seemed uncomfortable when I asked him to agree to things. Heathfield and McGahey were a little more inclined to follow the reasoning – but Arthur remained silent for long periods. Then suddenly he would break in to what the rest of us were discussing with some remark that would vitiate all our efforts. It was a fairly frustrating experience. Jimmy too noticed how withdrawn Arthur was and how close together McGahey and I became. He thought it was a sign that the pragmatic McGahey now believed the time had come to settle; that continuing with the strike was not going to win them anything. He could see we were probably going to be able to produce coal in Nottingham, no matter how long the strike lasted, and that therefore the strike was effectively lost. Perhaps he had realized that the best tactic might be to settle now on reasonable terms and come back to fight another day.

There were articles appearing in some of the communist and left-wing press at the time which were critical of Scargill's handling of the strike. When we broke up Jimmy said to me: 'I think the Communist Party is ready to settle.' I thought about it and said: 'I think McGahey is – but I don't think Scargill is.' It was the only time McGahey moved out from behind Scargill. Between then and our next meeting five days later he must have been pushed back into line. It may be that Scargill just temporarily lost his grip on the situation, but the old obduracy was back there by the time we gathered in Rotherham on 13 June.

Not only was the stubbornness there, but open hostility too. It seemed that everything went wrong that day. The meeting was supposed to be secret, but the hotel was being used as the headquarters for a lot of the media people covering the ongoing battle at Orgreave. One of them heard two of the staff discussing Scargill's arrival and in minutes the cat was out of the bag. Needless to say, before the meeting even started, Scargill blamed the NCB for betraying the venue. He also claimed to be upset by an interview I had given to *The Times* the day before which had appeared under the headline: 'After the strike: the hope of a coal bonanza'. I could not understand what there was to find offensive in this optimistic view of the industry's future, or in the article itself, which merely reiterated all the things I had been saying about what was needed to put the industry right.

Indeed, in my briefing notes prepared before the meeting, there was an item which said: 'The NUM may wish to pursue in some detail the chairman's statement in *The Times* on future output, markets, etc., over the next ten years.' I was hoping the interview would draw them out, so that I could show them how good a future the industry had – if only we could get our costs right. I wanted them to realize that there was a market for our coal from Scandinavia to the Mediterranean.

However, it seemed to me that, whatever the cause, the climate for intelligent discussion was missing and there was no point in pursuing that line. Clearly nothing constructive was going to be said, so there was no point in staying there. Jimmy was convinced that there was tension between the three men on the other side. All our previous meetings were, at least, well mannered – but there was open hostility on this occasion. Before we started, Jimmy reminded Heathfield politely that, since we had come here at their request – they had union business in Rotherham that day – we would want to adjourn in time to catch our train back to London. Heathfield snapped, 'Kindly address all your questions to the president.'

As usual Scargill went straight on television and radio afterwards and blamed us for the breakdown in talks. There was very little I could do to stop him, apart from instructing our PR department to counter his ridiculous assertions. Later I learned that Peter Walker was 'furious' that I had not contacted him to let him know what had transpired at the talks. He had never indicated to me that he wished to be briefed every hour on the hour about what we were doing – and I had seen no reason to start now. There were no new developments to report. We had merely adjourned the meeting. I sensed he was no longer as relaxed as he had been, nor as happy to leave things to me. But I felt confident that the prime minister was still supporting my conduct of affairs. However, the strike was now three months old and there were mounting concerns on all sides. People at all levels were just not acclimatized to the idea that this dispute might take a really long time to settle and they were becoming edgy.

Could this be the first tiny sign that Peter Walker was beginning to get worried?

Three weeks later we had our next series of negotiations – on 5 and 6 July in the Rubens Hotel in London, on the 9th in Edinburgh again, and on the 18th back in the Rubens. It was said at the time that Arthur Scargill never got a better offer from us than he did during the session on the 9th. Indeed that day we came quite close to settling. But it was now becoming quite clear that his total intransigence and his unwillingness to consider any compromise would always get in the way of a settlement.

Two days before these talks began I was asked to Downing Street to brief the prime minister. She seemed anxious that the dock strike, which had come out of the blue, could have a damaging effect on the country. She also wanted to know what the situation was in my 'corner' and what the prospects were for a settlement in the coming talks. I explained to her that our position was considerably stronger than it had been a month before, that Nottingham was now settled down and the back-to-work movement, though still a trickle, was showing progress. In the negotiations I was still willing to give ground on the timing – if, and only if, I could get a clear assurance that the NCB had the right to manage the industry.

Once again I formed the impression that she must be getting nervous signals from elsewhere and wished to be reassured that it was not really my intention to give away the store. I assured her that this was definitely not the case, but that obviously we had to be seen to be willing to trade something in order to get the miners to settle. However, I added that I was beginning to come to the conclusion that Scargill was now locked into his position of total victory – death or glory – and I did not think that anything we offered short of a total climbdown would satisfy him.

She seemed satisfied with this report and wished me luck in the negotiations. I left feeling it was a good job that she understood the nature of the problems and the need to take a firm line, while always being ready to trade on the lesser details. I am sure that many people around her – both politicians and civil servants – did not fully appreciate what was at stake, how to handle these matters, or the true nature of the struggle with Arthur Scargill. Many of them still believed this to be an ordinary dispute, which would normally have been solved by now were it not for the strange unwillingness of the management to come up with enough compromises. After all, in their view, most major industrial disputes in the last forty years had ended with the management making some valued gesture to the unions, so why not now? Yet there was also an odd anxiety in some of them. On the one hand they wanted Scargill beaten; but on the other, they wanted it done without any pain, nastiness or confrontation. This led them into curious, schizophrenic sort of frame of mind. For example, whenever Scargill made one of his speeches at this time, saying that the Coal Board was about to collapse and give way on everything, they seemed to believe him and rushed to ask us what we were up to and how long this agony was going to go on. But my message to them was the same as it had been to the prime minister: it would be over quicker if we planned on it going on forever. She had understood that. But not many others seemed to.

This lack of understanding of our position pervaded the July round of talks. It was characterized by the remark that a senior trade unionist from outside the industry made to Jimmy at the time: 'You've gone 80 per cent of the way to meet Scargill. Why don't you go the other 20 per cent and get the thing settled?' He thought Jimmy was being unduly aggressive when he replied: 'Why doesn't

Scargill come up with the other 20 per cent – then we'll get it settled!'

In those long hours of discussion we started by exchanging a series of documents, which slowly focused once again on the principal area of disagreement between us. Our final version on the morning of 18 July offered to keep open the five collieries which Scargill had made his 'front' issue – but any 'future decisions relating to these (and other collieries) will be dealt with in accordance with the guidelines under section three below'. Section three had three clauses in it – including the crucial one containing the problematic word 'beneficial'. It read:

In order to establish more clearly the parameters in respect of exhaustion of reserves, in line with the principles of The Plan For Coal, the following categories and procedures will apply:

(a) Collieries which are exhausted in line with the principles of The Plan For Coal will be closed by joint agreement.

(b) Collieries facing severe geological difficulties, again in line with the principles of The Plan For Coal, will be closed by joint agreement.

(c) The NCB and NUM agree that where a comprehensive and in-depth investigation by their respective mining engineers shows that a colliery has no further mineable reserves that are workable and which can be beneficially developed, such a colliery shall be deemed exhausted.

That was it. We talked for thirteen hours on that last day. The atmosphere was not hostile, but Scargill would not move. His belief was that no pit should close unless and until it was either unsafe or the last ounce of coal had been dug from it. My belief was that we had to have the right, however it was couched, to close pits for sound economic reasons. Nevertheless I felt it my duty to go on and on to the point of everyone else's exhaustion (I don't usually get tired in such long meetings – perhaps I have the constitution for them) to see if there was not some tiny scrap of willingness on Scargill's part to move. But I found that, while he was very skilful in the use of words and thought very quickly, as a negotiator he saw only victory for himself in absolute terms. He had just had a heady extraordinary annual conference of the NUM and the dock strike had brought the country as close as it ever came to a standstill. He clearly thought he was still on course for a major triumph. There were no compromises at all coming from him that night, so again there was no further point in talking.

It also emerged in this period that among those who least understood the dispute – the reasons for it, the nature, length and bitterness of it, and the failure to settle it quickly – were many of my colleagues in Hobart House. To start with, it interfered with their ordered world. They quickly came to the conclusion, I gather, that these new disruptive elements, as represented by me, might not be around for all that long and that life might soon return to normal. When life failed to follow the pattern they had ordained for it and the strike went on, the pain they felt was almost palpable. There were periods about this time when some of the staff felt that we were crazy, that we should settle quickly and get everything back to normal. Some were frankly disloyal; some uncooperative. But the atmosphere settled into a sort of sullen hostility. As I have said they were not accustomed to people at the top making major decisions and taking responsibility without long and involved committee meetings to agonize over every alternative. All-day committee meetings had gone and had apparently left a vacuum, a feeling of nonparticipation and frustration over the exclusiveness of the executive policies. As the strike went on through the summer with no sign of ending, their unhappiness and bewilderment seemed to grow with each day.

Jimmy and I led a fairly solitary existence at this time. We worked together and delegated tactics to the area directors. But in Hobart House even Ned Smith, and the others closest to us, oscillated between enthusiasm and despondency, hope and fear. I don't think they really understood the full nature of the struggle either.

There were to be no more talks until September. As long as Scargill was not prepared to move, there was little point in further discussions. I had, by now, considerably revised my thinking on two counts: I did not think that he was capable of any compromise and I began to realize that he was going to lead those poor men to the gates of hell rather than admit what I thought was now staring him in the face. Nor did I think, as a consequence of this, that there was much prospect of the strike ending in 1984.

This thinking was highly provisional, however, and dependent on there being no surprises or slips on our side, which might severely damage our position. There were, however, to be two such surprises or 'near misses' which, at the time, caused considerable anxiety and concern at all levels.

11

Where Are the Reinforcements?

The most interesting aspect of the great fuss which followed the prime minister's celebrated remarks about 'the enemy within', which she made on 19 July to the Conservative backbench 1922 Committee, was the inverse ratio which existed between those who protested about her remarks and the amount of practical support they were prepared to give Arthur Scargill. Generally speaking, my observation was that those who shouted the loudest were doing the least.

But this curious phenomenon reveals a fascinating side of the strike, one which was put privately by more than one trade union leader and by many Labour politicians in the summer and autumn. In summation it would be: 'We have to find a way of making sure Scargill is beaten without the miners losing.'

The truth was that, as the dispute progressed, the trade union movement in general found itself talking more and more about the need to support the miners, but doing less and less to help Scargill. I understood from my contacts that the 'establishment' of the movement was frankly embarrassed by his antics, worried by the damage the violence and mayhem was doing to the image of trade unionism in Britain, and, increasingly, unable to see any way of getting him out of the corner he had talked his way into. There was very little they were willing to do to help his struggle, but in order to keep up the front of brotherly comradeship, they found themselves constrained to offer a lot of verbal support. Hence the overblown expressions of outrage from all quarters at Mrs Thatcher's quite modest remarks aimed at the man who had, after all, vowed to sweep her away in his revolutionary tide. To my mind it was a form of guilty reaction to their unwillingness to do much to help their comrade.

When I examined the record, as far as it was made public, of his contacts with the other trade unions both individually and collectively, I found it easy to understand their reluctance to throw their weight behind him; for his approaches all seemed to be characterized by the same arrogance with which he treated his own members. In the early months of the strike he spent a fair amount of time running around trying to get support from various other trade unions, but with very little success.

It was not until the strike was four months old that he got any significant help at all and the July dockers' strike was the first of only two occasions when such aid arrived. On each occasion, however, the widening out of the strike – to the docks and through NACODS – caused a great deal of anxiety at all levels. The first of these ancilliary issues, the dock strike, was not really my affair in that it never directly involved the NCB at all. However, the events that led up to it demonstrated to us all the tightrope we had to walk all the time to keep the miners' strike from becoming a national trade union issue.

Scargill's constant efforts to play to a wider audience than the miners, to involve more workers in the struggle, and to take on the mantle of the whole militant left, while not directly our business, nevertheless had to be paralleled within the NCB by equally strenuous efforts on our part to correct his falsehoods, to draw the sting of his allegations and to make joining him as unattractive a proposition as possible. I had to take into consideration the likely reactions of people inside and outside the NCB.

There were several occasions during the strike, for example, when I thought it might be constructive to write to each member of our workforce. The first of these caused a great deal of derision in the media because I addressed each man as 'Dear Colleague'. It was difficult to persuade the people in Hobart House or elsewhere that I regarded the men who actually did the job as colleagues. It took some time for people to realize that I relish my trips to the pits and enjoy meeting and chatting with the men. The purpose of these letters was not so much to persuade the men to go back to work on the spot, but more to plant in their minds the idea that going back was possible – other men had done it – and that we were doing all we could to negotiate a settlement, but we were not going to cave in.

From the publicity these letters attracted, the public at large also got the message that there was another side to Scargill's story. It was also necessary to counterbalance directly a lot of the virulent propaganda that was pouring out of the NUM offices. One letter, written from the Yorkshire area office, complained of the 'unprecedented levels of brutality by organized police militia' which were preventing 'our right as trade unionists to picket trade unionists and explain our case'! I was left wondering what explanation the 10,000 men at Orgreave really wanted to quietly chat over with the lorry drivers, or how the brick and the baseball bat helped the thugs debate their case with the working miners' wives and children in the middle of the night in the villages of Nottinghamshire.

I was lucky to have advice and help in all aspects of communication from Tim Bell, who was chairman of

Saatchi and Saatchi, Compton Worldwide and had been the inspiration behind the Conservative Party campaigns in 1979 and 1983. Early in April I had sought out David Young, chairman of the Manpower Services Commission, and close to the prime minister, to talk over the problem of our public relations. I was aware that the existing set-up in Hobart House could not have either the enthusiasm or dedication required for what might be a long and gruelling campaign. Nor had it the imagination and breadth of vision that was clearly going to be required to counter Scargill on all fronts. Geoff Kirk, head of the NCB's PR department, I was proudly told, was the industrial PR man best liked in Fleet Street. That set all my alarm bells ringing. This was not going to be a dispute settled in the classic way in a week or two, after which Mr Kirk could go back to his cosy chats with his friends in the media. This had all the makings of a gloves-off job and I wanted a man who could handle the rough and tumble. David came back to me within hours with Tim's name and I could sense, as soon as I met him, that he was the right man for the job. For three months we met regularly and I was impressed with the way he worked his way quietly into the bones of the dispute. However, it was not until July that I felt the time was ripe to begin to go on the offensive in PR terms too, with a series of advertisements in the papers explaining our case. Then he came into his own and became an invaluable member of the team.

I suppose that I should not have been surprised by the row that his presence as a member of our team caused when it first came to light. Inside Hobart House there was consternation at all levels and near hysteria from Geoff Kirk, who shouted: 'You can't use him . . . He works for the Tories!' I thought that, since they had won the last two elections with Mr Bell's able assistance, that was probably quite a good recommendation. All sorts of alle-

historically at least, totally the wrong time. As we have seen, BSC's finances, while they were considerably better than they were when I took over in 1980, were still in a precarious state. This was principally due to two inter-related factors: the decline in demand and the excess of capacity in Europe. We had still not yet seen any upswing from the bottom of the recession and this had produced a situation where the three major light gauge sheet mills – at Port Talbot, Llanwern and Ravenscraig – were, in effect, competing for a decreasing amount of home business. Thus, while it was deemed politically imprudent to shut any one of them, it nevertheless made business sense to do so. BSC managers, and most of its workforce, were only too aware, however, that if one of them were shut down by outside forces – particularly by Arthur Scargill – there would be little opportunity or desire on anyone's part to open it up again. It would remain a rusting monument to the triumph of Arthur's fight for jobs.

Since the 1920s there has been in the trade union movement a sub-section – a sort of separate baronial fiefdom of common interests – known as the Triple Alliance. The theory behind it is that together the unions of the mining, steel and transport industries could clasp the nation firmly by the throat at any time they wished to and extract from it whatever they wanted. It was long ago christened the Cripple Alliance on account of its consistent failure to come together and act concertedly on behalf of any of its members to any great effect.

It was to the alliance that Scargill went first for support in his fight. On 29 March he met representatives of the steel, rail, seamen and transport workers, which included the docks, and called on them to instruct their members to block all movements of coal. Over the next six months their failure to implement his request in the steel industry was a harsh blow to Scargill, and in the patchy areas where they did show their support, much bitterness and recrimination followed as many union men saw themselves making sacrifices for a union that had given them little support during the steel strike of 1979.

At the start of the strike, BSC switched to importing as much foreign coal as it could and, where they could not get British union-crewed ships to carry it, they moved to foreign flags. There was sporadic trouble at the docks where this coal was unloaded, but the enterprise was never seriously threatened by the actions of dockers. It was getting the coal to the steelworks – with the exception of Port Talbot, which was on the waterfront – that caused some problems.

Bill Sirs of the ISTC was the most vociferous in his refusal to accept the Scargill call to battle. He could perceive clearly the threat to his own men's jobs. In the first three months of the strike numerous local deals were struck to make sure sufficient supplies got through to the steelworks at least to keep them running. Many of these fell apart under NUM pressure and amid much acrimony. At the centre of this action were, first, the rail unions and, second, the transport unions.

Many NUR and ASLEF (the traindrivers' union) members cooperated at first in the blacking, but then, when the local deals fell apart and BSC turned increasingly to road transport to get the ore in and the steel out, they too began to worry about their jobs and their resolve weakened. The TGWU, with its 1.6 million members, found it too had little control over the armies of owner-driver, or small non-union firms of lorries which replaced the work normally done by British Rail. At one stage this fleet of lorries was completing 25,000 journeys a week for BSC and the NCB.

The threat to their own jobs was indeed the key to the

reaction of the men in other unions. British Rail lost £250 million of business during the strike – £70 million of it on blacked coal trains – and it was clear to all but the most militant that Scargill's fight for coal-mining jobs was now likely to be at the expense of their own and their mates' jobs. Also the strike showed that their long-time near monopoly of the transport of coal and steel was not sacrosanct and might be very vulnerable. For example, it emerged that it cost more to transport coal by rail from the docks at Hunterston to Ravenscraig a few miles away than it would to ship that coal half the way from America to Hunterston.

No better illustration of the nervousness of the men in other unions existed than in the story of what happened one summer morning near Sherwood Colliery in Nottinghamshire. The pit was working normally after all the upset in the area, but had in recent weeks found itself challenged by an unexpected problem. The NUR signalman on the single-line branch which ran to the pit – and along which all its coal had to be delivered – was enough of a Scargill fan to refuse to let the trains through. Consequently the coal was piling up at the pit and there seemed to be no other means of moving it because the premises were serviced by tiny and heavily picketed access roads.

Both management and men were faced with the threat of closure, simply because of the actions of this one man. Early one morning a group of men in yellow coats and safety hats appeared in the field next to the signal box carrying surveying equipment. They worked their way slowly across the field towards the signal box, marking a path with stakes in the ground as they proceeded. The signalman, with nothing much to do, was obviously intrigued and, when they arrived close to him, he asked what they were doing. 'Oh,' said the leader, 'didn't you know? We're surveying this field for the new road that's coming through here to the pit. The Coal Board are fed up with the rail unions, so they are going to close the branch line here, and your signal box, and use the new road instead.'

Next day the trains were running again. John Liptrott says that his group of working miners returned the yellow coats, safety hats, theodolites and the other surveyors' equipment they had borrowed and laughed for days after.

I watched the skirmishes between the pickets and members of other unions with great interest not only because they diverted attention – as at Orgreave – away from pits where we were trying to keep men working, but because they also demonstrated to the strikers that all was not unity in the trade union movement over the NUM's decision to call the strike. This was particularly true in Scotland, where McGahey found himself tied up in an insoluble dilemma, trying at one time to obey the Scargill edict to stop coal getting to Ravenscraig, then working with the local ISTC man, Tommy Brennan, to make sure some got through, then supporting the pickets to try to stop it, then trying to explain to the miners at Polkemmet pit, which had no other function than to serve the steelworks, why he was trying to shut it down. Poor Mick had his hands full and it was a great credit to his versatility that somehow he claimed to be working on a consistent NUM programme.

Our decision to abandon the route of injunctions against the miners did not stop other leaders of nationalized industries, who were suffering as a result of the strike, considering such action – particularly against secondary picketing. Not only was British Rail losing heavily, but BSC lost about £100 million in the twelve months of the dispute. As we have seen, I spent a good deal of time with the chairman and chief executives of both enterprises – Bob Reid and Bob Scholey – persuading them that any action which could escalate the strike into other areas was not to their advantage. I was lucky that both were exceptional leaders and were prepared to bite the bullet and resist their instincts to go after the troublemakers throughout the strike. Bob Reid at BR had a particularly difficult time, since he had to negotiate his way through a big wage demand just as the strike was starting. He managed to do it without a major confrontation. He also managed to keep the pressure on his unions without them ever walking out. In many cases he sent home drivers who refused to take out blacked trains and went down the roster until he found one who would cooperate.

By mid-summer the prospects of either the railwaymen or the steelmen blacking all movements of coal *en masse* had receded considerably. Indeed on 29 June Scargill made one final appeal to Bill Sirs, who turned him down. A fortnight later he wrote to the ISTC man accusing him of having a 'disgusting' and 'diabolical attitude' to the miners' strike. He added that his behaviour in not falling into line had been 'in violation of every principle understood and accepted by the trade union and labour movement'.

As the use of road transport increased, I was pleasantly surprised by the lack of hold the TGWU had over this section of its activities. I don't think anyone quite appreciated the extent to which the pattern of heavy lorry ownership had changed. Single owner-drivers were unlikely to be union men – and the big firms, faced with an encroachment into their market from the smaller owner groups, were able to persuade many of their union drivers to ignore the picket lines. While the TGWU was proud of its new militant leader, Ron Todd, none of his philosophy seemed to be translated into action on the ground.

We also found the TGWU less than totally behind Scargill in the area of our open-cast operations – which accounted for over 12 million tonnes of production a year. Not only is open cast a sizeable part of our output and quite profitable, but it is also very valuable coal. Open-cast coal tends to come from the upper parts of the coal basins and does not have so many impurities in it, such as sodium chloride, which are often found in much of the deep-mined coal from the lower measures in the basin. Open-cast coal is used extensively to mix with deep-mined coals to help improve the overall quality, so it is a vital part of our total production. The TGWU, not the NUM, represents the men in the open-cast operations which are usually carried out by contractors to the NCB. There has been, since the arrival of Scargill, some friction between the two groups and their unions. Scargill, in his wisdom, wishes to abolish open-cast operations which does not endear him to our contractors' men. During the strike George Henderson, the TGWU man in charge of open cast, apparently asked Scargill for a little *quid pro quo* on his demands to close down open cast, in return for their fullest cooperation in the dispute. Scargill was outraged at this grotesque lack of spontaneous loyalty and Henderson was forced to watch as Moss Evans, then still the leader, wrote to the NUM leader to apologize.

However, open-cast coal was dug throughout the strike – and, though its movement was severely restricted at first, the situation eased somewhat towards the end of the strike and increasing quantities became available to consumers.

It was out of this tangle of irregular, sporadic and often contradictory secondary picketing arrangements that the July dock strike suddenly blew up, like a genie from a bottle, and threatened for a few days to do what all the huffing and puffing of the Triple Alliance had failed to do – to bring the country to a halt. Only the fact that there was patently no real excuse for it and that, in the end, the men themselves could see that its whole exercise was undertaken not for their benefit, but to aid the miners, caused it eventually to collapse.

It did not concern me directly, but I found myself puzzled that a man could pick up a load of coal in a dumper truck in a docks area one minute without any problem – and the next minute, when he does exactly the same, the explosion of forces that the act provokes leads to the closure, within a few days, of every major port in the country. Yet that is precisely what happened at Immingham at around 10 a.m. on 6 July. In the byzantine complexities of the dock labour scheme, the dispute was thus born, and translated in a matter of days into a national issue. Everybody concerned apologized for whatever had been done wrong. The transport minister assured the House, the militant TGWU docks man, John Connolly, and the public at large that there was no intention whatsoever of altering the dock labour scheme in any way. There was no reason left for the strike – but still it went on. Preparations were made to bring in the troops and for a few days it looked as though Scargill's friends had, almost by accident, managed to get their hands on the nation's throat.

But then, as suddenly as it had come, it was gone. It was the stranded lorry drivers who put the genie back inside the bottle. There were hundreds of them, of all nationalities, stuck on each side of the Channel and becoming, with every day that passed, a little less enchanted with their brothers in the British trade union movement. Finally they cracked and, with a mounting succession of threats about what would happen if they were not allowed to move their lorries, they persuaded the dockers in Dover that, in Scargill's words, they too had a contractual arrangement, which they intended to honour come hell or high water. In two days the whole strike was over –

but not before it had given the government a considerable fright, which, incidentally, made Mrs Thatcher's Channel Tunnel decision eighteen months later even more surprising.

Peter Walker was particularly perturbed by the incident. He thought it would mean the end of the whole of our strike as well. It must have confirmed all his fears that we would never win. Over the first few months of the strike I had asked one or two political associates what his position was *vis-à-vis* the strike. They indicated to me that he was very much a captive of his cabinet colleagues' resolve but they suspected he had no real enthusiasm for it himself.

Scargill made one more major attempt to win the physical support of the brothers – this time at the TUC conference in Brighton in September. But here too he ran into difficulties. By this time many of the delegates were only too aware that most of their members had been frightened off by Scargill's rantings. They were not the revolutionary material he imagined them to be. So the delegates came to the conference – anxious to be seen to mouth the right words for the support of the miners' leader, but keen not to let it go any further than that. They knew they could not commit their members to any major supportive action.

The union leaders – particularly those on the TUC council itself – had a further reason to ensure that their support did not lead to much action. They did not like or trust Scargill. He had never shown much regard for any of them. Earlier in the dispute he had virtually told them to keep out of it. Now, in the build-up to the conference, he tried to impose on them a motion which would commit the entire constituent membership of the TUC to a 10p a week levy – raising more than a million pounds a week to keep the pickets out in force and the mayhem going at full pitch. The motion and its proposed amendments called for all unions to respect the miners' picket lines and for all material connected with the dispute to be blacked if it was delivered by non-union men or by the armed forces. It was estimated that the miners, who had started the strike with £10 million – but had moved £8 million of it abroad as soon as the strike started – had gone through most of the remaining £2 million, as well as some of the £5 million which had been raised for them by fellow trade unionists. But much of this £5 million was earmarked for welfare and hardship cases and was not supposed to go to help the picketing.

It took all Len Murray's considerable skills to defuse the various bombs in that motion and render it, on the day, strong on rhetoric and weak on action. A major crisis in the TUC was thus averted, for there was an awful lot of face-saving to do. The strong feelings from the more militant leaders also had to be considered. At least Scargill was the only one among them who was attacking the hated Tory government head-on. The members of the TUC at Brighton that week might be described in exactly the same way as John L. Lewis, the great American trade unionist, described the merger of the AFL and the CIO. They were, he said, 'bound together by strands of sand'.

However, Scargill got his moment centre stage. And he certainly roused the rabble. The motion which was passed to great acclaim promised total support for the NUM's struggle, a major fund-raising drive and detailed discussions by the TUC general council about the proposed blacking of all NCB products or substitutes for them. But as Eric Hammond, of the electricians, said: 'Either this means a complete cessation of civilized life, or it doesn't mean what it says and it is a con trick on the miners.' Thankfully, to the great credit of the TUC, it looked to me like the latter.

One important development, with amusing consequences on the side, came out of the deliberations in Brighton. I was sitting at home quietly late one night during the conference when the phone rang. A deep gravelly voice introduced himself as Robert Maxwell, the publisher, who had just taken over the Mirror Group. I had met Cap'n Bob, as he is known, on a number of occasions around town and I had always had a sort of sneaking regard for him. He didn't wear a black eye-patch but there was a lot of the buccaneer about him – I recognized all the symptoms. But he was amusing with it; and in his own strange way his heart was in the right place.

Anyway the deep voice said: 'I am sitting here at the TUC conference in Brighton in my suite in the hotel and I have here Ray Buckton [ASLEF] and next door to him is Peter Heathfield and next to him is Arthur Scargill. I have been talking to them and I think we should try to find a solution to the strike. What I would like to do is to arrange a session to see if we can sort it out.'

I was a little bit leery of this for two reasons. First of all, I did not see Cap'n Bob as a natural harbinger of peace – though he clearly thought that was his mission. Secondly, on the whole, the Mirror had been very much pro-Scargill for the last six months and I didn't want to become a patsy for one of its stunts. Geoffrey Goodman, the paper's industrial editor, was related by marriage to Ken Sampey of NACODS, and was fairly strongly committed to the miners' cause, so I was concerned about getting tangled up in this sort of deal. Goodman might just take my willingness to talk as being a sign we were ready to cave in and we would be off on the same old roundabout again with the NUM and the consequent problem of getting men to return to work.

However, I agreed to meet a few of the TUC people – Ray Buckton, David Basnett and some others – to see whether there were any grounds for talks. We met and talked over in generalities what the problems were. Meanwhile I also had some private chats with Bob to let him know where we stood before he took it any further. I said to him: 'You know, one of the problems standing in the way of me getting involved with you in trying to find a solution is your paper. It has been highly critical of me throughout this strike. If you stop the *Mirror* attacking the NCB, I'll work with you to try to mastermind a solution to the strike.' I don't know whether or not it was sheer coincidence, but from then on the *Mirror*'s coverage ceased to be uniformly hostile.

His interest in the strike did, at least, lead to my first meeting with some of the TUC people who were to figure largely in things later. I found it quite amusing that in the meetings we had I should be sitting there with them and we should all be talking around trying to find a solution, not so much to the strike but to the problem created by Arthur Scargill. They understood the nature of the difficulty just as well as I did.

12

NACODS Enter the Fray

With a mixture of self-deprecation and resentment of their role both in the industry and in the union world, some members of NACODS had, for years, humorously referred to themselves as the 'National Association of Can-carriers, Obedient Dopes and Suckers'. It was a reflection of the inferiority complex this 15,000-member union of the pit deputies had when standing beside the mighty National Union of Mineworkers and equally when examining their status – as neither 'management' nor 'workers' – within the hierarchy of the NCB. It reflected their historical position as the all-too-often whipping boys of the industry – since they were in charge of safety in the mines, they were most often blamed when things went wrong. In more recent years it had also come to reflect an anxiety about their continued existence, not only in the conventional terms of pit closures and the shrinking industry, but also because, in the age of the hand-held instant gas detector and high-technology coal-winning, there was some doubt as to whether there really was a role for that many of them.

For all that they were happy gently to mock themselves (lest others do it for them), although their attitude also concealed a great deal of resentment, which, if fuelled properly by those who wished to see the NCB defeated, could cause the explosion which would bring that victory about. This had not escaped the notice of many of those in the TUC, who could not bring themselves to support Scargill but equally could not bear to see the miners lose. Thus it was at the TUC conference and afterwards that NACODS were ushered on to the centre of the stage and, to the applause of the crowd, given their moment of glory. Their 'performance' lasted altogether for nearly ten weeks of the dispute and caused a great deal of anxiety at all levels.

The NACODS row – after the docks strike – was the second of the two 'side issues' which brought Scargill near to victory. It was the issue on which relations with the secretary of state became very uptight as his political worries – and my apparent reluctance to respond – caused his frustrations with me to boil over. I for my part had become alarmed that we were near selling out on all the principles we had stuck to all these months. It was the issue on which the government collectively seemed to develop the jitters for the first time. It was also the issue over which my relations with the prime minister came nearest to being strained and caused her to give me the only direct order I received from her in the entire twelve months of the strike.

For some months before the NACODS issue blew up, I had been warned by friends and political associates that Peter Walker was not all that happy with me whenever the subject came up for discussion. I suppose that in the early days he had felt that I was the wrong man for the job. I doubt whether he would have appointed me. But by now I began to get rumours he was considering talking to union leaders to try to find a solution to the growing labour problems of the NCB. I felt he was concerned not to be seen to lose the strike, and whispers from friends in Whitehall all suggested that if there was a chance of it going against us, he would consider compromising and be seen as the man who brought peace to the industry. None of this helped my worries and from then on I always had the uneasy feeling that there was some kind of screen between us and that I was not a trusted member of his team, which was, of course, an extraordinary position for the head of the industry to be in.

The NACODS dispute began on 15 August, but it had its roots in the strikes of 1972 and 1974. Many of the duties of the NACODS men are defined in the various mining acts of parliament, in that miners may not go underground unless certain tasks and safety checks have been carried out by the pit deputies and they may not go down to work unless accompanied by the appropriate NACODS men. In the two strikes of the 1970s, when the whole industry was at a halt, NACODS members had continued to go to work, but for the first time some of them had met with large-scale picketing and intimidation. In such cases the management agreed that the men should return home, telephone the manager, explain the extent of the problem which had prevented them from getting to work and they would still be able to draw their wages.

But the guidelines agreed a decade before were scarcely applicable in Scargill's strike – particularly not as the back-to-work movement began to gain momentum. NA-CODS men in Nottingham, for example, were expected to make their way through the violence and intimidation of the picket lines, but in Yorkshire, at pits which were completely closed by pickets and where there was no work being done underground, the management had allowed most of the NACODS men to stay at home and still be paid, whether they went near the pit or not. Between these two positions, some area directors would not pay the men unless they turned up at the pit, whether or not there was work being done, and others paid them after they had rung in – even though other personnel, such as the canteen ladies, were getting to work through the picket lines.

By early August the situation had become quite acrimonious – with the tougher area directors complaining that it was difficult to hold the line when so much was being given away by others. Bert Wheeler and Ken Moses felt particularly strongly about Michael Eaton in North Yorkshire, who was not insisting on his NACODS men coming in before being entitled to pay. Jimmy Cowan asked Ned Smith and Merrick Spanton to sort out the situation and in the middle of the month they announced to a meeting of the NACODS executive that where other workers were going through the picket lines so would NACODS men be expected to go – or they would not be paid.

To them it was a simple and formal re-statement of the 74 guidelines, albeit tightened up slightly in the light of the present circumstances. They believed on that day that there was general understanding from NACODS of the problem of the disparities that had arisen and that they had the agreement of the NACODS executive. However, two key members of that body – the president, Ken Sampey, and the general secretary, Peter McNestry – were away on holiday. McNestry's absence was to prove particularly awkward. He had only been elected a few months previously and had 'come from nowhere' to the post – the expected reward for a man who has worked long and hard for the left-wing caucus of a union. Not only had he, in a few short months, managed to generate more fire and militancy in the NACODS stance, but also he was beginning to put pressure on Sampey, who was coming up for retirement.

Both men felt slighted on their return that such an important issue had been resolved while they were away and, I gather, both were intrigued that Scargill and Heathfield had already been in touch and a meeting had been called for to see what they were going to do about it. In the meantime also, the problem had been further exacerbated by Bert Wheeler's enthusiastic interpretation of the new guidelines and his refusal to pay any NACODS men – unless and until they actually presented themselves inside the pit gates, whether miners were working there or not. He felt it demonstrated the management's resolve to keep the industry going, but the union saw it as unnecessary extra provocation.

Bert's enthusiastic attitude I suspect may have been somewhat coloured by the adulatory attention he was getting at the time from various people at the Department of Energy and elsewhere. He was persevering with his back-to-work movement and was getting a fair amount of TV exposure in Scotland. I have no doubt that those in political circles were anxious to encourage him and feel they were doing their little bit to help. But such intervention made it difficult to exert management control in the running of any kind of business; even more so in this case, because it was the running of a successful war. The last thing you want in either business or war is to have enthusiastic amateurs telling your field commanders behind your back what they should be doing. Perhaps too charitably, I put such interventions in the conduct of the strike down to examples of overenthusiasm – but maybe tinged with occasional malice. Whether politically or bureaucratically inspired, these interventions were often unhelpful and usually damaging to our cause. I was frequently reminded of that old saying: 'With friends like these, who needs enemies?'

The NACODS problem did not really come up on my radar screen until the end of August, when Sampey and McNestry suddenly returned from holiday and demanded

a meeting. I had not been involved in the earlier decision
to revise the guidelines – I had merely been told that the
lack of uniform NACODS practice had been tidied up and
had been approved. At the meeting on 30 August it
rapidly became clear that, far from this being the case, we
had real trouble on our hands. The NACODS attitude was
aggressive, to say the least. McNestry made a string of
demands which followed the Scargill line and demanded
that the new guidelines be withdrawn.

Then the real mischief started. The following week was
the TUC conference in Brighton. My own reconstruction
of what probably happened there is that some kind of
brainstorming session was held one night in which some
of Scargill's more left-wing brothers in the TUC, in response to the castigation he had given them for their
failure to follow his revolutionary banner, had looked
around for some other way in which they could show
their support for him. I presume that any such session
must have included McNestry so they had eventually
lighted on NACODS. Here was a mining union group who
not only had a ready-made grievance, but also offered
the tantalizing possibility that through it the miners might
sneak a win – without Scargill necessarily being victori-
ous. The theory was that no work could be done underground without the deputies and therefore the entire
underground operation would be brought to a halt overnight if the NACODS members could be persuaded to
come out on strike. They could do in three weeks what
Scargill had failed to achieve in six months. Thus the left
in NACODS must have reacted with joy to the idea of the
union being the chosen instrument of the TUC, though
the much more thoughtful and cautious Ken Sampey was
clearly considerably more reluctant.

Before we knew what was happening the smouldering
NACODS grievances were fanned into flames and we had

a potential strike on our hands. Scarcely had the union's officials returned from Brighton than they were formulating demands on which to base a strike call at a special delegate conference in Doncaster on 12 September. They asked among other things that the NCB abandon its pit closure plan and withdraw the 15 August guidelines. The motion was passed unanimously and the ballot set for the last week in September. The NACODS issue was thus set off and running on a course to win this dispute once and for all.

That, at least, was what Arthur Scargill clearly thought. It was what the NACODS high command themselves had come to think. It was what the TUC and the Labour Party must have thought with a great sense of relief. It was also quite probably what Peter Walker thought and I am sure he must have lost no time in passing his concern on to the prime minister. I am certain he felt that I had made a grave error and, as a result, that the government was about to lose the strike. But that was not what I thought. Jimmy and I took some soundings in the very early days, as the trouble was brewing up, soundings which remained constant throughout the entire NACODS crisis, and they were telling us a very different story.

The grouping of the issues together on one strike ballot form was rather like asking a man if he wanted to win a million pounds. It was bound to produce an overwhelming 'yes' – especially since the vast majority of people who were being asked if they wanted to strike were not working anyway. It was not surprising therefore that 82.5 per cent of them voted in favour. But while this public setback worried me – and really worried the politicians – I felt confident we would prevail. My confidence flowed from a conviction that, if NACODS were to strike, it would hardly affect us at all over most of the country – since there was either no work being done at the pits or only a tiny handful of men back at work. The only place it could seriously have affected us was in Nottingham. However, according to our careful soundings, men who had fought so long and bitterly for the right to go back to work would not stand by and let their own NACODS people go against their convictions and reverse the hard decisions they had made. At the local pit level, I was assured, the NACODS men would be persuaded very quickly that the strike was neither their concern nor in their interests, and that they must throw in their lot with the working miners. Thus, I came to believe, we could keep Nottingham going and therefore live through this new strike threat.

It was a high-risk strategy, but one I was convinced could be successful. However, I did not take one thing into account. From the moment McNestry took charge of official NACODS policies, it began to emerge that he was in touch with Peter Walker on a regular basis. The theme of these conversations was, I gather from the 'coincidental' media speculation, that if only the government could find a way of getting rid of MacGregor, then the way to peace was a clear and open road. I was the villain of the piece who was threatening the whole future of the industry and holding up the prospects of a settlement. Alas, the message seemed to have fallen on receptive ears and I am sure that, as a minister, Walker felt duty bound to pass it on to Downing Street.

At about this time the media began to reflect some official attitudes, which were naturally 'confidential', along the McNestry line that the deputies were really moderates at heart and it was all the Coal Board chairman's fault that they had been forced into this unnaturally aggressive posture. It was also widely stated that, if they voted to go on strike, it would: (a) be my fault for handling the issue in such an insensitive manner and (b) would be catastrophic and lead to the collapse of the whole six-month strike. The emergence of official whispers from high places did a much better job for Scargill and McNestry than any rumours that could have been created by their own PR men.

The truth, however, was somewhat different. McNestry's election was not a sudden development. There had been a shift to the left in the union and that, coupled with the genuine sense of grievance they felt at being trapped between the NUM and the NCB, as well as the impossibility of voting 'no' to the carefully structured ballot proposition, would ensure that they came out. The ground had been well prepared for them.

When, very early on, I put my view to the secretary of state that the NACODS dispute, even if it led to a strike, should not worry us as long as we could keep Nottingham going, my view was met with a somewhat amazed response. I was asked in somewhat incredulous tones: 'You mean you're prepared to let them go on strike?' When I replied in the affirmative, he said: 'You must be out of your mind!' Any arguments I put forward about our need not to be seen to be weakening or deviating from our purpose were poorly received.

In very short order I was summoned to the prime minister, where it soon became clear that the bad news had already been delivered. I was not sure to what extent this could undermine my position and, at the same time, create differences between the prime minister's stance and mine. The differences, as it happened, were small and stemmed principally from our need to address separate 'audiences'. My principal concern was with the industry and I had no intention of settling on any terms that gave away the right to manage. As such, I did not see the threat of the NACODS strike as being totally crucial, nor did I believe it would in the long run weaken or damage our position. The prime minister's principal concern remained steadfastly the need to get the industry right and, especially after all these difficult months, she too had no intention of giving way on the principles. Nevertheless, she had to think of the public's view of things and whether it would accept another strike in the industry.

I was afraid that now there were others in government who did not realize the damage that could be done by widening this marginal gap between us with a mistaken campaign to 'sell' NACODS to the media as a group of downtrodden moderates, who would not have been in such a ferment were it not for my activities. However, this strategy would be attractive to some politicians – for it would achieve three objectives. First, it would undermine, or perhaps eliminate MacGregor, who was seen by many as a barrier to a solution. Second, it might put pressure on the prime minister to settle the strike and soften her intransigent stance. Third, it might put those achieving an end to the strike in the advantageous light of seeming to be the moderate peacemakers.

The atmosphere in the prime minister's study on this occasion was very different from our earlier meetings Clearly the enormous anxieties of her ministers had been passed on. She too indicated her great concern about the NACODS situation, especially from the point of view of the public who, she felt, would not accept that the NCB was blameless if NACODS struck. Therefore it should be averted if at all possible.

I started to tell her that I thought we were beginning to see our way towards a successful solution to the main dispute, and that I was confident the NACODS dispute was not critically important. The prime minister cut in sharply: 'Well, I'm very worried about it. You have to realize that the fate of this government is in your hands, Mr MacGregor. You have got to solve this problem.'

It would have been nice to have had a chance to talk over all the aspects of the case with her and take her through what we were doing and to reiterate that this was the sort of danger you faced in a long strike, but with the secretary of state and other staff there, it was simply not the forum for a reasoned debate. I felt the atmosphere between us had changed. The impression I got was that she thought I was showing a cavalier disregard for the perils she and her government faced. It was clear that she must have been under great pressure from the members of her cabinet, including, I presumed, my immediate boss. I began to realize I was no longer talking to a prime minister who was free to make all the decisions and was confident of success. Her attitude as a master politician was, naturally, more coloured and sensitized by public opinion than mine. She was very concerned about maintaining the government's support. But she was also beginning to see a picture painted for her of defeat if NACODS came out on strike and it must have been painted for her very vividly indeed.

The good soldier always accepts the commander's orders so I promised to do my best to settle with NACODS on reasonable terms. As it happened, after many many long sessions we were able to come up with a solution which I believe avoided us giving away the store – even if it added frustrating steps to the process of shutting a pit. But I am still firmly convinced that we could have succeeded just as well, if not better, by letting NACODS go on strike – especially if my own minister had not indicated a willingness to listen to McNestry.

I went back to my office and called Jimmy in. He asked how my meeting with the PM had gone and I said: 'I got a pretty rough ride. It appears as though the owners are getting nervous. We have to change tack and get down and resolve the NACODS problem to counter the growing fear there is in the government. Don't ever tell a soul why we did this – it is just you and I who are going to have to see this one out.' To his eternal credit he never did. We went on pretending that all was normal and started to try to set up some negotiations with NACODS.

For all that I may have incurred the prime minister's concern and wrath professionally, she showed shortly afterwards that on a personal level she bore no resentment. She heard somehow that my wife had gone off for the winter to our home in Florida and that I was living alone during this crucial phase of the strike. The phone rang one night and I was invited to Chequers for a 'family night', which I was told would be just her and Denis. Work was hardly mentioned – certainly no reference was made to our recent *contretemps*. Instead we had a delightful, relaxed evening during which Denis and me fell to talking about golf. After a while she intervened to say that people who played golf were crazy – if Denis was anything to go by – because it did terrible things to their backs. I said, to the contrary; it was very good for you and suggested she took it up – adding that I thought she would be very good at it. Well, we got into an almighty argument about the game, which ended with Denis and I pulling her leg unmercifully and all three of us laughing a great deal. It was a wonderful evening, for us both I suspect – away from all the problems – and it gave me a surprising glimpse of the well-concealed, decent, sensitive and amusing person that she is. As I drove home that night I couldn't help but think how sad it was that few people could have the chance to see the prime minister as I had seen her that Saturday evening.

However, there was no evidence that attitudes towards me at the Department had either softened or changed and McNestry was at no pains to conceal his frequent discussions with the minister, who, while he was convinced he was helping the situation, was, in my view, actually hindering it considerably. There was also a growing official desire to settle with NACODS, whatever the cost – even if it meant compromising all our principles. I became quite philosophical about this. A number of politicians and bureaucrats, whose anxieties showed clearly, were now, I hope unintentionally, beginning to harass me. I am sure these were people not used to being involved in issues where there were very strong convictions and so it was understandable that they should be wavering. I was reminded of the famous Harry Truman saying: 'If you can't stand the heat, get out of the kitchen.' In my case, I had gone into the kitchen with my eyes open. Meanwhile I had my job to do, which was to make sure we recovered the right to manage the coal industry. All these official waverings made it more difficult now, but then I had never anticipated my task being easy.

For me September and October were the months of maximum pressure in the strike. All the balls were in the air – the back-to-work movement, the negotiations with the NUM and NACODS, the publicity campaigns, the political pressures, the TUC – and Jimmy and I were running around trying to keep them there. The Robert Maxwell initiative did yield two results – one more set of abortive negotiations with the NUM and, as we have seen, my first contacts with the panjandrums of the TUC, which were later to prove quite useful.

Norman Willis took over from Len Murray as general secretary of the TUC at the Brighton conference. It was a job for which he had obviously been carefully groomed, in that he seemed to be well schooled in the ways of avoiding controversy and was careful not to step on the territories of the individual union barons. I don't know whether he was behind the NACODS move, but it bore all the hallmarks of a TUC gambit. They were quite happy to use NACODS to win on a technicality. They didn't want to be seen to help Scargill win, but if NACODS could do it for them, they would be happy. In the byzantine world of TUC politics you do not necessarily win by persuading people to your cause, you win because you play the rules better. This was their playing of the rules and I had to expect something like it from them.

I already had a number of contacts within the union movement, stretching back to my days at British Leyland. It was there that I had come to know and respect John Boyd of the engineers and, when I was at BSC, I had asked the secretary of state to put him on our board. He has been one of my most important confidants on union matters and has always been a sound adviser. Throughout the strike we met at board meetings and other sessions and I always took advantage of these opportunities to have a chat with him about the latest state of play and what he thought about things. Through him I also had come to know and respect the AUEW president, the late Terry Duffy, for whom I had as much regard. In fact there were a number of trade union leaders with whom I could communicate and talk frankly – including Gavin Laird, Gerry Eastwood, Alan Tuffin of the Communications Workers, and of course Frank Chapple of the electricians.

Thus I was not surprised to find David Basnett and Ray Buckton, with whom I came to have a number of dealings, quite approachable and open on the subject of the NUM strike. Basnett takes life very seriously and was really worried about finding a solution to the Scargill problem; Buckton, on the other hand, has a certain amount of charm but must be a bit of a pirate, if I understand some of his dealings with British Rail. Nevertheless I found him as interesting character.

The Labour Party also began to try to get in on the act at about this time. I had met Mr Kinnock for an introductory chat before the strike began, but it was not until the summer that Stanley Orme, the shadow energy spokesman, came to see me to plead Scargill's case. However, I didn't feel it was with any great conviction. I had known him since my days at Steel and found him pleasant, if a little low key. You end up marvelling at how someone with his quiet personality is such an important man in such a robust part of the political arena. As industry minister he would have to approach the task of revitalizing the business life of Britain with great fire and drive. I think, at heart, he understood that we were not going to surrender the right to manage the coal enterprise and, on the other hand, that Scargill was not going to settle for anything less than total victory. Nevertheless he kept on trying and came up with a flurry of activity in late August and early September with the 'Orme initiatives', which, alas, did nothing to tackle the fundamental question. He persisted gamely throughout the autumn, but I could sense that, in the face of Scargill's intransigence, his heart was progressively less and less in it.

All these opportunities were, however, useful to us, for they must have slowly built up in the minds of what you might loosely call the 'opposition' – the Labour Party and the TUC – the idea that, for all the public adulation of Scargill at their annual gatherings and the wild rhetoric with which the extreme left supported him, there was another side to the story. They came to realize that there were fundamental issues at stake; that we were willing to trade, but could not budge on our right to manage the industry. In making them all welcome to join in the search for a solution and watching them trip one by one on the stumbling block of Arthur's obduracy, we hoped that the message was being planted firmly in their collective subconscious that the real problem was not so much with us, but with Arthur. It was good to plant the seeds of that idea in their minds now, for the day was not far off when we would need them to recognize the fact fairly publicly.

The set of negotiations with the NUM which arose out of Robert Maxwell's intervention took place on five successive days from Sunday, 9 September, to Friday, the 14th. We started in Edinburgh and worked our way slowly south – chased and harassed by the media all the way – until finally we arrived at the old Steel building next to Hobart House in London. The sessions were supposed to be secret, but wherever we went the media turned up. In the end just about the only thing Scargill and I agreed on was a joint, but ineffectual, plea to the press to go away. On the first day I had had to use my fairly extensive knowledge of the back roads of Argyll to escape the attentions of a group of reporters who had camped all weekend outside my Scottish home – only to arrive in Edinburgh and find more there.

It was on this occasion that I made a joke with them which probably fell flatter than almost any antic I have pulled in my life. I got out of the car and, taking a Harrods bag which had some of my wife's knitting in it, held it up in front of my face and said: 'Gentlemen, don't you know this meeting is so secret it is not actually taking place? Can't you see I'm not here?' Not only could they not see, but they were not interested in seeing the joke either. I suppose it is my fault for trying to be funny with a bunch of people who either took themselves far too seriously or saw a chance to exercise their personal political preferences. It may have been a pretty feeble attempt at humour, but you would have thought that they would either have seen the joke by now or forgotten it. However, it is obvious that these were people who would never have seen any of my actions as light-hearted. I fear I am doomed, long after the strike is forgotten, to be remembered as the man who held a plastic bag in front of his face on the way to a secret negotiation!

Once again in the negotiations we came quite close to a settlement: this time it was during another late session, at the British Ropes Works in Doncaster, on the Wednesday night. But the stumbling block was the same. We offered a total package deal. We would stay the execution of the five pits and put them back in the Colliery Review Procedure. We would phase the cut of 4 million tonnes of capacity over a longer period – in view of the length of time the strike had been going on. But in exchange for these two items, we had to have some form of words – any form of words – which meant that there was, as there always had been, a third category of closure which was neither safety nor complete exhaustion of the coal reserves. I told them: 'Gentlemen, it comes as a total package. You don't get the first two things unless we get the third. If we can agree it – then I will give you some things you can use to go off and claim a great victory, provided we can still genuinely say that we have retained, at the end of the day, the right to manage the business.'

They kept hanging their hat on The Plan For Coal, saying that the industry should have expanded to 135 million tonnes a year, which had been Tony Benn's fairytale forecast for the year 1985. We continued to point out that the demand for coal was nothing like that today, that the government and the NCB had delivered in terms of investing in new capacity, but the unions had not delivered in terms of shutting old, or improving productivity. We had to be able to shut uneconomic pits. The argument went round and round in circles again.

In the early hours of Wednesday morning, I thought there was a chink of light through which we might see our way to settling. We got them as far as accepting that there had been third-category closures in the past and that 'in accordance with the principles of the Plan it is acknowledged that this procedure will continue to apply'. But we came unstuck on the exact wording of the definition of such a closure. They would not agree to the word 'acceptable' in the sentence which stated that closures would take place where engineers from both sides established that there were no further reserves 'which can be developed to provide an acceptable basis to the Board for continuing operation'.

We spent hours trying out different phraseologies, talking endlessly trying to find common ground. In the past I had found these all-night sessions a useful technique in labour negotiations, because some people get tired and reach a stage where they want to make a settlement just to get home to bed. Going on all night engenders a spirit of wanting to find common ground – especially if you keep people working with their minds. It tires them mentally and they become more ready to try to settle, but you must remain alert and indicate a willingness to sit around the table for as long as it takes to reach a settlement. You have to be careful, of course, that your own negotiating people don't get mentally tired and start trying to give everything away – just because they are also weary! This was essentially what happened at the British Ropes office in Doncaster where, by 1.30 a.m., I felt my own crew was beginning to waver.

We left the session then and came back to London, arriving at dawn. We met with them again the following morning to carry on but the atmosphere of cooperation and the apparent willingness to settle had evaporated. I suspect Scargill might have heard some news during the night which made him scent victory. The NACODS delegate conference, with its decision to hold a strike ballot, had ended after our meeting started on Wednesday. It could have been that news which caused him to stiffen his resistance; but whatever it was he was in no mood to settle on Friday. By then he had read into 'the principles of the Plan' exactly what we had meant it to mean – that the industry had to be economic – and he wanted to drop that too. So, once again, we broke up with no further plans to meet.

I think that, for the time being at least, the decision to adjourn was better for both of us, since we both now, for different reasons, had our eyes on the NACODS dispute, which was escalating nicely from the union's point of view. I also had one further problem at this time, which a temporary respite from the negotiating table gave me a chance to begin to consider. For a while I had been worried about relations with Ned Smith. He had a serious back problem and was in pain much of the time and consequently was, I thought, unable to concentrate on his job to the full. Out of loyalty to the NCB, he had insisted that he carry on, but by the autumn it was clear something had to be done – especially since, as the strain on him mounted, he was becoming increasingly critical of our conduct of the dispute. We had several major disagreements – notably over a television 'confrontation' with Arthur Scargill on Channel 4.

In fairness to him, he was very professional at his job, but our differences in approach and ideology were fundamental. I saw the need to hold the line to re-establish the right to manage as paramount; he thought the need to compromise was paramount. He was old-style Hobart House. I was the new alien breed. The list of things he disapproved of in our conduct of the dispute grew by the day, and he made no secret of his views. He didn't like some of our back-to-work tactics. He didn't like our advertising, and, like Geoffrey Kirk, was quite obvious opposed to the use of Tim Bell to help with it. He wasn't keen on my slate of non-executive directors, nor what he called 'government involvement' in the strike.

It was on this last point that matters came to a head. He was severely critical of me after the breakdown of the September NUM talks in Doncaster and London. After so much work on his part, so much effort put in to try to reach an agreement when he was often in so much pain too, he could not see why we would not make more concessions and presumed it must be because the government was 'pulling the strings'. I think that he could not believe that I didn't get secret orders every night in a sealed envelope from no less a person than the prime minister herself. The evidence was to the contrary, but he could not accept it. Another of the effects of his genuine, but over-enthusiastic, desire to see peace was that he tended to give the other side the impression that we were ready to search for compromises, which would avoid the difficult issues. The union took this to mean that we were about to collapse and fall at their feet. Not only was this rather far from the truth, but it could have damaged the very good results we were beginning to get from the back-to-work movement.

In the end, in early October, I ordered him to take some time off and rest. He was mentally and physically under a great deal of stress. He had already written to Jimmy saying that he wanted to pull out from the end of the year and retire to his home in Kent. We therefore made all the arrangements for him and it was planned he should go at Christmas. In the meantime, in order to avoid as much stress as possible – to help him and to help me – it was made clear he was 'on call' should we need his invaluable experience in any of the talks. As it happened his services were of great value at the eleventh hour of the NACODS dispute, when things began to look very dicey. It did not seem as though we could avoid the deputies going on strike, despite the prime minister's concern about such an eventuality.

From the start the NACODS issue was a muddle and, for the ten weeks it lasted, it was never easy to handle. As we have seen, it was hindered by increasing government worry and their inability to conceal it. Later things were further complicated by the intervention of the TUC and ACAS. Pat Lowry, an old colleague from British Leyland days, had us all running hither and thither for a week in October while he tried to make some sense of it all. Eventually the TUC even brought the NUM into the talks in the vain hope that Lowry could solve the whole issue in one go with some magic compromise formula. But many others had tried and failed with Arthur Scargill. He was not able to make much progress and became quite disillusioned.

We had spent a good deal of September trying to get NACODS to the table to talk, but naturally they dragged their feet as much as possible until they had a pretty good idea of how their ballot was going. We finally got together on 26 September, just before the announcement of the result; but already the indications were that they were going to get a pretty massive 'yes' answer. The meeting was difficult and acrimonious. I went through much of the same procedure that we had been through with the NUM, outlining where there were areas for negotiation and where we had to take very firm positions. We did of course quickly indicate that we wanted to work out an agreement with them on the 1974 guidelines and were prepared to listen and to negotiate with them on all the other issues they wanted to raise. However, it began to emerge that the strongest demand, on which they were launching their attack, was the difficult business of the Colliery Review Procedure and their unhappiness with it.

The CRP is a process which was introduced in the 1960s at a time of substantial closures to give unions the opportunity to challenge the management's decisions. It became agreed practice to go through it before any pit could be closed. The procedure has several steps. First, at pit level, a review of unsatisfactory performance. After a full debate over what steps might be taken, or equipment used, to improve performance, the manager could recommend closure if he could see no economic solution and if the unions agreed that ended the matter. If there was no agreement, the manager's recommendation was followed by an area review with the unions. If no agreement was reached then, the area director made a recommendation to the NCB top management. Before they endorsed his closure decision, a full review was held with both unions and the area presenting their case. Finally the full Board then looked at these presentations and on the advice of the management either rejected or endorsed the closure. As we have seen the problem with the NUM was that they were not prepared to accept any such closures on economic grounds.

NACODS approached the pit closure issue from a somewhat different direction. They complained that the CRP itself was inadequate. In particular, they expressed the view that the NCB had been high-handed, had taken to rushing through the CRP. In many instances, they claimed, the NCB had failed to give the unions notice or time to rebut the management's arguments. Finally they complained that the NCB was treating their objectives in the last stage of the procedure as though they were a mere formality and giving them the most cursory attention.

At our next meeting, with the ballot result in their pockets and a mandate to call a strike whenever they wanted, the NACODS negotiating team became even more critical of the CRP and insisted that it must now be modified to the extent that the final recommendation must be referred to some jury completely independent of the biased judgements of the top management and the Board.

Patiently we pointed out that they were proposing that decisions on the fundamental operation of the business were now to be subject to nothing short of independent arbitration. They wanted a system which could require the board to accept the verdict as a binding decision. This, however, would completely vitiate the instructions clearly laid down in the Coal Industry Nationalization Act of 1946. This act gave the NCB clear responsibility not only to operate the industry effectively but also to make a profit.

Despite our telling them this, NACODS continued to press for an independent review. Finally we suggested we could contemplate such a body if it functioned like the public inquiry in a planning issue. There would be an inspector to ensure that all parties had the opportunity to state their case and to determine whether there were errors in the facts that lead to the decisions that had been recommended. However, we pointed out that all we could do was to give 'full weight' to any such independent review and that, unless there was evidence of error or miscalculation in the assessment of the viability of a pit, the NCB would have to have the final say. We explained that evidence or arguments on the social cost or impact of closure or costs were not within our remit.

There, with a few other variations, we stuck, while ACAS and all the rest did their best to resolve the situation and the strike deadline of 25 October drew nearer and nearer. When we brought Ned Smith back on the 23rd, however, things began to look brighter.

The proposal we made that day restored the conditions for NACODS members pre-15 August. We discussed the fact that NACODS did not have a legally constituted closed shop but that the board would continue to recognize their present *de facto* situation. We agreed to withdraw the five pit closures and that they would now be considered all over again with all others in the new Colliery Review Procedure. We also said we would carefully reconsider the 6 March proposals to take out our 4 million tonnes of capacity, in the light of the loss of output during the dispute. Finally we hammered out an agreement to insert an independent review body into the CRP. The agreement did not mention economic closures – but it talked of 'plans reflecting both market and production opportunities', and it promised 'full weight' would be given to the new body's findings.

During the later stages of this negotiation, I began to see some of the usual signs exhibited by union negotiators who are ready to settle. Although McNestry continued to press for things he must have known we were not prepared to give, the attitude of the others on the committee meanwhile began to seem much more conciliatory.

However, an annoying but nevertheless useful delay then occurred while Norman Willis tried to intervene and to persuade NACODS to wait while he got Arthur Scargill to the table to take a hand in shaping the final agreement. Pat Lowry was furious – and rightly so, too. But he need not have worried, for I knew what Scargill's reaction would be. It didn't matter what was on the piece of paper. He told the NACODS negotiators they were fools. In his view they should not have accepted 'reconsideration' of the 6 March proposals – they should have demanded outright withdrawal and, similarly, they should have demanded the total and permanent reprieve of all the five pits. I was glad he was so uncompromising: it was yet another sign, for all to see, that he had no intention of settling. It also indicated to me that perhaps he now knew he was losing.

I do not know to this day whether the NACODS men felt they had got something in the agreement which subsequently turned out not to be there – after all, we had made it absolutely clear that we intended to retain the right to manage the business at all times. Nevertheless considerable acrimony subsequently developed over the working of the independent review body. I believe that some of them thought they had won a form of independent arbitration of our actions on pit closures, only clothed in other words. However, this was not the case. We were not, nor could we be, bound by the findings of the body. We had promised to listen to any new evidence of identifiable errors of fact in our decision-making process that the body might consider important and to give that due weight. NACODS were, I am sure, not the only ones who, at the time, thought I had given away the crown jewels and their subsequent disappointment must have arisen when they realized they had misinterpreted the situation.

In the end we had to go to the High Court to prove that our interpretation of the words of the agreement was correct and that we had not given away our right to run the business. Eighteen months after the agreement with NACODS was signed we finally got a verdict in the High Court.

The case concerned the bitterly argued review of the proposed closure of the Bates Colliery in Northumberland. In this the independent lawyer had concluded that, while he was willing to concede that the colliery would never make a profit, he nevertheless recommended the NCB keep it open for a variety of reasons, none of which was connected with our responsibilities to produce coal economically.

As was our duty I held a special meeting of the full Board to review his findings. We had a long session and the directors unanimously decided that they had to reject the findings of the independent lawyer because they were based on the idea that the NCB should take into account all sorts of other factors besides the economic issues. The Board was sadly unable to accept this expansion of its responsibilities.

Our decision resulted in a furious response from McNestry, who at once called a delegate conference to seek authority for strike action and rushed to the High Court to get an injunction to stop us from closing the pit. But their case did not stand up and the court ruled against them. McNestry went back to the High Court to argue that we had to obey the findings of the independent review body. However, the court ruled that the actions taken by the NCB were entirely within our remit. The NCB has retained the power to decide which pits are to be operated and which are to be closed, even if it has an independent review of the steps taken in reaching those decisions.

It is ironical that since the High Court judgement not one of the people who, at the time of our negotiations, complained that we had sold out to NACODS has apologized for his mistake. We knew then that we were right and it was a difficult time for us. At the end of October, Jimmy and I felt very much alone in what we were doing and we were more determined than ever to drive on with our back-to-work movement.

We had seen a great degree of concern in various members of the government and even the anxiety of the prime minister. I went into the winter feeling that the government's support behind me was no longer totally unqualified. I felt I was sure I was still on the same strategic wavelength as the prime minister, though my tactical approach might be different. However, I could feel the tremors of growing unease in official circles. It was giving me increasing problems in my attempts to lead the team with a strong and commanding image.

As time goes on and events such as Westland, General Motors, Sunday trading and so on occur, I cannot help reflecting that we were witnessing then the first signs of the emergence of challenge in the cabinet of the dominant role of the prime minister. It would not be long before this situation would go a stage further and politicians would be publicly scrapping with each other – even at the expense of allowing other parties to take advantage of their brawling.

For the moment, though, I had one consolation: now Scargill had nowhere else to go.

13

The Battle for the Media

The meeting which was held at my flat in Eaton Square on the evening of 18 October will be perhaps the most difficult for outsiders not privy to the day-to-day details of the dispute to understand. Here we were, a close circle of people all involved in managing the dispute, deciding, after it had lasted eight months, what to do about our conspicuous lack of success against Arthur Scargill in one of the most vital areas of it – our public relations. The truth was that, while each one of us, drinking our coffee or sipping our Scotches late into the night, was confident that we were now beginning to gain the upper hand in the struggle and that we would in the end be successful, however long it took, we were were all aware that our PR was a disaster.

Part of the reason for this was my fault. I do not suffer fools gladly and I had met quite a number of them during the previous year's high pressure media attention. At the best of times I react badly to aggressive questioning in front of TV cameras, particularly when it comes from people who are seeking confrontation rather than infor-mation and who clearly have a limited understanding of the issues they are talking about. During the dispute, I found this all too often to be the rule. However, now and again there was some relief. I was interviewed by David Frost, and I enjoyed my chats with him because he was courteous and seemed to be both intelligent and interested in trying to find out what it was we were up to and how we thought. For the most part, however, I found myself forced into an adversarial position in TV sessions so that it became very difficult to contribute anything constructive in an interview. I am sure that as a result the public were left with very little understanding of our side of the issue.

Scargill, on the other hand, had been the darling of the media since long before the strike began. Most reporters, whether they be in newspapers, radio or television, rate themselves and their performance not by how well they communicate the content of the interview, but by the amount of space their material gets in the paper, whether it is on the front page or in a prominent position elsewhere, or, in the case of broadcasting, by the amount of time it gets on the air and whether it is the 'lead' item on the news bulletin. So, it seems to be a fact of media life that the man who has a plausible quote, or a fresh line to peddle every day, or a new shock to rock the audience, is the man who is going to get most coverage in the media and therefore is going to be the recipient of the reporters' grateful thanks for helping them achieve such prominent success. Hence much of Scargill's popularity and apparent dominance of the public relations battle throughout the early months of the dispute came from his willingness to help reporters to make news and provide entertainment.

The reason for that meeting, at which Jimmy and I, Tim Bell, David Hart, and later Ned Smith and his deputy, Kevin Hunt, were present, was partly to discuss how to arrest the tide of bad publicity we had been receiving, partly to work out how best to assist the back-to-work movement in the face of Scargill's continuing barrage of propaganda, and partly to work out how to profit from the distinct feeling we were getting that Scargill's media stardom was beginning to wane.

We had also been under great pressure from Peter Walker, who always carefully handled his own PR, to do something about ours. In fact I noticed that he was always aware in his political activities of the public relations point of view. I suppose this is appropriate for a twentieth-century politician. For months now he had been expressing unhappiness at the Coal Board's bad PR. Every time a mistake was made, or we put up a poor performance against Scargill, there would be recriminations – not so much that Scargill had trounced us, but that his Department might be implicated in that trouncing by its connection with us, and that therefore his own carefully groomed public relations image might be diminished by our inadequacies. My attitude towards PR was much less sensitive. I realized the great value of the public knowing what we were up to – indeed we had a duty to inform them. After all, it was their money we were spending. But I did not believe public relations should play such a dominant role.

Nevertheless, all our discussions that night very quickly boiled down to the urgent need to find a presentable, personable and knowledgeable 'spokesman' to put our side of the case against Scargill's constant barrage. Geoff Kirk had, as I had feared, proved unable to supply an operation of the scope that was now required, and he was increasingly hesitant, if not unconstructive, in supporting my efforts. What was needed, it was felt, was for us to find someone who could undertake the task on a day-to-day basis of countering Scargill on radio and particularly on TV; someone who would take the pressure off me by being readily available to give frequent interviews, since I had never enjoyed the role of being a very visible public figure.

Scargill's principal ammunition against the back-to-work movement was simple, effective, and constantly repeated. His message was: We are in negotiations with the Coal Board. They are about to collapse. The government is nervous – we know Peter Walker is talking on the telephone to McNestry every minute of the day begging him to come and make a deal. MacGregor is in trouble. Nobody trusts him any more. The skids are under him – it's a matter of days not weeks before he goes. So in a few days (or weeks) we'll have won. We'll all be back at work and you will be the one who looks silly if none of your mates will speak to you because you returned to work and were a scab. It was a very persuasive argument and it went right to the core of the loyalty to the union that existed in many of the men.

We had to find a man who could counter that message day by day, always refuting the arguments, always putting the facts over, always reciting the progress that had been made and, above all, putting the pressure on and keeping it on. We had started off a few weeks earlier by looking outside the NCB at a couple of professional people – but the problem was that by the time they had studied and learned the complexities of the industry and its disputes over the years, the strike would be over. So that night we got down to finding someone from within our own ranks. It was fascinating to me as an outsider in the communications business to hear Tim Bell's professional view of certain of my colleagues as 'media performers'.

Jimmy, we all agreed – including Jimmy – looked a dour old curmudgeon. So did I! One area director always shut his eyes on television and therefore, despite being as honest as the day is long, looked shifty. Another paused to qualify his points too much and came over as though he wasn't sure which side he was on. From the NCB's point of view Jimmy and I also had reservations about some names that were suggested. One or two of the area directors who might have done a good job were too heavily involved in their own back-to-work movements to be spared. Jack Woods, from Nottingham, would have been very good – but we felt that he would have been in danger of being lured away from the main topic of the coal strike into controversial discussions about his own area. Finally a name came up against which there were no fundamental objections; indeed there was a lot to be said in favour of it. It was North Yorkshire area director, Michael Eaton.

It is to Geoff Kirk's credit that he welcomed Eaton's appointment warmly. But it was a sad irony that our decision that night should have led directly to his ultimate departure from the NCB after so many years of service in the PR department. Sadder still that he should have met his death in a boating accident so shortly afterwards, just as he was beginning to enjoy the retirement he had looked forward to for so long. I do not relish the task of asking people to leave an enterprise, particularly if I have worked closely with them. It is never pleasant or easy and I am aware now that I should, perhaps, have done it earlier to spare both of us difficulties and embarrassments we could ill afford the time for in the heat of battle.

However, rather than diminishing, Geoff's antagonism to Tim Bell's close relationship with me, and his alleged influence on me grew as the months passed. I learned only later that after Tim's first presentation of a media strategy to us in the early days of the dispute, he had made a point of saying to Geoff: 'I hope you don't feel put upon by us appearing out of the blue like this. We are not here to take your place, but to help. I hope we can get along and work together.' To which Geoff had replied: 'I do resent you being here and I am not going to speak to you or cooperate with you in any way, shape or form.' He never changed his attitude but, for the sake of peace, I tried for many months to find ways of working around the problem. At one stage Tim was having advertisements drawn up and I would then take them to Geoff Kirk, telling him that they were ideas of mine, and ask him to get the Board's agency to put them out. He must have marvelled at how I became such a brilliant copywriter overnight!

Throughout the summer Tim reported directly to me, but as the role of public relations became more central to the conduct of the dispute in the autumn, so he was unwillingly brought more and more into conflict with Geoff Kirk. I am sure Geoff was a staunch Labour supporter and therefore found it especially difficult to accept that Tim was paid by us as an advisor, and was limited in his activities to just that. I am sure he was convinced, quite wrongly, that the Tories, and particularly Downing Street, were now running the show.

Tim's expertise was concentrated on advertising, addressed both to the miners and to the public at large. It was necessary to run a fairly sustained campaign to put the record straight about Scargill's outrageous claims, and to point out that the industry had a future if only we could get it down to size and get our costs right. I think in the end the campaigns worked and one of the factors in the swing against Scargill during the winter was that the public came to realize he had not been telling the truth about many things. By now they had seen many other industries undergo painful but necessary change. There was a feeling among them in the end that Scargill wanted everyone to dance to his tune and to pay for the band as well! A growing number of ordinary people decided that it was simply not acceptable, and the credit for this shift in attitude is due in no small way to Tim. In the first series of advertisements we ran, which was in July, each one had the headline: 'How The Miners On

Strike Have Been Misled'. These caused a tremendous row, with Arthur Scargill complaining that they had cost the taxpayer £500,000 and that he could not afford the right of reply. I am sure the public at large would have welcomed him taking half a million pounds out of the funds used for financing the thugs and bullies on the picket lines, and using it to explain his case with words rather than iron bars and half bricks.

Tim also had good access to the media and was able, through the summer, to explain our case in a series of regular briefings of interested editors. I took part in some of these. Once again I found that, away from the artificiality of set-piece interviews and their tendency to be conducted in an atmosphere of confrontation, most editors relished a chance to learn how we saw things and what we considered our problems to be. From my point of view I found it valuable to learn their perception of us and what we were up to – and, most importantly, how they felt the public were reacting to us and to our case. This role, played particularly by Tim, helped us more as the strike went on. It was from his contacts that I also learned about a campaign to persuade the media that the NACODS dispute was all my fault and that my dismissal was on the cards. There is nothing like the wish being father to the thought.

Both Tim and Tommy Thompson, from Opinion Research & Communication, did regular field surveys of opinion for us. Tommy did attitude surveys in the mining areas and came up with a lot of useful material at the beginning of the strike, which helped confirm much of what we had been thinking about those who wanted to work and those who would die rather than be disloyal to their union. The depressing thing about these surveys was how slowly attitudes changed through the long months of the dispute. However, by the end of the first six months we were beginning to see signs of confidence waning among the miners on strike. Fewer of them believed they would now win and fewer of them had absolute confidence in Scargill.

By Christmas, despite all our efforts, the one factor above all others that kept coming up in the surveys as the reason for the strike was still the fear of closing pits. But there was good news in other aspects of the polling we did at that time; there was a large increase in the number of men who now thought they would have to go back to work with no victory. Tim drew up a strategy for the vital months of the early New Year, based on what turned out to be a correct assumption that the return to work could turn into a flood. We concentrated even more on the message that the industry had a very bright future in which all our people should participate. The conclusion to his report has stood the test of time: 'We must make miners who might go back to work believe that our offer is final. We must make them see that our industry can and will carry on, that the opportunities are enormous and that it is unrealistic to believe that all this must be held back because a group of people, who are not faced with redundancy, will not consider a move to other areas.'

He also played a part in the presentation of our case on television. When I gave interviews he would be on hand to brief me and help me prepare for the occasion. On one occasion his friend Gordon Reece, who is best known for his work with the prime minister in her election campaigns, had come in to see me in connection with the American oil magnate, Armand Hammer, for whom he had gone to work when he left Downing Street. As we had limited time together I invited him to come with me in the car that was taking me to a TV studio and to stay, if he wished, to see my performance that night. I thought that, at least, it might be valuable to get his professional comments. Yet within days the story was out that the PM's 'image maker' had been hired by the NCB to do a whole rework on me. The entire extent of his advice to me that night, as I recall it, was to say, as he was known to say to Mrs Thatcher, that I perhaps needed some powder on my nose!

I suppose it was a measure of the collective anxiety of the media – that the strike was not going according to plan, that they were getting bored with their 'hero' and needed a new one, that the whole thing had not yet been settled with a dignified sell-out at No. 10 – that they reacted so excitedly and unpredictably to the most trivial of items. The Gordon Reece incident was one of many at this time, but none of them caused as much fuss and brouhaha as the appointment, and subsequent short career, of Michael Eaton as the NCB spokesman. The publicity around this period not only contributed to Geoff Kirk's departure, but caused more lost tempers and frayed nerves than almost any other aspect of the dispute.

To begin with, the media, I suspect with ample encouragement from those who were hoping to undermine my position, heralded his appointment as only slightly less significant than the Second Coming. Within days the Michael Eaton bandwaggon was rolling. He was not only going to speak for the NCB, he was going to take charge of the negotiations. He and Peter Walker were going to solve the strike together. It was heady stuff for Michael Eaton – and I am sure he played no part in all this speculation at the outset – but of course none of it was true. My belief is that it came about through the coincidence of two factors. First, the media needed a hero. Scargill and MacGregor had been punching it out for eight months now with no result and they wanted someone who looked like a winner. Second: those within the system, who found my presence irksome, saw this as a glorious opportunity for mischief and malice and built the poor man up until he was about to be appointed chairman.

He was a fine person and just right for the role. He had an easy manner on television – a sort of rounded, pipe-smoking charm. He had spent all his working life in the industry and knew both it and Arthur Scargill inside out. He had been rapidly promoted in the NCB and became our youngest area director, but he was pretty relaxed and somewhat easy going and was not destined, in any of the organization plans, for any future major promotion. However, all the sudden rush of publicity created a number of problems, of which I am sure his avid promoters knew nothing and cared less.

Not the least among these difficulties was the state of near mutiny in the ranks of our other area directors – some of whom had worked themselves to the bone for months trying to get men back to work. They saw a man, whom some of them blamed for the NACODS dispute and who had not achieved much in their view to get the men in his own area back to work, now getting all the glory and being talked of as the next chairman. They were pretty upset and bombarded Jimmy with phone calls. What particularly concerned them was the thought that Eaton, whom they did not rate as tough in business terms, might now be put in charge of negotiations. For all that Jimmy tried to assure them that this was not the case, they were reluctant to believe him. Of course the media went wild when they discovered he would not be included in the negotiating team. But we took the decision to exclude him to emphasize to everyone, on *all* sides, that the batting order at the NCB had not changed.

The situation was further complicated by the assiduous wooing of Eaton that went on at the highest levels. It was as though people wanted to believe the myth they had seen created in front of their eyes. In the end, I suspect he too started to believe in some of his own publicity. He was known to have contacts with Michael Allison, the prime minister's PPS, who was his local MP and an old acquaintance. This may have led the media to surmise that he had a direct route to the lady herself. He was wined and dined by politicians and ministers, until it was hardly surprising that the poor man came to believe that he could, and was indeed probably going to have to solve the strike single-handedly.

I fear many of these stories must have originated from within the government. It was reported that, in early November, he and David Hunt, who was junior minister for coal at the Department of Energy, were discussing the strategy for the coming months and that 'Eaton gave it as his firm opinion on the strength of more than a decade across-the-table experience, that Scargill . . . would never compromise,' and that it was from these meetings that the two of them had decided on the policy of no more talks and back to work, which was subsequently to end the strike. When some of the other area directors heard this – after all their efforts and ingenuity in wooing men back to work and all their pleading with us to follow just such a route and to try to have Eaton make more of an effort in North Yorkshire – some of them were nearly apoplectic with rage.

While they and the area directors were angry, the press and politicians were nearly hysterical with delight. At last they had a hero, after waiting so long, but you could tell, by the events of the last few days in October, how distorted was their view of the situation. Eaton's appointment was announced on the 20th and he arrived in London that weekend to start work. By the following weekend the press and TV interest in him was enormous. Then, on the

Sunday morning, the *Sunday Times* broke the story of Arthur Scargill's attempts to get money for the strike from the Gadhafi regime in Libya. Assessing the situation on Monday morning, it seemed foolish to us that Michael should be giving a whole string of personality interviews at this time, when we should have been leaving the field clear for the media to exploit the Libyan story to its fullest. Accordingly, I told Geoff Kirk to cancel the interviews that had been set up. This he did, with such zeal and lack of tact that the story of our 'gagging' Eaton replaced Libya at the top of most of the media's coverage.

For a while Eaton did a good job as our spokesman. He was indeed the right image of a man to dispel the Scargill myths and by Christmas we had pulled back a lot of ground in terms of public opinion. But he was progressively less happy with the role he was being asked to play, at the same time as being the object of much public, and private, speculation about the roles he should perhaps have been playing. In the end, I believe the pressure of the hectic media and social whirl that went with it became too much for him and, exacerbated by a bout of flu, he collapsed at a senior management meeting. He was sent off to rest and, shortly afterwards, Jimmy came to me and said that he had had a talk with Eaton who was now in a mood to leave altogether. I did not try to prevent his departure.

The Libyan adventure surprised me in two ways. First, that Scargill would even consider contacting Gadhafi, through the union's chief executive, in his desperate search for funds, but also that the British public were so excited by the news – considering all Scargill's other well-known contacts with, and love for, revolutionary parties and groups the world over, his regular trips to the Soviet Union and his union's contacts with the Sinn Fein in Ireland. I suppose it was because people were still very aware of the brutality and terrorist nature of the Libyan regime – it was only a few months after the murder of WPC Yvonne Fletcher outside the Libyan People's Bureau in central London.

What didn't surprise me was the way Scargill twisted and turned to avoid the truth. Nor was the horrified reaction of many of his more moderate members unexpected. The story did a great deal to confirm to them what we had been saying all along. Right through the winter many of the men returning to work told us the Libyan affair was one of the things that contributed to their disenchantment with the NUM leadership.

It also prompted the final exodus of Geoff Kirk. The differences between us had been growing for some time. His lack of enthusiasm for nearly everything we were doing had developed until it was nearly impossible for me to work with him. I finally came to the conclusion that it was time to call it a day. On his side, I think he could not bear to find his previously happy and relaxed activities with his friends in the media now subject to close direction from people whose beliefs were alien to his own. On the day it seemed no particular effort was made to explain the reasons for curtailing Eaton's interviews. Geoff Kirk just walked in to the assembled media men and pulled the plug, so to speak, and, when asked why, he said: 'Orders from the chairman's office.' I decided that we couldn't possibly afford a situation any longer where, in the middle of a major labour confrontation, we had a PR department which was sulking. So he had to go. In the end he wasn't dismissed; the sad episode ended with Jimmy working out the best possible terms for his early retirement.

The whole Libyan incident, with all its aspects relating to Eaton and Kirk, revealed a lot to me about the media, its attitudes and needs. It also revealed a great deal about

Scargill and his attitudes to the media. He nursed the media, like a true professional performer, while all the time professing to hate it. It was his stage; but he could not bear the fact that he didn't own it, nor was the audience captive. Our media are not like *Pravda*, or any of the other Iron Curtain organs where all that the tame audience gets by way of information is what the central committee decides it will have.

Distorting the facts is a fundamental and acceptable tool of the revolution. For example, Scargill stated frequently and flatly that all violence in the strike was caused by the police. While it may not have gained much credence as such, it planted a seed in the minds of the naive and the gullible in the media and elsewhere. Very soon you found that the police were having to defend their actions in stopping groups of miners on their way to create mayhem and violence, having to defend the use of horses to control rampaging mobs of brutes bent on stopping men going to work or lorries passing through gates and, worst of all, having to defend their policing of the villages and their protection of the families of men returning to work.

This last attack on the police was made by, of all people, the National Council for Civil Liberties, whose so-called 'independent' inquiry into the policing of the dispute strongly criticized the use of numbers of police to protect what is, in my view, one of the most fundamental civil liberties of all: a man's right to go freely to his work. The criticism was on the grounds that it was 'an inappropriate use of scarce police resources such [as would] promote disharmony and discontent among those picketing'! The big lie, told often, may not convince many. But it brings numbers of people, particularly in the media, well down the road towards acceptance of half-truths.

Perhaps it was only natural that I should find the

media's collective willingness to report so much of the Scargill line completely naive. In some cases of reporting there was deliberate bias too, even in some of the so-called right-wing papers, and certainly in a large part of the television coverage as well. It was widely accepted that Scargill had a group of strong supporters among those whose job it was to report his activities regularly. Some of this willingness to follow his line was born of conviction; some, as I have said, out of his ability to help the reporters concerned to provide excitement for the front pages and for the top of the nightly bulletins. The Industrial Correspondents' Group has both these elements in it. I suppose it is not surprising that in many cases their sympathies lie with the unions, since so many of their stories originate from that side of the fence. The situation is further aggravated by the fact that many of them are now, if not encouraged, then at least not hindered from editorializing within the columns of their 'fair' reportage.

The attitudes of most major newspaper editors were easier to 'read' during the strike since the stance of their papers was fairly well established before it began. However, one or two, who originally supported us, shifted their ground somewhat towards the finish to the conflicting Walker line which caused a certain amount of confusion and, in the end, helped delay the process of reaching a satisfactory conclusion to the dispute.

As far as the radio reporting of the dispute was concerned, we are indebted to Nicholas Jones, of the BBC, for making us privy to his beliefs and theories in a book on the subject called *Strikes and the Media*. Mr Jones is clearly a believer in the conspiracy theory of history and sees sinister motives behind the most innocuous of events. He makes a great play of the management of the news that went on during the strike, conceding grudgingly that towards the end of 1984 we began to redress the balance in news management and became better at handling the media. But I believe his complaint is that it was somehow unfair for us to be doing this. I get the impression that he regards the use of people and resources like Tim Bell and his company as something immoral. You end up feeling that his view is that we should have let Scargill dominate the scene and that we were not supposed to take any steps to oppose him.

Needless to say the most powerful medium involved in the reporting of the strike was television. Sadly, in my view, it also turned out to be the most biased. The great claim always made by the folk who run the news and current affairs departments is that what they do is 'balanced'. Unfortunately one has to be pretty naive to accept that view. There can be no such thing as balance when one side is defending a static position against someone who is prepared to do anything to destroy it. If you give the two sides five minutes each on one night then, yes, you have balance. But the next night, which television station is going to bear repeating the same message from the man defending his position, when it has a fancy new tale to show from his opponent?

What is more, news is created out of imbalance. It comes more often than not out of the presentation of an attack *on* something: an attack on prejudice, an attack on the church, an attack on the prime minister, an attack on Neil Kinnock. It is adversarial. If the defence has the same position each day and the attack is different, then the attack will get the media attention. In the first six months of the strike Arthur Scargill played television's 'balance' game beautifully, with a fresh 'line' every day. The television people seemed to swallow it gratefully. We had very little to say which was fresh, because we only had one position to defend: our right to manage the business.

Worse than this was the way in which, after a while, even 'balance' was flouted in the interests of good television. 'Good television', I must stress, has nothing to do with providing information. Good television is what makes you turn one particular programme on and watch it. Good television is entertainment. It is an extension of cops and robbers. Also, most of it is excitement, not education. In news and current affairs terms 'good television' shows dramatic pictures of violence. In the strike good television was pictures of the police hitting strikers, which were worth ten times more than pictures of strikers attacking the forces of law and order. Good television was not the orderly presentation of each side's case so that the public could make up its mind. Good television was a slanging match, or better still a punch-up, in the studio while live on the air.

Hence, for all his complaints to the contrary, Scargill got the lion's share of television time throughout the strike – and particularly in the early days. Indeed his complaints that he was being hard done by were probably deliberately designed to make sure that he continued to do as well as he was. For he did indeed do marvellously. Buried away at the back of Alastair Hetherington's analysis of the coverage of the strike in his book *News, Newspapers and Television* is a shattering statistic, which should disturb our television elite in their complacent adherence to their profession of 'balance'.

Professor Hetherington examined all the television coverage of the strike on each of the three major news bulletins – Channel 4 News, BBC Nine O'Clock News and ITN News at Ten – from Monday to Friday for one week in each of the first eight months of the strike. He showed that the strike and related issues took up one quarter of all the news coverage of that period – but that coverage of the NUM pro-strike side amounted to 89 minutes, whereas the NCB and working miners' side got only 49 minutes.

What is more, he says that even in the amount of time given to the NCB side – only just over half that given to Scargill – 'the urgency and drama of each day's events . . . tended to leave little time for extra information.' Nor in his view was the NCB's pit closure case (or the NUM's response) fully covered. In addition, the vast majority of 'background' features on the strike were pro-NUM.

Clearly the needs of 'good television' took over from fair and accurate reporting. And the fact that the nation was patently involved in a civil war seemed to have been ignored altogether. Hence it was fair game to edit and select favourable shots of one side and unfavourable shots of the other. Were the more revolutionary sections of Scargill's speeches ever given the air play they deserved? Or were they kept out, lest they reveal to the public the true nature of the man and his objectives?

Were the hours and hours of stoning and missile-throwing at the police shown? Or the few seconds of the occasional angry retaliation by an individual policeman under severe provocation? The ratio of the former to the latter must have been 100 to one – if not 500 or 1000 to one – yet Professor Hetherington's book shows us that the TV time devoted to violence on the two sides ran at a ratio of eight to one.

Not that I can – or should – complain about it, but how many times has the shot of me with the plastic bag been edited into films about the strike, not because it adds anything to the argument, but because it is 'good television' and would perhaps help discredit me and my cause?

I am sure that the end result of this overall presentation of the strike in favour of Scargill's propaganda helped prolong the dispute considerably. I believe it may well have doubled the length of time it took to get it settled, in that for the first six months Scargill was projected as being totally successful and the back-to-work movement as being totally unsuccessful. This delayed the resolution of the strike, by either negotiation or return to work – because both were impossible as long as Scargill was portrayed as winning. In that time the union was seen as more powerful than the NCB, superior in its arguments and in its ability to sabotage and destroy all that stood in its way. All this created a public image which either encouraged support from others who never thought about the issues that underlay the struggle, or discouraged those who might have wanted to go back to work.

A large proportion of the public, however, plainly did not accept what they were being shown on television night after night. They began to take the coverage with a pinch of salt – especially when we began to show that we could get people back to work and when it became clear that Scargill had no intention of settling. Indeed I formed the impression, as did many others, that the whole purpose of the strike was not to win through negotiation, but to win by inflicting more pain on the NCB and the government than they could take. Unfortunately, in Margaret Thatcher and myself, Scargill had picked the wrong two people on whom to try this tactic.

This sense of my being the underdog – the guy taking a pasting from the bully – earned me some popularity which was quite noticeable in those people who chose to ignore the message the media was projecting. I was approached many times in the street, or on planes or in trains, and asked by complete strangers where my bodyguard was. People were amazed to find me wandering about on my own, and some of them seemed to want to look after me until I got to my destination! They were all so full of encouragement too – telling me to hang on in there and not to let Scargill push me around, making it clear they understood I was fighting for all of them.

The point I think the sophisticates in the media missed was that, for all it was good television and he was good copy, Scargill scared a lot of the ordinary people of this country. I got the feeling too that a lot of them were even more scared because what they were being shown on television every night was no longer their country. It was not a place they knew, or wanted to know.

On many, many occasions I became dispirited by it all. I would ask myself: what am I doing all this for? I felt particularly downhearted after some of my more unpleasant sessions with Mr Walker. The inability to develop a feeling of confidence in each other marred our relationship and made me feel extremely uncomfortable. It was at times like this that I was thankful for the support I got from all sorts of ordinary people in all sorts of quarters. Some union leaders would occasionally drop a word of encouragement my way, and Dr David Owen, from the SDP, was quite supportive. He came in once or twice to see me and his discussions of the issues couldn't have been more constructive.

Fortunately, in the end, the media collectively appeared to get bored with Scargill when they saw he was losing. It was as trivial as that. In addition, our efforts to improve our communications – with Tim Bell's guidance – began to bear fruit. We found a 'winner' for the media for a while with Michael Eaton. Soon he was providing the media with something fresh to talk about every day. We had men going back to work. We had a success story to tell and the tide was seen to be turning.

14

Desertions in Scargill's Army

On the morning of 8 November a lone miner was taken under police escort past 'The Alamo', the pickets' hut which had become a national symbol of the strike to millions of television viewers, past 700 stunned pickets and into work at Cortonwood pit, the South Yorkshire colliery which was at the heart of, and indeed in some ways the cause of, the dispute. When he emerged that afternoon a gallows had been erected by the side of the pickets' hut with a sign on it saying, 'This is for scabs'.

No single event in all the dispute can have had a more devastating effect on Scargill's morale than this breach of the strike at Cortonwood by a twenty-three-year-old married man with two young children. Indeed the following night the miners' leader addressed a rally of 5000 of the faithful in Sheffield City Hall and had them raising the roof as he whipped them into a frenzy with promises that victory was theirs and that all scabs would become like lepers – total outcasts, unable to work or live in the locality. Less than five hours later many of them, their ears still ringing with their leader's promises to smash both me and Margaret Thatcher and to wreak terrible vengeance on men who returned to work, assembled outside the entrance to Cortonwood pit a dozen miles away to stop, at all costs, that one brave man going in there again.

A measure of the sensitivity of the strikers to this affront to their solidarity at the very core of the dispute could be seen in the succeeding days when thousands of Scargill's troops rampaged through the area. This was not like previous battles with the police. Here we saw catapults, barricades, blazing vehicles and petrol bombs. It was the blind hatred and raging madness of hooligans who knew the game was up but wanted to smash indiscriminately until it was finally over. The police took the brunt of their fury. Many of them were injured. But they held their ground.

A similar measure of the mounting courage of those who had been forced unwillingly to strike, and of those former Scargill followers on whom the truth was slowly dawning, could be seen on the following Monday morning when not one, but four men went defiantly back to work at Cortonwood. A month later there were eight. Two months later there were 15. Out of such small, brave, lonely beginnings was the back-to-work movement born.

After the NACODS dispute was over and the NUM had refused to settle at the same time, we made it clear that there would be no more negotiations unless there was acceptance of a formula for the closure of uneconomic pits. In the meantime we announced that we were going to concentrate on the back-to-work movement, thus indicating to the miners that we were preparing for a long haul and there was going to be no easy way out or quick victory.

Thus November was the month when we began to show that there really was an alternative to the compromise and climbdown being so strongly touted by some sections of the media and many anxious politicians who could no longer bear the agony generated by a long dispute. Many of the bureaucrats both in government and in Hobart House – and many of Scargill's supporters – all began to realize in their heart of hearts that there was now no way for him to avoid defeat.

The fact that one man elected to return to work in Cortonwood was highly symbolic in itself. But there were many, many other similar acts of defiance taking place right across the coalfields. For the myth of Scargill's invincibility was now being dissipated even among his own men. To more and more of them, victory was no longer the certainty it had seemed in the heady days of spring and through the summer. More and more of them were now worried as to exactly where it was he was leading them. What was his real intent? Did he really want to win them better wages and conditions without pit closures? Why wouldn't he settle the strike on the terms offered? Did he really want to? Was he fighting a political war of which they wanted no part? And why was he disgracing their name by dealing with Gadhafi, the Libyan madman? Failure to come up with satisfactory answers to these questions was at the root of many of the men's desire to return to work.

Our new strategy would at last give a chance for the area directors to prove, as they had been saying to us all along, that negotiating with Scargill was pointless and that getting the men to return to work was the only way to a successful conclusion. Every time we agreed to new talks I had to listen to their anguished cries that it was defeating their efforts. But as I had explained to them many times, we had a number of 'audiences' to address – and the public would not have forgiven us if we had made no attempt to negotiate with Scargill, however fruitless an exercise it turned out to be.

Now, however, we could set about turning the second front into the main theatre of war. Although our field surveys showed distressingly little change throughout the strike, one in November did reveal a drop in the number of miners who thought they would win – paralleled by a similar fall in their faith in the various methods by which Scargill had promised victory. Other soundings by our area management people also showed that attitudes were changing. Miners were becoming more anxious about the level of violence being perpetrated in their name. They were becoming anxious for their families – especially as Christmas approached – and were beginning to think about the personal consequences of what Scargill had demanded of them in the name of loyalty. The arrival of winter also gave them less opportunity to help make ends meet with casual work. Many of those who had made some money by taking Scargill's shilling and joining the army of pickets found there was less – though still a surprising amount – in the kitty to pay for their activities. In addition, the new influx of outright hooligan elements beginning to join Scargill's cause was making such activities more and more repugnant to them.

We had aimed much of our advertising in a similar way to the way in which cars are sold in the US. It was a form of saturation media coverage where you sold the product on the general attractiveness of the vehicle – enough to get the public into the showroom – but left it to the local dealers themselves to make the final pitch and swing the deal. Similarly, the text of our advertisements was on the broad sweep, making it clear that we were not going to compromise our right to manage, but that there was a great future for the industry. There was no further point in negotiating so the only thing to do was to go back to work. That was the background. The real selling of the idea was done at local level. We had learned early on that the best trigger for a man's final decision to go back to work was if that man talked to one of his working mates.

The second best was to arrange for a colliery official, whom he knew, to talk to him, but this had progressively less effect as the organizational distance between the two men increased. Nevertheless, we used every avenue we could, even if only to prepare the ground for someone who might possibly return to work much later.

There were, of course, considerable obstacles placed in our path. Scargill on the defensive was even less of a pushover than he had been on the attack with all guns blazing. He kept up a constant barrage of propaganda that we were failing and he was winning. Nor had his contacts with the media entirely evaporated and a good deal of time and space was given over to pooh-poohing the very suggestion that any significant numbers of men had actually abandoned his camp and returned to work.

The struggle was essentially for the hearts, minds and pockets of those who neither supported the strike all out, nor had settled to return to work early on. And everything we did at the local level was aimed at redressing the balance of fear – making the men in this group feel that it was prudent, wise and safe for them and their families to run the gauntlet of the pickets.

It was especially galling to us that, having persuaded a man to return to work, to overcome all his fears about disloyalty and the violence and his long term-security, we then had to take his NUM dues out of his pay packet each week and hand them over to the union.

Many people in Hobart House, in the Department of Energy, and in the ranks of the political parties were sceptical of the idea that a back-to-work movement could succeed. Nor indeed at first did all the area directors or those below them share the conviction of their colleagues like John Northard in the Western Area, Ken Moses, Bert Wheeler, Albert Tuke and David Archibald. These men had been working for more than six months now and, although their successes could be measured only in terms of a trickle, they had had a significant effect in broadening the front and attenuating Scargill's lines of supply.

However, these doubts among our commanders in the field had been laid to rest at the end of June when we arranged for the regular meeting of the area directors to be held in Moses's north Derbyshire district and he was asked to give a talk to his colleagues about how he had developed his efforts to get the men back. The meeting, as it turned out, was one of the most important of the whole strike for us. It gave a lot of encouragement to the doubters and generated a certain amount of professional competition which quickened the individual local efforts to get men back throughout the summer and into the autumn. It laid the foundation for our major national back-to-work push in November and, eventually, played a significant part in terminating the dispute.

Ken Moses explained that detailed hard work and as much personal contact as possible was the only way to convince men to go back to work. As we have seen, his results were slow to come – his numbers had gone from 52 NUM men back to Shirebrook at the end of May, to 89 at the end of June. They were to go to only 100 by the end of July, 130 by August, 167 in September, 194 in October, and 1085 at the end of our big push in November. As he told his story that day in June, with maps and charts showing where each of his employees lived, I could sense some of the other directors showing a great interest. Since May he had added refinements to his system of 'rolling it back from the edges'. His wall map, showing the house of every man at the pit was now dotted with coloured pins: red for the location, replaced by orange if there was a chance the man might want to come back, green if he would – and blue if he had.

Only a few days before the meeting, he had phoned

Jimmy one day and said, in his usual blunt fashion: 'I want the authorization to buy twelve buses and to cover them with protective armour.'

'Why?' Jimmy asked.

'To get men back to work,' he said.

'Go to it,' Jimmy said.

'But what about the money – it's £5000 each?' he asked.

'Never mind that,' Jimmy told him. 'We'll work out how we pay for it later.'

When Jimmy told me later what he had done, I endorsed his decision immediately.

Those buses, fitted in his own workshops with metal grilles and protection for the drivers, ran throughout the strike, giving the men who rode in them a feeling of security they would never have got if they had had to make their own way to the pit.

The buses were frequently attacked and great efforts were made by the strikers to find out where the pick-up points were and who the drivers were – but they were never forced off the roads. Indeed, on one occasion, one of the drivers taking an early morning shift into the pit saw through his rear-view mirror that he was being followed by several carloads of strikers. He had a short discussion with the men about the situation, then, the story goes, diverted the bus up a quiet country lane and stopped and waited while the men leapt out of the bus and gave a sharp 'return bout' of the violence they and their friends had been suffering all those weeks at the hands of the mobs. Then they climbed back on board and continued on to work. Such actions were not condoned, but were understandable when Ken read off the long list of shocking personal attacks on his working miners. On one Sunday alone five of them had had their houses set on fire.

The real key to his success at Shirebrook – and at the rest of his 11 pits as they began to get men back – were the 'profiles' of all the men he built up with the help of the colliery management teams. Then each man was approached personally by someone he knew well to talk the whole issue over. No scrap of information was too small to be considered and to provide a lead to be acted upon to persuade a man who might be thinking of coming back. Ken used to swim on Saturdays at the local baths and made a point of chatting with the men – little tips he picked up here and there helped him to get two or three back to work. Tips flowed in from contacts made in pubs and clubs – one even from a chance meeting of two wives at the hairdressers! Regular letters were sent both by him and by the pit managers – they even designed their own Christmas card, which attracted hundreds of letters and calls of thanks.

One day, to his surprise, after a fair number of men had returned at Shirebrook, the manager at Warsop, next door, suddenly started to get men coming back. They were led by a twenty-eight-year-old man who told Ken, when he went to see him at the pit: 'I came back, because I got your letter, sir, and I suddenly realized that Scargill couldn't stop me working.' It was quite common to find a feeling of great relief among the men returning – that at last they had been able to clear their minds of all that Scargill had been telling them and to see the issue in true perspective. North Derbyshire's figures for returning miners at the end of each month – from May to the end of the year – were 343, 520, 542, 404 (holidays), 818, 863, 3772 and 4056.

It was not just Ken Moses's efforts which were showing the way to some of the more hesitant area directors. Bert Wheeler was having a battle royal with the notoriously militant strikers of Scotland. But he was helped enormously by the arrival, again, of several hundred Durham miners who stayed at the gates of Bilston Glen for almost a week. During that week, immediately after the pit's holiday, one of the most savage skirmishes of the entire dispute was fought out to stop his thirty-odd returnees going in. But the mistake the Durham miners made was to shout abuse and use the taunt once again that the Scots didn't have the stomach for the strike. Bert went on television and said that it was a sad day for Scotland when the only way the NUM could keep the strike going was to bring violent striking English miners in to stop Scotsmen going to work. More men came back after that and by the beginning of September there were 205 men at 12 of the NCB's sites in Scotland. The November push saw that figure rise to 2242.

Many of the men returning faced terrible intimidation and violence. Bert's management team helped them where they could – sending people to repair damaged houses, arranging for cars to be repainted and damaged tyres replaced. Some men were attacked in their homes and their families threatened. One man had a howling mob of dozens lay siege to his home and the police had to rescue him and his wife. But it was also the humiliation they and their kin suffered – the constant spitting and other degrading forms of abuse. A man who decided to return to work in Scotland was very much more on his own than a man who lived in Nottingham, or next door in Derbyshire.

Bert also found that the first day back was crucial. In the early months he used to try to meet as many of the men as he could on the day they actually came in for the first time. He found that the ordeal of that first time had a distressingly similar effect on them all. They had steeled themselves to it. They knew it would be an ordeal, but nothing had really prepared them for what it would be like. He saw men come through the gates, where they were told, in effect, by the pickets that that was the end of their normal lives. No one would ever speak to them again, no one would drink with them. Their wives would be ostracized, and nobody's children would play with theirs. When the strike was won they would never work again and until then they would be hunted down and abused, or worse, wherever they went. Tough, grown men, hard Scottish miners, arrived inside the gates ashen-faced and shaking and some would be physically sick. Bert reckoned if he could get them over that day, they would be all right.

Individual acts of bravery in the face of the mob were legion. Paul Wilkinson went alone into Easington pit in Durham on 20 August and did the same every day for two months afterwards until others began to join him. That takes both stubbornness and courage; but what it did to him and his family was terrible – just because he had the conviction that Scargill's strike was neither in his interests, nor in the interests of the miners in general. They didn't let up on him after the strike was over, and, like so many others who had been so brave, he eventually had to leave the industry.

Much of the intimidation that went on was carried out by militant miners and other hooligans – but nearly all of it was at the instigation of union officials. Our intelligence was that orders were passed down the chain locally to the thugs on the ground who did the dirty work. It was rarely ever spontaneous violence. For example, in the Western Area, John Northard very quickly got Point of Ayr pit back working – even though there was much bitterness between the two sides throughout the strike. I went back there recently for the ceremony launching the new coal liquification plant and I noticed that, in the absence of the local NUM hierarchy, who had refused to meet me, members of the local NUM, UDM and NACODS all mingled freely and happily together both with men who had worked during the strike and men who hadn't. They told me there were no problems between the men in the pit. The trouble had been instigated and orchestrated all along by the absent NUM officials who were, I hoped, too ashamed of their disruptive past to accept an invitation to come to meet me.

The national back-to-work drive in November was boosted considerably by the decision to point out to the men how much they could earn before Christmas in pay, bonuses, holiday allowances and so on. These advertisements were among the best of the campaign. Under the headline, 'It'll Pay Every Miner Who's Not At Work To Read This', the copy pointed out that negotiations had ended, there had never been a ballot and more and more miners were now voting with their feet – 54,000 NUM members were no longer on strike and 56 pits were turning coal. It ended with the words: 'By returning to work now miners can earn up to £1400 by Christmas.' This figure was arrived at by calculating what the average miner would pick up in that time. We stretched a point or two on the timing of the offer's closing date – but not to the extent of putting in any extra lump sums, and by the end of the period we had 15,000 new 'faces'.

Needless to say we were accused of bribery. I don't think it is bribery to tell a man what he could earn at work. The figures were quite genuine and aimed to give each striker a chance to make a sober assessment of his own and his family's position. A bribe would have been seen through by most straightaway for what it was – a few might have fallen for it – but in this case I think our appeal made many thousands of men pause and give serious thought as to what they were doing and why. At about this time the accusation that we were starving the miners back to work also started to surface. My answer to that was that we had done all we could to settle the dispute, but it had been their personal decision to go on strike in the first place and it was their own personal decision to stay out now. It was not I who was starving them – if they were starving – they had chosen that course of their own free will. A well-paid job was there waiting for every single one of them who wanted it.

There were now significant numbers of men back in every area and, as they came, so more and more of their mates could see less and less reason for hanging on. At Ellington pit in Northumberland John Cunningham, an NUM official, led 107 of his men back to work one day. At last we got the feeling that the men were realizing that Scargill's battle was certainly not for their benefit. The pickets became fewer and more spread out; but the acts of violence were becoming more vicious as the desperation of the hooligan element among the strikers grew.

At Hobart House we monitored progress day by day, with a meeting every morning to go over the detailed reports from the areas and to discuss any new thoughts or actions that might be needed. Sometimes Jimmy or I would decide to go and visit one area if we felt things needed pushing along a bit. We also built up a marvellous information network which fed intelligence, from chatter in a pub, or 'moles' among the union officials, or observations of pickets, right up to Kevin Hunt and Ned Smith and then, if necessary, on via my office to the daily meetings at the Department of Energy, where representatives of all the other ministries involved met at 10 a.m. every day.

The assessment of intelligence in our personnel department became pretty good and we could predict fairly accurately where there was going to be trouble. They could 'smell' a target pit coming up, often days before the first sign of any gathering of the mobs. Scargill was convinced that all the NUM's phones were tapped – I do not know whether they were or not – but his decision to switch over to issuing picketing orders, like bomber targets during the war, in sealed envelopes handed out on street corners did not interfere at all with our expanding sources of intelligence of what he and his minions were up to.

The police also developed their own intelligence system and the two networks together became a formidable force in the battle of wits that developed in the coalfields. No praise can be too high for the work of the police – from the very top in coordinating the whole operation through the National Reporting Centre, down through the local senior officers, particularly the chief constables, many of whom, as I have said, faced considerable harassment from local left-wing police committees and councils, right down to the policemen on the ground. Many of these young men – a large proportion of whom came from country areas and had no experience of this sort of duty – courageously took all the abuse and violence with commendable calm and forebearance day in and day out. They were often living in uncomfortable conditions, going out in the small hours of the morning to face a whole day of front-line duty in the cold and the wet, yet they rarely complained. It gave me great confidence in the young people of this country to see these brave men face some of the most savage civil disorder we have ever witnessed – and to do it so willingly and with so much restraint, control and dignity in the face of enormous provocation.

As we planned to get men back at a particular pit, so we would notify the police, both locally and through our links with the Energy Department daily briefing sessions. Then a senior policeman would work out with the colliery manager the exact details of the operation and how to avoid the mobs. We found that a large police presence early on in a back-to-work drive at one pit tended to inhibit mass picketing, and that once we could establish a regular pattern of attendance the in-depth police support could be scaled down. After the first few weeks we were seldom surprised by the sudden appearance of huge numbers of pickets. Even when they tried diversionary tactics, we were quickly able to work out which were the feints and which was the main thrust so that the police would be there in time to stop it. There were occasional slip-ups but by and large the system worked progressively better and as a result major battles were avoided because the policing anticipated trouble and thus prevented it.

Obviously, there was little that the returning miners could do at first by way of actually producing coal – there had to be substantial numbers back at a pit before even one shift a day could work on a face. But in the vast majority of cases there was ample for the men to do simply clearing up the damage and mess caused by months of neglect and preparing for the day when work could start. Nevertheless, by the New Year we had 71 pits turning coal – 47 of them working normally. Some work was being done at 68 others and only 35 were still on strike or picketed out.

It had become clear long before this, however, that Scargill's last great hope, his last great ally – General Winter – who, he had told his men hundreds of times, would soon be riding to their rescue – was not going to appear quite in the form, nor to have the devastating effect, he had promised. The first half of the winter of 1984–5 was exceptionally mild and the second half, though more severe, was not of the Siberian nature the strikers had prayed for.

But, more importantly, the CEGB was getting better and better organized to meet the crisis. At no stage in the winter did the level of consumption threaten to exceed

the supply of electricity so that power cuts – the politicians' nightmare – were never even contemplated. This
takes us back to the very beginning and the puzzling
question of why Scargill chose to strike when he did. His
error was more fundamental than merely to ignore the
fact that there was more than six months' supply of coal
available in stocks, more fundamental even than to fail
to get Nottingham out, and hence allow the big coal-fired
power stations on the Trent to keep working. It was an
error of simple mathematics: the UK has capacity in
various forms – nuclear, oil, coal fired – to produce just
about twice as much electricity as there is normal demand.

The reason for this was partly shifts in technology and
partly shifts in demand. The electricity supply industry
had once been coal dominated. Then nuclear power had
been developed and it became a sort of status symbol, a
sign of technical virility, for a nation to have a chain of
such stations. I am sure Tony Benn's great enthusiasm
for nuclear power was born in part out of this
strong desire to be seen prominently and publicly in the
vanguard of the technological revolution and privately,
in all probability, by his politician's fear of being held to
ransom by the miners. The long and dramatic fall in the
price of oil in the 1960s also gave the UK the incentive
to build more oil-burning stations, while the continuing
power of the miners had led to coal maintaining a large
share of the market. Thus, by 1984, with the demand for
energy still well below the level of the days before the oil
crisis – and massively below the level that had been anticipated – we had an embarrassment of energy riches, more
and more varied power plants than the country needed.

As the winter wore on the CEGB still had a wide choice
as to how it allocated its energy production – obviously
still with one eye on the coal stocks. But there was no
longer any great urgency to preserve them. The dispute

ended with 11 million tonnes still in stock and enough being produced to hold that figure. Ironically, during the strike, a certain amount of foreign coal was being imported by coal dealers and retailers, and a fair amount from Poland. Scargill's lavish praise of the Warsaw regime and scathing attacks on the Solidarity movement clearly transcended the miners' dispute in ideological terms and his voice was strangely muted when it came to picketing Polish ships or calling their crews scabs. It was interesting to note that he seemed to consider his loyalty to the Polish regime above the needs of his own members.

Thus, by Christmas, he was recognizably hard-pressed. He began to show every sign of being a man in a corner. His troops were becoming more vicious, though their attacks were more sporadic. Two assaults in particular shocked the nation and caused yet further revulsion among the miners not only that the acts should take place at all, but also that their leader should refuse to condemn any violence other than that shown by the police. Michael Fletcher was beaten to within an inch of his life by a mob wielding the local equivalent of baseball bats who chased him into his own living room, while his wife and children cowered upstairs, and a taxi driver, David Wilkie, was killed when strikers dropped a block of concrete on his car from a motorway bridge as he drove a miner to work.

In my view neither of these stupid, mindless acts would have taken place were it not for the constant emotional and extreme oratory that Scargill had been keeping up for the duration of the strike.

Our intelligence was also telling us that Scargill was in trouble with his own executive council. While he still completely dominated it, there was growing concern at where he was leading the union. It often puzzled me how it was he managed for so long to muzzle criticism from this body of 24 men. Could it be only Roy Ottey who had dared dissent? We knew there were others who did – but why weren't their voices heard more often and more openly?

One reason perhaps could be found in an interesting item in the *Spectator* at the height of the strike. It discussed all the conditions and benefits that a member of the NEC is entitled to.

All National Executive members earn approximately £25,000 per annum. Each receives a free house which he can occupy until the death of him or his wife (whoever dies last). He has the opportunity to buy this house from the union at an artificially low price. His heating, lighting, telephone and rates are paid. He is given a car, and he benefits from a curious system of allowances which allows him to claim three nights' subsistence allowance (at £40 a night) for a meeting which only lasts a day. These arrangements, though generous, are not very unusual. But the Executive's pension scheme is. There is a fairly small pension administered in the ordinary way but on top of it is added a grace-and-favour bonus. This was invented by Lord Gormley, and is very valuable. Its distinctive feature is that its rate, and whom it is paid to, are at the discretion of the NUM President. This helps to explain the continuing 'solidarity' of the Executive. (*Spectator*, 11 August 1984)

We ran an advertising campaign at this time to point out each of Scargill's prognostications and how they had failed to come about. This too was successful in keeping the pressure on. It was important to remind the striking miners that they were getting nowhere and that they might as well come back to work. Our strategic responses to warfare on the Scargill battle ground were working. The economic warfare was beginning to constrict his resources. His friends could no longer help him. I knew it would not be too long now.

This, of course, was the very question I was asked almost daily by the secretary of state. How long would it go on? I could feel his frustration and annoyance every time I said I didn't have an answer and implied that we should plan on the strike going on forever – being the best formula for ending it quickly. For a politician who was used to feeding pretty firm news to the media, this was not good enough. I sometimes thought he wanted a date and a time for it all to end. Just as he appeared irked by the slow and uncertain grind of the back-to-work movement, so I am sure his political instinct for compromise was made distinctly uncomfortable by the absence of negotiations. There was an atmosphere which constantly implied that something should be done, but few suggestions were made for any initiatives which would fit within the bounds of our strategy.

I can understand some of his unhappiness – and that of many other politicians, who clearly felt that what was going on was perhaps alien to the British desire for compromise and that I was being annoyingly stubborn and intransigent. It was and I was. The normal British approach to this would have been for the NCB and the government to have backed down long ago. I was not prepared to give ground, because, under the terms of the task I had been set, there was no more ground I could give. Indeed it was at this time that I speculated that Mrs Thatcher probably only had two other people in her cabinet who really accepted the fundamental issues of principle that were at stake here. From my initial discussions I knew that Nigel Lawson was fully aware of what the struggle would involve and I got clear indications that Norman Tebbit was too.

I learned with great concern in early December that

the secretary of state had been 'negotiating' with the TUC. For some time I had been puzzled as to why our back-to-work drive, which had been so successful in November, had suddenly lost momentum. I had hoped, with all the factors involved clearly going our way, that the water which was trickling through the cracks in the dam would suddenly burst through and it might be all over, bar the shouting, by Christmas. But suddenly no new 'faces' were reporting for work. The whisper was going around the coalfields, yet again, that the NCB were about to collapse and so there was no point in being a scab for just a few days before the NUM finally won. I paid little heed to it at the time, believing that it was just another, more virulent, bit of Scargill propaganda. Nevertheless I continued to puzzle over it – and to be unhappy that the strike was not going to be over as quickly as I had tentatively begun to hope.

Then in mid-December it all became clear. The TUC announced they were going to have another meeting with Peter Walker on the 14th. I had not even been aware that there had been a first meeting, which it subsequently transpired had taken place on the 5th. I was pretty upset. This was why the whispers had started to go round the pits. I am sure this was principally why the men were not coming back to work; and I had not even been told. Apparently Peter Walker and the 'TUC Seven' – the congress's negotiating panel, with whom I had had dealings in October – had got together and were working on a new deal to put to the miners. Arthur Scargill had, apparently, graciously agreed that he would not oppose them having talks!

My next meeting with the minister was not cordial. I did my best to suggest to him the danger in what he was doing. He was playing right into Scargill's hands. For nine months the NUM president had been trying to get the government involved directly in the dispute. Now the secretary of state had stepped right into it and Scargill could run to his men with the message: 'Don't worry, boys. It's nearly over. The government has taken control. MacGregor has been moved out of the way and they are about to cave in. Just hang on, victory is ours!' It also had a disastrous effect on the early talks to set up the UDM. Jimmy Cowan was helping and advising Roy Lynk and his men, but every time there was a whisper of government intervention they turned to him and asked what the point was of sticking their necks out if there was about to be a sell-out to Scargill.

Perhaps we can put Peter Walker's actions at that time down to anxiety, lack of previous experience in strikes of this magnitude – and to the fact that he had no one around him with the necessary experience to advise him to do anything to the contrary. In my view he was simply unaware that, by agreeing to these meetings, he had probably stopped the back-to-work movement, and as a result the length of the strike was extended by what turned out to be a further three months. This was, of course, the very opposite of what he intended to achieve. I tried to prevent this from happening but my efforts were not effective. When I went to see him he seemed uncomfortable in my presence – perhaps concerned that what I was saying may have had some truth in it, but his political instincts made him unable to accept it.

However, he did seem to grasp one important point: that, above all else, the TUC must make it clear to Scargill that there could be no settlement without an agreement to close pits on economic grounds. I gather that at his meeting on the 14th he did make this point and, predictably, the TUC men stated that they saw little hope of peace because they correctly presumed that Scargill would not accept it.

One other interesting exchange took place during that meeting with the minister on the 11th. I wished him a Happy Christmas and said I would see him in the New Year. He asked me why I was doing that now, to which I replied that in a few days' time I was flying to America for my annual Christmas vacation and would be back on 2 January. He was horrified that I should be leaving the bridge, at such a time and for so long. I explained, yet again, that the back-to-work strategy was a long haul, that there was no prospect of the strike collapsing while I was away – and, in my view, even less of Scargill suing for peace. Walker was, I think, aghast. He *still* clearly hoped for some great coup, some compromise that would get everyone off the hook.

When I got to America the following week I had a chance to think quite objectively and used the vacation to review carefully what had happened. I was deeply disappointed that so much of the work to get men back had in a way been vitiated by the secretary of state's initiatives. The November effort could well have turned into a flood by Christmas if it had not been for the uncertainties raised by the discussions with the TUC. I was now nervous of what might be done by the government or others to try to settle the dispute – though I could hardly believe that attitudes had changed at Downing Street.

I also took the opportunity to look over my hand. I thought about all the cards that had been played, all the ones I had left and all the ones Scargill had left. In the end, I reckoned that unless he had a few wild deuces in there, which I was sure he hadn't, there was no way he was going to win this one. That cheered me up and I remembered an off-the-cuff answer I had given to a question from reporters in Paris in November. They had asked when the strike would be over: now, I concluded that the answer I had given then was, despite everything, more true than ever.

'When 51 per cent of our people are back at work the strike will be over,' I had said. 'The men are having their own ballot and are voting with their feet.'

15

Laying the Final Trap

At 7 a.m. on 1 January 1985 Arthur Scargill and his wife Anne joined the picket line outside Thorpe Marsh power station, near Doncaster. He proudly told the small group, their numbers swelled by a party of German trade unionists, that the dispute had so far cost the government £5 billion and 77 million tonnes of lost coal production and that together these factors had helped the pound plunge by more than 20 per cent. 'The only difference between now and March 1984,' he said, 'is that we are more convinced and more confident of winning now than we were then.'

That week we had 70,026 of his members back at work – representing 37 per cent of the NUM workforce. We were producing coal at 71 of our 174 pits – 47 of which were working normally. Men were in and work was being done at 71 other collieries. At only 32 pits was Scargill's strike still solid. A month later nearly 10,000 more men had returned, making a total of 43 per cent of the NUM working.

If he had looked around him, in the first light of that frosty New Year morning, he would have seen all the evidence he needed in order to know that the game was up. Where were the flying pickets? The dozens of tiny legal ropes of David Hart's Gulliver concept had tied the NUM to the ground and it was now incapable of mounting the mass movement of pickets. It was a month since Scargill and his executive had lost all control over their financial affairs and all their assets were in the hands of the receiver. Yet he still believed he was above the law. His attitude was that nobody could do this to him.

Why weren't hundreds of local pickets there with him? Many of the men who supported him had been sickened, first, by the widespread violence on the picket lines, and, second, by his repeated and nonsensical insistence that all the violence had been caused by the police. Most miners, like most ordinary citizens, were law-abiding people who were shocked by what they had seen and preferred to stay at home than get involved in the sort of mayhem that was going on. Three thousand five hundred of his own elite – the Yorkshire miners – had already gone back to work, defying the abuse from their colleagues in the heartland of the dispute.

Why was the Thorpe Marsh power station working? All the support from other unions, on which he had banked, had evaporated in a rancorous cloud of recrimination and accusations of betrayal. His colleagues at the TUC were publicly silent and privately shamed by the way he had scorned negotiations. His propaganda alleging that the winter would bring chaos was rebounding on him. The Coal Board and the CEGB still had 36.35 million tonnes of coal available.

Scargill's switch of emphasis, which we saw that morning, from the certainty of victory to the inventory of damage he had succeeded in inflicting on the government, was to become more noticeable in the coming weeks. It did, I suspect, reveal his true motives and illustrated the only shred of pride he had left in his achievements of the last year. For, although he could not admit it, he was now trapped with nowhere to run. Some, particularly in the media, felt sorry for him. But I felt no such emotion; he had set out to destroy democracy in his own union and in the country. The tragedy was in the havoc he had wrought in both. Nor was he yet finished.

Five days later he attended a meeting of the inner left-wing caucus of the NUM, a group of about fifty militants who had met regularly throughout the strike to assist in its execution. The main function of this 'union within a union' was to supersede the national executive committee as Scargill's principal advisory body and sounding board. Just as the special delegate conference, packed with militants, had taken the place of the ballot of all the members, so had this group come to be the forum at which policy was first presented by the president and then the means of getting it implemented decided upon.

At the meeting in Birmingham decisions were taken – presented by Scargill and ratified – which were to make the union a totally centralized national body and to expel the Nottingham area branches. On 10 January, with scarcely a murmur, his executive agreed to this and a delegate conference confirmed it on the 29th. Thus was democracy in the NUM finally hijacked. The Union of Democratic Miners, formed six months later, was the natural consequence of the decisions made that day.

Nor had Scargill finished trying to make capital out of the negotiating game. As we have seen, one of his most powerful weapons against the back-to-work movement was his ability to persuade men who might be thinking of returning that the NCB was on the point of collapse and that there was no reason to risk a lifetime's obloquy as 'scabs' for the sake of a few day's wages. We had to be careful not to make any negotiating moves in his direction that he could misread and translate into clear signs that the strike was about to end in victory for the miners. At the same time, we had to maintain our posture of always being willing to negotiate. The public would not forgive us for stubborn intransigence. That is why I had decided on the policy of not negotiating with the NUM without a guarantee from them that they would first accept pit closures for reasons other than exhaustion or safety. I believed this made it clear to everyone exactly where we stood. But it was not so; as I was to learn.

In the meantime, in January, I continued with the policy and out of it came several skirmishes with the negotiating procedure – but nothing that looked like getting talks off the ground. Scargill would try to draw us out so far – then claim he had made 'new initiatives' and that it was only our intransigence which prevented the two sides discussing them. Far from it. We were willing to talk – but saw little point in doing so if he was not going to recognize the basic right of the management to run the enterprise.

One of these sallies arose because Ned Smith, who stayed with us until the end of January, met Peter Heathfield to see if there was anything for the two sides to discuss. In order to pre-empt Scargill's usual announcements suggesting that we were about to give in, Michael Eaton expressed our doubts about the long-term value of the talks as soon as they had finished. The correspondence between the NUM and the NCB which arose as a result of this was acrimonious, but it shows clearly that Scargill had no intention of conceding our right to manage and our fundamental responsibility for the bottom line. The advantage of continuing to stick to this fundamental point was not only that it aided the return to work, but also that it stopped Scargill repeating various versions of statements to show that on day 'X' we had said one thing and on day 'Y' another. If we made it clear now, once and for all, he would be robbed of further propaganda planks.

Norman Willis and the good Pat Lowry also had attempts during this period to get the ball rolling, but

Scargill's position was frozen in place. I made it clear to both of them where we stood – in fact I told Pat he was welcome to try to get Scargill to move and, if he succeeded, to get in touch. But if he expected us to shift on the issue of the right to manage, however it was couched, then it was a case of: 'Don't call us. We'll call you.' Willis must have been in an uncomfortable situation. He was the new boy at the TUC – no great reputation for anything in particular preceded him – yet the first item to come down the pike at him was Scargill. Scargill spotted the potential here very quickly, I believe, and had Willis running around much more than any of his predecessors would have done. Most of them, by this stage of the game, would have told Scargill to shut up and settle. But the unfortunate Willis was still feeling his way and obviously had to be seen to try everything to help the miners.

As January drew to a close a scheme was already forming in my mind to assist him in this process. There was obviously a fair head of public steam for a settlement to be attempted. There was, more obviously, political pressure for it too. Willis was clearly willing to try anything. All these factors combined began to suggest to me a way in which everyone was satisfied that everything reasonable that could possibly be done had been done. It would be a sort of 'play within the play' – the end result of it being that Scargill would finally be revealed as a man who constitutionally was quite incapable of moving one inch from his demand for total victory. I wanted no inconclusive negotiations. This time the result had to be clear cut.

At the same time as I was pondering this, I began to hear whispers, yet again, that the secretary of state was 'having talks' with the TUC. They may have concluded that they might get nowhere with me and so they thought they might have another go at the politicians to help them

345

get Scargill off the hook. I was surprised to think that such a step would even be contemplated after what had happened to the back-to-work movement last time. The first I heard of it was when Ray Buckton sidled up to me at a party and, with a nudge and a wink, hinted that something might be happening. Within days the coalfields were awash with rumours that the government was ready to 'cave-in'.

My discussion with the secretary of state had to be more frank this time. In fact I am sure it was an unpleasant experience for both of us. I told him that I thought it should have been clear to him that talking to Willis was not helpful and that if the TUC wanted to talk to anyone they should be talking to me. They could not talk to both of us, because both Scargill and the TUC would drive a coach and horses between us. Surely he could see that? I also regarded it as extremely unhelpful that he should have had these discussions without at least informing the head of the industry concerned that he was doing so. The relationship between Walker and me could hardly have been more strained. It seems like a confession of failure to say so, but we seemed to be circling round suspiciously, looking for the opportunity to prevent each other taking initiatives, instead of working closely to bring the strike to a successful conclusion.

However, it was eventually agreed that the NCB should handle the negotiations from now on. I asked him what they had been talking about. Had there been any new contribution to the thinking? This time, he told me, the TUC seemed to think they could find a way out which was acceptable to Scargill if we agreed to understandings on the closure of the five pits which were discussed in our negotiations, as well as the question of the reduction of industry capacity. In addition, we had to agree to an important initiative which was to rewrite The Plan For

Coal. I said I would be happy to talk about that, providing it was clear in this document that we would have to retain our basic rights to manage and decide on the size and capacity of the industry. There would be no point in finding ourselves back where we started from in six months' time because it hadn't been made clear to Scargill that we had to have the right to shut pits on economic grounds. However, I agreed to meet the TUC people promptly, for it would give me the opportunity to test out and determine Scargill's real motives. I hoped to use Willis's enthusiasm for a settlement to force Scargill into declaring his hand.

I was sure that we could put together a document based on the normal rights of management with the help of Willis and the TUC 'Seven' which would be, and would be seen publicly to be, a fair deal by normal standards on which to settle the dispute. In usual industrial relations terms what we were seeking from the NUM was nothing more than existed in most of the agreements with which most of the unions in the TUC were operating. If we could frame an understanding with the TUC on terms on which they thought Scargill should settle, it had to be made clear that there would be no further negotiating on it. It was not a basis for further talks. It was what a group of Scargill's peers, having immersed themselves in the subject for five months now, having had endless meetings with all sides, and having taken the matter as far as it could be taken with the NCB, were prepared to recommend to the NUM that they should accept. It had to be seen as our last and final offer. If Scargill then accepted it, the strike would be over and the TUC would have made a valuable contribution.

But my betting was that Scargill would in the end refuse to agree. By constantly studying Scargill's actions, I had now come to believe that I knew him fairly well. I was convinced that no matter how reasonable the understanding with the TUC, he would be unable to make any concessions. I believed that once this became clear, within days we would have more than half his men back at work. We could then with justification declare the strike over.

This was the concept, the 'play within a play', which would establish the final set of negotiations in the strike. Obviously I could not share these innermost views of mine with the TUC, though I had a suspicion, by the end, that Willis realized what was going on. It did not seem prudent to rehearse these ideas with anyone, not even the secretary of state, but of course I shared my thoughts with Jimmy Cowan before we met Willis the next day, Wednesday, 30 January. With a certain amount of malice aforethought, I had chosen, for the venue of these secret talks with the leaders of Britain's trade union movement, the Ritz Hotel!

We had two sessions that week, then went away to consider our position. We started the serious work of drafting the document on Monday, 11 February. There were just four of us: Willis and Ken Graham, his sharp and capable deputy, Jimmy and me. Over the next three days we worked mostly at my apartment in Eaton Square, where, in addition to the serious business of negotiation, I also made the tea and poured the whisky. It was convenient for us all to meet there, since it was secret and we were undisturbed. My wife was away in Florida at the time.

You will remember that we had failed to reach agreement with the NUM on the issue of the third category of pit closures – those we had to close for economic reasons. We had been unable to find a form of words which was acceptable to them and which allowed us to retain the right to manage the industry in this crucial area. On the other hand, our agreement with NACODS had side-stepped and, by implication, resolved this issue and concentrated instead on the consultative procedure whereby we came to a final decision to shut down a pit. Eventually we had agreed to set up an independent review body, which would be a sort of 'public inquiry' for the unions on the matter of the closure of any pit before the Board itself met to confirm, or otherwise, a recommended closure. However, the last word on the matter, after the independent review body had reported, would continue to lie with the board of the NCB, who would nevertheless give its findings 'full weight'.

Fundamentally, what we sought to do in these talks was to find a way of bringing these two approaches together in a form that the TUC would feel Scargill should accept. The device we used for this – indeed at their prompting – was to put an 'umbrella' over the whole issue in the form of agreeing to a joint rewrite of The Plan For Coal. The timing was convenient because all the basic projections in the original plan only went as far as 1985 anyway – so here was a golden opportunity for the NCB and NUM to state together how we saw the industry's future. However, there were many problems – not the least being that any deal we did with the NUM had to be compatible with that done with NACODS.

We went through a number of drafts, edging slowly towards something that was acceptable to both us and the TUC. At one stage the secretary of state, perhaps unaware of the subplot I had in mind, became alarmed that we seemed to be willing to give too much away. Funnily enough, I am sure he thought I had become too anxious to compromise. However, his objections, when they were boiled down, were largely a matter of semantics. After a certain amount of amendment to satisfy his concern, and a tightening up of the details, in the end we all felt that the paper was right. It was sufficiently robust and it clearly retained for us the management's right to close uneconomic pits and hence to maintain our responsibility for the economic health of the industry.

The final wording, agreed on 13 February, consisted of eight paragraphs and an annex of the agenda of items to be included in the discussions of the new Plan For Coal, which had a target date of six months set for its completion. The eight paragraphs covered the following areas of proposed agreement between the NCB and the NUM.

First, for us to look to the future success of the industry in an atmosphere of reconciliation. Second, for the NUM to recognize that we had a duty to manage the industry efficiently, while we recognized the union's duty to represent the interests of its members. 'In this regard the NCB is firmly of the view that the interests of the membership of the NUM are best served by the development of an economically sound industry.' Third, a return to work and an immediate start on the new Plan with full cooperation on both sides to complete it in six months. In the meantime collieries could be referred to the old review procedure. Fourth, for both sides to accept the value of outlining at this stage how it is envisaged modifying the Colliery Review Procedure. Fifth, for both parties to hold talks on incorporating an independent reference body into the CRP. 'Until such time existing procedures will apply.' Sixth, the future of all pits will then be dealt with under this new CRP. Closures for safety and exhaustion would be by joint agreement – 'and in the case of a colliery where there are no further reserves which can be developed to provide the Board, in line with their responsibilities, with a satisfactory basis for continuing operations, such a colliery will be closed.' Seventh, in the new CRP the independent body would provide a further review and consultative stage for cases where agreement could not be reached in the earlier stages. All parties would give full weight to its findings. Eighth, 'At the end of this procedure the Board will make its final decision.' This was not seen as a no-strike agreement.

There it was. We had documented the form of our final agreement. There would be no more talks, no more alterations. This was not a basis for further discussions or negotiations. This was what the TUC had worked out with us as being the best possible deal and they were now committed to recommending it to the NUM. We shook hands on it and Willis and Graham went off, planning to deliver it to the miners the following morning. I thought that if Willis could lean on Scargill, or the other members of his executive, and get them to accept it, he would have my sincere respect and admiration for life. However, I suspected his belief that Scargill had the wish to settle on any but his own uncompromising terms was misguided. The NUM president was, after all, not a 'normal' union leader by any stretch of the imagination. He was a Marxist revolutionary with a romantic streak – he would listen to the voices of reason from the TUC, but he would be hearing his heroes saying those fine ringing words: 'No compromise! No surrender!'

In the meantime, I had other problems on my mind. My wife had been taken severely ill in Florida and, while we were concluding our discussions on the Thursday, I had been on the phone organizing doctors to see her and a hospital bed for her in Florida. I made plans on the Friday night to fly out to be with her – as soon as I had heard Scargill's reaction to the document.

It came fairly quickly and it was, predictably, 'No'. Well, I thought, we have laid down our markers. Everybody could now see what Scargill was like. As I went to the airport on Saturday morning I felt confident that we had everything lined up now for a swift return to work.

This, however, was not the end of it. The first I knew that something was wrong came early on Sunday morning in Florida when the phone rang. Jimmy was calling to say that he was under great pressure from Peter Walker to see Willis and that Willis now wanted to change the document. I could not believe it. We had all agreed this was the final document and that there would be no alteration and no further negotiations. What sort of a pantomime was this?

Scargill had apparently had a meeting with his executive in which he had criticized the document from top to bottom. For once, he had failed to carry them with him; and, led by the moderate Trevor Bell, they had insisted that, in view of the weight of the august body which had brought the document to them, they should not shred it line by line, but merely make a few points of criticism.

This they did: finding fault in the wording of the points about the interests of the NUM members being best served by the development of an economically sound industry, the continuance of the existing CRP while the new one was worked out and the fact that the NCB wanted to retain the right to close a pit which could, in line with their responsibilities, no longer provide a satisfactory basis for continuing operations.

For what reason I don't suppose I shall ever know, the TUC saw some hope in this response. Perhaps it was because, for once, Scargill did not entirely get his own way with his executive. Or perhaps they thought, since there were so few points in number (but not in substance), we might be prepared to move a little, despite our mutual agreement that this was the full and final document. Whatever the reason, they had gone to Peter Walker, who, I was led to believe, had agreed to their request, but did not attempt to get in touch with me instead. He started pressing Jimmy to agree to meet Willis and Co. and get to work on the changes.

I was furious. I told Jimmy there were to be no changes and he was to make this clear to the minister. What was more, he was to tell him that if he tried to change it behind my back, I would resign and make public my reasons. I was so upset that perhaps I took too much of my anger out on Jimmy and it took a while for him to get the point through to me that he could not very well refuse the minister's instructions for him to meet them, but he would stonewall until I could get back. I told him to be very, very careful and not to agree to any changes whatsoever. I spent an agitated Monday morning, making rapid arrangements for my wife to ensure she would be completely looked after, and then made my way back to the airport.

In the meantime I thought the situation over carefully. To my mind the main point was that we had agreed this document. We had given Scargill all the excuses he had needed over the months for endless rounds of debate and we could not open this up for yet another one. Knowing his determination to take the miners on to the bitter end, I felt this could mean a delay of yet more months before we got more than 50 per cent back to work. I was amazed that people in London could not see, even now, that he was in no hurry to settle. I supposed there were some at the Department who thought that this was their chance to be seen to solve the strike and that just a few changes might mean victory for them. Victory, I suppose, to some of them meant being able to settle – no matter what the cost.

Over the weekend Willis had clearly realized that he was not getting very far with Jimmy, who, true to his word, had stonewalled. The Department, also, had had no success in persuading him to move. An extraordinary piece of collaboration then took place between Walker and Willis; together they had persuaded the prime minister to spare them an hour on Monday morning – just before she was herself due to leave on a trip to America. This too staggered me when I learned of it just before I left for the airport. What propaganda ammunition would Scargill make of this? I could hear him saying: 'No need to go back now, lads. The prime minister herself is about to get into the act and negotiate. There you are, I told you all along she was behind it!'

I am sure they were all trying to be good politicians and be seen not to be intransigent – but clearly none of them saw the same dangers in the situation that I could. Obviously my 'audiences' were narrower than those the prime minister had. I can only guess at the political pressures on her. Nevertheless, I was amazed that a politician of her stature agreed to the meeting at all. I assumed that Peter Walker had urged her to do so. I was as near to a total sense of failure as at any stage in the entire dispute. We had soldiered on all this time. We had taken all the flak and the sniping, yet we had stuck to our battle plan and we were within sight of success – only to have this extraordinary turnaround. Had the country wasted £3 billion for nothing? Could they not see it was only a matter of days before it would be over anyway?

As it happened, I needn't have worried too much. I gather Mrs Thatcher was courteous to them all, but firm that the Coal Board must retain its right to manage. When the question of the status of any changes in the document came up, the prime minister asked if the TUC agreed that, once the changes were made, the NUM would accept that they constituted the final document and there would be no further alterations, nor would they become an agenda for further talks. Willis agreed and the rest of his team nodded their assent. It was then left to them to sort out.

I went more or less straight from the airport to Peter Walker's office on the Tuesday morning. It was a fairly stormy meeting. Fundamentally there were two irreconcilable views. He explained what had happened and how Mrs Thatcher had reacted and that the changes the TUC were seeking were not all that significant. I was somewhat mollified – though still surprised at her apparent willingness to skate on such thin ice. Once again I insisted that one or other of us had to conduct the meetings with the TUC. They could not be seen to be dealing with both of us. He agreed that I should continue and then, with the heat of our arguments dissipated in a more relaxed atmosphere, we went out to a Soho restaurant for lunch with David Hunt and Tim Bell, and Walker went over the changes the TUC had asked for.

That afternoon Jimmy and I cloistered ourselves away to work on the document. In fact the changes to be made were not substantial. The TUC, in response to the NUM and despite the agitation of NACODS, who were concerned that their agreement with us was being undermined, wanted only a few changes. We amplified the part of paragraph five which referred to the existing CRP staying in place until the new one was ready. Early in the paragraph we added a clause which confirmed that the existing CRP had been operated by both sides for many years. Then we added on to the end of the paragraph:

Until then, existing procedures will continue to apply to closure proposals which are not disputed. In the case of a disputed closure proposal, as under the procedures that will be operating in connection with any such proposed closure, it will take more than three months before the point was reached where there was a need for either party to make a reference to the independent review body, all parties will endeavour to reach an agreement upon the details of its establishment before the First of June 1985. In the event of a failure to reach agreement on the independent review body by that date, the existing procedures will continue to apply until agreement is reached.

They were also worried that paragraphs six and seven, in the order they were given, could be taken to imply that we had in mind closing pits without the unions having had the opportunity to refer a case to the new independent review body. Therefore we merely changed the order of the two paragraphs, thus making the point clear.

In the covering letter to the new document which I wrote to Mr Willis I made the following observations:

The secretary of state confirmed that [at the talks with the prime minister] it was the view of the TUC that the document that we had prepared subsequent to discussions with you was a document, that, if agreed to, would for all of the matters dealt with in this document be the final agreement, and was in no way a document which would be an agenda or form the basis of, any further negotiations.

We note also that the TUC confirm that the executive of the NUM had accepted the Board's duty to manage the industry efficiently; had confirmed its acceptance of a modified Colliery Review Procedure; and had accepted that the Board would take the final decision on closures after completion of all the review procedures.

It ended with the words: 'Having given careful consideration to your views, I wish to make it clear that this must now constitute our final wording. We hope that the NUM executive will accept this as a means of ending the present damaging dispute and allowing all sides of the industry to concentrate their attention on the future success of the industry.'

We had one last meeting with all seven of the TUC people on Wednesday morning at the Goring Hotel in Victoria, where I handed over the letter and the new document. It was quite a pleasant gathering, though they were anxious about the NUM's reaction. I reminded them, as was laid down in the letter, of the assurances they had given the prime minister and said it was up to them. That afternoon they went off to see Scargill, who, I gather, played some silly games with them before a meeting with his executive was finally convened. Willis described to them the talks of the last few days, answered a few questions, then left. Apparently, Scargill took the document, flipped through it, then dismissed it contemptuously. The following day, obedient as ever, a special delegate conference followed suit.

The curtain thus came down on my 'play within a play' and all the audience could now see clearly the nature of the man we had been facing for nearly twelve months. On the following Monday, 25 February, having had time to think it over during the weekend, nearly 4000 miners came back to work. It was, I think, at last clear to everyone that Scargill had no intention of settling. I believe even Norman Willis realized in the end what we had done was to expose Scargill and, to his credit, I don't think he objected to it. He too appeared to have lost all patience with the man.

On Thursday 28th, 50.75 per cent of the men were back. Five days later it was all over. They were five extraordinary days in that, to the end, Scargill and his friends tried to wriggle and squirm their way out of what was staring them in the face and to put a different complexion on the catastrophic damage they had wrought on their members. On the Friday, for example, in the middle of a television debate with Michael Eaton, Scargill pulled out a copy of the NACODS agreement and offered to sign it on the spot. It was the same old story. But it alerted me to the very real possibility that we were going to have problems when the strike was over – not least with those who thought that, once it was over, things would be just the same as they had been before.

Already the bandwagon was rolling. We were told in the media that we should not punish the miners too much. We should be magnanimous in victory. There should be an amnesty for all those miners who had been sacked – no matter what heinous crimes they had committed on their fellow men or on NCB property. Last, and quaintest, was the concept that the remaining strikers, now a minority, should march back to work with their heads held high and banners flying. I don't know what this was going to prove to anyone, beyond demonstrating to the world that these poor loyal men, who had been led such a song and dance for a whole year by Arthur Scargill, were still held in vassal thrall by him. It was a pathetic gesture born of a derision and contempt for most of those men. They deserved better from their leader, having given their all to him in blind obedience.

It also revealed to me that there were a lot of people in the industry who did not understand what had been going on for the last year; that, now we had succeeded, we were going to exert our right to manage the enterprise. From now on there didn't have to be a ritual genuflection to the NUM every time we wanted to do anything. If they thought they were marching back to where they had left off, then they had a very rude shock coming to them.

Our first task was to make it clear that we were not

going to take back all the men whose thuggery, vandalism and violence had helped shatter so many lives of those who had wished to work, nor those who had done so much damage to NCB and other people's property. There would be no general amnesty. It was extraordinary the way sections of the media seemed to think that we should instantly forget what had happened in the last year, not only to the country or to the NCB but also, more seriously, to all our loyal employees who had braved so much to keep the mines going. We should not forget that we and our working miners had just been through twelve months of the most concentrated mayhem the country had ever seen.

As the dispute drew to a close, a further, sinister, aspect of this lack of will for any kind of sanction or punishment for the miscreants was confirmed in my mind. It seemed as though widespread pressure was being put on the courts of summary justice to 'go easy' on pickets brought before them on charges relating to the strike. First of all there was the obvious plea in the court that these men were not natural law-breakers and, were it not for the unusual circumstances of the dispute, would not have thrown the brick at this policeman or kicked in the door of that working miner's house – and therefore they should not really be punished all that much. But behind this type of plea there also began to emerge a pattern of leniency right across the coalfields, especially where local councils were of militant-left complexion and, hence, perhaps many of the justices were more likely to be broadly in sympathy with the strike.

I heard numerous stories of the frustrations of police, particularly senior officers, who, having faced great danger from the mobs, having exposed their men to hours of violence and missile-throwing, having apprehended, perhaps, a few ringleaders or a few of the worst offenders, brought them to court on evidence which would have been perfectly satisfactory elsewhere – only for the case to be dismissed or the most paltry of fines handed down. I never thought I would see this in Britain. But it was happening.

I was particularly upset because I felt the working miners were owed something. They were the ones who had broken the bonds of serfdom with which their union had tied them. They were the ones who needed to be shown that their struggle had not been in vain. They should have been allowed to see that their tormentors were at least reprimanded for what they had done. But no; instead, in many cases, bullies and thugs walked away free with no forcible reminder of the terrible things they had done.

Also in those last few days Jimmy and I sat down to examine what was clearly a huge task in front of us. Not the least of our problems would be to make provision for those many men and their families who had suffered, and were still suffering, intimidation. Sadly, but understandably, many of these courageous men elected to leave the industry and take the generous redundancy terms on offer. We moved many hundreds of the rest to other pits or areas where they might have peace and arranged new housing for them. Thousands more were counselled and helped with their problems. However, one or two cases became the darlings of the media and enjoyed the exposure. I got the feeling, as we were forced to attempt to resolve their problems in the full glare of media attention, that nothing was good enough for some of them. It was sad but predictable that the press ignored the vast majority who are now happy and settled.

I was subsequently staggered to be taken to task by the prime minister because of my failure to do anything for these people. She had apparently been fed a malicious story of our unfeeling attitude towards all the suffering former working miners, which was based on one particular case – that of Mrs Irene McGibbon. Unfortunately, as is the way of these things, nobody had told Mrs Thatcher about the great efforts that had been made for most of those we took care of, nor that, if the extraordinary demands of some of the malcontents had been met in full and applied universally, the £3 billion bill for the cost of the strike would have been increased astronomically. Nevertheless I was fairly sanguine about her criticisms. I didn't expect the efforts of those who wished to undermine my position to cease just because the strike had ended.

It was also clear to Jimmy and me that we were going to have to do something about the NACODS agreement fairly quickly – but that, in the meantime, since the NUM had rejected our final document, we had no obligations to them and should therefore declare a state of emergency while we assessed the damage and got the show back on the road again. In some areas, because of lack of people for maintenance, the underground workings had been damaged irreparably during the year of the dispute and we began to work on what we would have to do, which pits would have to shut, which faces to close and where men would have to be moved. In the end this exercise led to the closing of nearly 40 pits and many more working faces. Some 38,000 people left the industry in a short space of time – in addition to the 12,000 who had left during the dispute.

We also knew that we would have to tidy up the matter of the wage claim and the overtime ban. Both of these were settled within weeks of the dispute ending, allowing the men to embark on a sustained period of high production and hence high wages. Union militâncy was not generally popular after such a long time out of work, though Scargill and his henchmen continued to strut about making believe they had won. It was inevitable too that the NUM should finally reject Nottingham and the working miners and so, in July, the UDM was finally formed.

In the last few days, while we waited for the men to go back to work, Jimmy and I discussed all these problems and how they were likely to affect us. One problem we did not discuss was the pressure I had been getting from Peter Walker to replace Jimmy himself. We had already set in motion a full-scale reorganization of the upper management, promoting John Northard and Ken Moses, moving Bert Wheeler to Nottingham, and several other key changes. I had never tried to hide from Peter Walker that because Jimmy had had heart surgery and was over retirement age, and had asked to go as soon as the strike was finished, I felt I should not impose on him for too long after the strike was settled. The minister seemed to take this to mean that I wanted him to go now. I knew he did not like Jimmy's efforts very much, but I had underestimated his strong feelings on this. But I was not in a rush and wanted to find some less strenuous job for him, so that at least we would still have the benefit of his advice on hand.

In the meantime I suggested that if any medals were being handed out for conduct over and above the call of duty in the dispute, then Jimmy should receive one, not only for his long years of service to the NCB, but also for what he had done in the last year. Jimmy's contribution to the industry exceeded by a quantum leap anything any of his predecessors or anyone else during the strike had done. Alas, it has not been recognized. When Jimmy ceased to be deputy chairman, he received the usual flowery letter of thanks for all his work, but nothing more.

I felt very sad. Look at the way medals had been passed

out to others in the industry for lesser contributions. Even if they had put in a lifetime's work, they had not made such a major improvement in the performance of the business as Jimmy Cowan had done in his short term at the top. I was more concerned that, apart from the prime minister and some members of her cabinet, there was, even at this stage, not a lot of sympathy for what we had been trying to achieve among the ranks of the politicians and the civil servants. There were 'enemies within' in many more senses than one.

On the last Sunday night of the strike, knowing finally that it was all over, I went out to dinner. Sibyl was still in America, so I invited my sister-in-law and an old friend from America, Dr Drucker, and his wife. The four of us went to a restaurant in Walton Street. We were pursued there by a group of reporters and photographers who wanted to take pictures of this great victory celebration and to chronicle every mouthful of our 'triumphant' meal. It was not a celebration. There was so little for so many men to celebrate. We chatted about other subjects throughout the simple meal. We drank the house wine. And when we left the photographers flashed off pictures of us in the street. I felt sorry that on this occasion I did not have a Harrods bag handy.

EPILOGUE

In the aftermath of the strike, as we were running around trying to get the business going again – inspecting pits, seeing the area directors, deciding where to cut our losses and where to keep things going – it was difficult sometimes to remind myself that this was my true task. In the week the dispute ended, my three-year tenure was half completed; yet it seemed almost as though I had done nothing in all that time but manage the dispute. I now had to remind myself, those around me and the public at large that I had not been brought into the NCB to have a strike, but to solve the industry's problems – of which the runaway labour relations situation was just one. We now had a job to do.

Nevertheless the year-long dispute had had a seminal effect on the industry and I began to take time to think about the good and the bad that had come out of it. Had the miners learned anything? To be wary of the demagogue? To distrust the militant? Some perhaps. I believe many more perceive dimly that all the shouting and bluster did not actually achieve anything for them and that there is truth in what I go around the coalfields saying, 'Produce and you'll get paid.' On these trips I am often asked by miners, 'How come American miners can earn £30,000 a year?' To which I reply, 'Productivity.' We have sent small groups of men over there to see the US mines. Many are equipped with British machinery, some of which is the finest in the world. But the crucial

364

factor is productivity. In one mine I know just 629 people
– some are women – produce three million tonnes a year,
sell the coal at less than $25 a tonne and make a profit. I
tell the men here I would be more than happy to pay
them £30,000 if they could match that.

I believe the message may be getting through – though
of course not to some of the union leaders – about
the economic necessity of getting their heads down and
working, but the strike reinforced the lesson for many of
the men. As it dawns on them that Scargill's type of union
activity is designed to keep them poor they will perhaps
be more reluctant in future to follow Scargill into war,
especially when it is so demonstrably clear that they were
not intended to benefit from this last struggle.

Has Arthur Scargill learned anything? I doubt it. Within
a very short while he was running round claiming it as
a victory, because the lessons learned from it by the
revolutionary left meant that next time they would win.
He also pointed out that the strike had cost the nation up
to £8 billion – 'thanks to Mrs Thatcher's intransigence'.
Indeed, only three months after it was over he chose his
union's annual conference to call for a repeat assault on
the NCB and the government. 'In the present climate
any industrial action, hopefully involving other mining
unions, can stop a pit closure programme.' He also casti-
gated critics on the left for deploring his failure to hold a
ballot and the violent nature of the picketing, and he
added: 'We are involved in a class war and any attempt
to deny that flies in the face of reality. We are entitled,
indeed obliged, to call upon our class for massive support.'
It was the same old song again.

Thus I fear he will be with us for a while yet, because his
strength lies in the fact that he recognizes how fragile
democracy is. As long as we allow Scargillism to happen,
it will. Sadly, even now, I do not think people are properly

aware of what he tried to do. The system provides too comfortable an existence. It lulls people into thinking there is no danger, that we shall go on as we are, without it being necessary to actively assist in preserving democracy. Until people everywhere recognize the threat, until the miners collectively see the danger too, then Scargill and men like him will continue to exist and flourish.

Some miners saw through him early on, particularly those in Nottingham. His denial of the membership of a say in the union's affairs, his centralizing all power on his office, supported by the special delegate conference and his ruthless repression of all opposition, made it inevitable that Nottingham would move slowly away from the body of the NUM and eventually secede, in the form of the UDM.

Needless to say, the very existence now of the UDM with its 35,000 members has made both it and them a constant target for every form of abuse, chicanery and outright thuggery imaginable. There is a concerted effort at all levels of the left to make these honest working men – many of whom have voted Labour all their lives – into pariahs, politically, economically and socially. Yet I believe they will survive as long as there are men, like their general secretary Roy Lynk, and president Ken Toon, who have the will to fight for democracy. We have helped them all we can to achieve their objective of a free democratic union. I hope my successors retain that commitment and are not seduced by arguments about bureaucratic 'untidiness' caused by having two miners' unions into letting them down.

For the existence of the UDM has a meaning far wider than merely being a union for those men. It is a symbol of the other argument, the other side to the case presented by Arthur Scargill. As long as it is there, it is a reminder that Scargill's word is not law, that there can, in a democracy, be dissent. Scargill would stamp the UDM out. The TUC would throttle their existence. The Labour Party would acquiesce in their demise. It is not in their nature to recognize that the day it becomes a crime to disagree is the day that democracy dies.

Many of the heroes of the strike are to be found in the UDM's ranks. Ordinary men, who, when their rights were being trampled on, said 'No'. It took guts and endless fortitude to put up with what those men suffered at the hands of Scargill's bullies. 'Randy' Florence was one of my heroes – but there was a legion of others in the working miners' groups whom he would want me to name first. Then there were those, particularly out in the more militant areas, whose bravery made it impossible for them to stay on in the industry afterwards. It is difficult to imagine the effect on the individual and his family of the day-by-day intimidation; how it eats into your confidence and saps the will to go on. It is a tragedy that so many of them were driven out as a result of the stand they made for honesty, decency and democracy. We helped many thousands of them. We moved more than a thousand. But it is a desperate comment on our times that many many more chose simply to walk away. To those men, who include in their number people like Taylor and Foulstone, we all owe, perhaps, the greatest debt.

It simply does not bear thinking about what might have been were it not for those brave fighters. Imagine if the bullies had won. Imagine if the thugs now had the industry to themselves. How much mercy would they have shown to those who dared to disagree? Sadly, many of them are still there, even now skulking in corners, waiting for the chance to put razor blades in a man's pit-bath soap, or ruin his street clothes or urinate in his snap tin.

There were heroes too among the area directors – men who grew in stature as they came to grips with the problems and took on management responsibility. It was a pleasure seeing such men broaden and mature during the strike and its aftermath. Some of them, I am sure, will go on to very high office. Without them the back-to-work movement would never have got off the ground. Their leadership did a great deal to boost morale among the managers fighting to open up their pits and among the men determined to work in them.

The managers themselves played a key role. I know we did not have all of them on our side when the dispute started. These men are usually ex-miners, or from miners' families, often born and bred in the locality, and even those with university degrees or other professional qualifications have served their time. Traditionally managers have seen their role in a strike as being, at best, neutral: to keep the pit in working order for when the dispute is over. Furthermore, in recent years, as the power of the union grew, many of them had a further incentive to keep their noses clean and not to put pressure on the local NUM chiefs by demanding any greater productivity: some of them had become enslaved by union blackmail, hesitant to do anything 'managerial' for fear of reprisals. When we asked them to abandon their neutrality and to play a positive part in getting a solution to the strike, there were many who were anxious about doing so. Perhaps another of Scargill's fundamental errors was to permit such mayhem on the picket lines, and rarely, if ever, publicly to condemn it, and so blatantly to deprive men of their simplest civil and democratic rights. In doing so he drove many of these managers and supervisors, who are by and large among the more intelligent members of the mining community, into our arms. We ended the dispute with a very broad base of support from these men, which I don't think we have lost. I watched many of them, too, grow in stature as the dispute went on and it was one of the very few pleasures the whole business afforded me.

I believe the future of this business, as a successful enterprise with a firm set of goals, lies precariously in the hands of a very few people. It will depend on the strength of character and philosophical beliefs of those few. I am only too conscious of the fact that in my three years I have not been able to swing all the people at headquarters away from a bureaucratic approach to the industry and round to a managerial stance. We have not yet learned in this country as a whole that there is a fundamental difference between administration and management. We produce excellent administrators but they are essentially guardians of the status quo and very rarely make good managers. Managers have to be ambitious for change, to be constantly dissatisfied with the way things are and looking for ways of improving them.

If British Coal is to be successful it has to have, from whatever government is in power, the political will to continue with the process which has been started. We have not sought, yet have not shied away from, confrontation in our pursuit of a high-output, low-cost industry. We have established at the very top and at area level a 'management' approach to the enterprise. There is a restlessness and enthusiasm in the management now, a continuing desire to improve results and to find new ways of doing things. Of this I am proud.

But, if British Coal is to be truly successful it also has to have managers right through the industry. The administrators still have too much of a role to play. We have to reduce the endless flow of paper, much of it created for the benefit of close government supervision, and about which I have been able to do little. We have decentralized much of the business, but there is still a large centralized mechanism, linked umbilically to the

Department of Energy, which seems to have a perpetual need to examine in detail every action, and every expenditure. The need to monitor every decision being taken, to collect information, is above and beyond that which would be needed to run any normal enterprise. Struggling through these rafts of committees and collections of statistics during the strike was bad enough; but, in addition, there was not a lot of enthusiasm for what we were trying to do from some of the men responsible. It is one of my regrets that I did not have longer in the job to reorganize properly the headquarters and its relations with government on simpler, more direct management lines.

Naturally, thinking back over those months, I have other regrets too – and feel sadness at mistakes that I made. As far as the conduct of the dispute itself is concerned, I believe we were wrong even to contemplate using the injunctive procedure. Fortunately we managed to back away from it in time, but it could have been disastrous if it had been granted, as I am now sure it would have done, as a rallying point for the whole trade union movement at a critical time.

We were also probably over-optimistic about getting a settlement in the June and July negotiations. We were criticized at the time for appearing to want to give too much away – but I had not recognized at that stage that Scargill was not going to move one inch. I still believed there to be a chance of a solution and therefore – as is the traditional role of management – we had to go as far down the road to meet him as we possibly could, without surrendering our right to manage.

Then, when it came to the NACODS negotiations, I believe we should have resisted their totally unnecessary demands. But we were victims of a real hold-up. I also made a mistake in that I did not identify the impending NACODS row earlier – before it blew up out of all proportion. Although, in all fairness, I really did not understand much about the debate that was going on among our IR people in August. It referred to past practices and obscure details which I thought, wrongly, need not concern me. By the time I got involved the horse had well and truly left the stables. It had also been saddled up by Scargill, mounted by the TUC and was off and running.

But perhaps my biggest mistake was in the area of presentation. In retrospect it would have been much better for me to have insisted on bringing in my own PR from the beginning. I had worked with Ronnie Melvin at BSC and wanted him to come with me. He was known for being dedicated to promoting the interests of the business, unlike Geoff Kirk who was known for being popular among the industrial correspondents. I should have spotted the problem far earlier and insisted on Melvin coming. Instead I was persuaded by officials in government to keep Kirk. It would have been better for everyone in the long run to have made the change at the very beginning and would have saved a lot of pain. None of the solutions we tried after the dispute started was entirely successful – not even Michael Eaton. In his case, I believe the problem was that the solution was just too simple. It looked good on paper – he was the bluff, pipe-smoking Yorkshireman who had not had much luck in getting the men in his area back to work and therefore had very little to do, so why not use him? In retrospect I suspect he might have considered our objectives with some reservations. His projection of the NCB case may have given the impression of a degree of softness which, I think, may have caused the NUM people to make a number of wrong assumptions about our position and intentions.

My last, and greatest, regret is that I didn't have longer before Scargill came running headlong at us. As it was I did not have time properly to assess where the weaknesses were in the organization or to start to do something about them. It is simply not possible to turn round a great enterprise like Coal in three years – at least not in all the detail required to have it perfectly tuned – so that you know, when you leave, that it is set on course as a successful business for many years ahead. It has been especially difficult at Coal because most of the first two years had to be spent on the runaway labour relations problem – only then could we really get down to driving for an efficient management organization.

Nevertheless a great deal has been achieved. In fact the industry has gone from an annual loss of £800 million to near break-even point. In the last quarter of the year 1985–6 the NCB actually made an operating profit on the deep-mine operations – the first time this has been properly achieved since 1977. Our costs are lower and our output per man is 40 per cent higher than before the strike. We have achieved all this by doing precisely what we said we would do – shutting high-cost production (about 40 pits and many production faces) and concentrating on high-productivity pits and faces.

Since the middle of 1983 some sixty thousand men have voluntarily left the industry. Yet not one of them has been made redundant against his will. We have very nearly the same coal production rate today as we had in 1983. That, if anything, should nail the Scargill lie.

Naturally the fall in oil prices has affected our position in the market – particularly with regard to electricity. Our principal customer, the Central Electricity Generating Board, is required by law to provide the consumer with the cheapest possible energy. The present, short-term, drop in oil prices has forced them to look seriously at the lower cost of using oil-burning plants instead of the higher cost NCB coal. The dangers to the NCB are immense. Just when we have begun to achieve a good tempo of production and improved costs a sudden drop in demand for coal would completely destroy our momentum. It became imperative for the NCB to retain its market and the question has been how much leverage can the CEGB put on the NCB to provide cheaper coal in the meantime? However, we have now settled the matter honourably, I believe, by fixing a long-term contract price for our coal. This has safeguards to ensure that during a period of five years the consumer gets cheaper coal, but if the price of oil goes up again, the coal supplier will get some benefit too. The idea of a long contract and a stable and predictable demand enables us to plan our production for the same period, knowing precisely what it is we have to achieve both in production and costs.

I leave the industry with its new name – British Coal – convinced that it has a bright future in front of it. The name was changed to indicate among other things that we are living in a different age and that the whole operation is based on a different concept than the one long associated with the NCB. I wanted our people to get more of a feel of the unity of the place. The National Coal Board – abbreviated as it was to 'the Board' – was a remote and confusing title for the employees. It promotes an image of a bunch of remote old men sitting in London making the decisions for everyone else all over the country. If ever I went to Nottingham, or Sheffield or Edinburgh or Cardiff, and the area director's NCB driver met me, I could ask him, for example, why he was driving a Ford – and he would say, 'The Board decided.' I want that man to be able to feel that the decision about what car he drove was not made by ten wise old men in London – but by that man he says 'hello' to each morning and talks to about football occasionally.

One of the most rewarding areas of the last three years has been getting down to the work of building the business properly and achieving the more efficient use of our people. This country still has the great problem of producing so little GNP per individual in the workforce. The skill and inventiveness we have as a nation, if combined with the dedication and efficiency of, say, the Koreans, would overnight make us one of the most successful economies in the world. But at last we are moving in that direction again and the prospects have become substantially brighter. In the case of coal, we are sitting on vast reserves and, as we have seen, it is a fuel which will come into its own in the next century. If the business is in a good enough economic shape to handle the opportunities, it will make the UK a powerful economic force, unique in Europe with a choice of energy sources.

Ironically I believe this is a view I share with Peter Walker. For all our disagreements, he too is optimistic about the future of the industry – if its costs can be got right. It was, to my mind, a pity – as indeed was inevitable in such a long strike – that he lost confidence in the management of the NCB. I feel that, if we had had greater mutual confidence and been closer, he would have recognized the impossibility of going through such a traumatic struggle without pain and loss of prestige, and the strike itself would have been over that much quicker.

I think the popular media, including television, is partly responsible for a sea change in our political life, which perhaps Mr Walker understands and knows how to use. Newspapers and television, by their very nature, trivialize an issue like the coal strike. Particularly television, where the image, not the content, more often than not dictates the story. Looking good becomes more important than being good. Having a quick answer which will satisfy the questioner today is more important than knowing what the answer is in the long term. Having a fresh line to give the chaps each morning for them to chew over for the rest of the day is more important than the hard, gritty and very unglamorous business of settling the strike.

This trivialization of our news has had two interlinking effects. It has meant a decline in the role of the editor. The editorial, like the rest of the paper, has become trivial too. In some cases it has even been reduced to the level of a piece of knockabout comedy. At the same time, the editorial function has been decentralized, in that every journalist is either encouraged or has elected to be his own editor out in the field, to make judgements about what he sees and hears instead of merely reporting it factually. In television the editorial function has been further devolved right down to the cameraman, who edits merely by where he chooses to point his camera and when. This process of editorializing is then refined in the cutting room, before the producer even decides what film is to be shown in a bulletin.

The effect of all this is to reduce the statesman – the politician who can see the long view and has the courage to be unpopular momentarily in its pursuit – to the level of the PR man. No longer is it deemed possible for many politicians to risk even a moment's unpopularity or to be seen in anything but the most flattering light.

Not so Mrs Thatcher. She is a remarkable woman in that, in an age where the instant and the trivial are rated so important, she should pay so little attention to either. She had the courage to take the long view most of the time in the strike and act accordingly. All politicians must, however, take some notice of public opinion and I could therefore understand the pressures on her when she exhibited nervousness on a couple of occasions over the direction of the dispute. Particularly in the period of the NACODS threat, I got the feeling that she really thought the house was going to fall down all around her. Nevertheless, overall she understood the principles involved. She stuck to her guns and had the courage to support us, even if, at times, she must have been more than a little nervous. She could be described as a stateswoman.

I also think that her leadership throughout helped the nation to understand the great issues that were at stake and the necessity of seeing it through to a successful conclusion, however long it took. If nothing else, the dispute did one thing for us all. It demonstrated that the power of the union movement, individually or collectively, is above neither that of government nor of the law. It is as recent as 1979 that a government (for the second time in a decade) was brought down, effectively because of union opposition to it. The miners' strike of 1984–5 showed us that it is possible to resist a determined effort to bring about the downfall of a government by the mere flexing of industrial muscle.

Public apathy had, over the years, allowed unions to presume that they were immune from the fundamentals of all British law – that they could use intimidatory mobs rather than just a few men to picket, for example. The dispute re-established the right of the individual to determine for himself whether or not he should be on strike. In doing so it has also reminded us that perhaps we need to examine closely in all future legislation whether we should, in fact, grant any further immunities, implied or otherwise, to the union movement and perhaps to examine more closely some of those they have presumed to adopt.

The fact that Scargill believed, to the end, that he was above the law, should warn us that concerted attempts will continue to be made to preserve this illusion. But the reality is that such arrogant assumptions end in mob rule. The strike showed us, as never before, how vulnerable we are to a determined assault on the forces of law and order. Our system of policing is essentially dependent on the consent of the populace. A sufficient number of men gathered together and raised to a high emotional pitch by a demagogue can threaten the very fabric of society. We were lucky we had policemen who served with dignity and tolerance. The process of undermining the forces of law and order by local political pressure through the far-left continues. We may not be so lucky the next time.

It is also clear to me that there are great gaps in education in this country. Not only are large sections of the populace economically illiterate and hence unable to comprehend the changes taking place around them, but we are also up against increasing technical illiteracy, which restricts our ability to take advantage of the job opportunities that rapidly changing technology will provide. Furthermore, by trivializing the presentation of our society, we are rendering people heedless to the dangers threatening democracy itself – which leads to the third handicap of constitutional illiteracy.

During the strike we came within a whisper of concluding, as a nation, that the thug and the bully were immune from the law because what they were doing was sanctioned by orders from a union. We fought it and we won. Many people would say that the price was too high. But to my mind that is the price you have to pay for freedom. The enemies of democracy are everywhere. If we are not to sink into soulless collectivism we must realize that we cannot rely on our freedoms always being there. We cannot assume that Scargill, or any other of his like-minded pals on the left, will not make strenuous efforts again to reduce us to the state of serfdom he tried to impose on the miners as a whole.

The lesson, above all lessons, to be learned from the strike is that we cannot depend on democracy. It depends on us.

INDEX